ETHICAL RELATIVISM

The Islamic College for Advanced Studies

The Islamic College for Advanced Studies (ICAS) is an educational and research institute offering undergraduate and graduate courses in Islamic Studies. The courses cover the Qur'anic Sciences, in particular, Qur'anic Hermeneutics, Hadith Studies, Islamic Law and Jurisprudence, Islamic Theology, Philosophy and Mysticism, Contemporary Islam and Arabic.

The Department of Research and Publications at the College undertakes the preparation and publishing of textbooks, as well as the translation of classic and contemporary Islamic works into English. A number of important compilations and translations are currently in progress.

This work by Dr Shomali provides an overview of ethical relativism, along with a critical study of the writings of philosophers Gilbert Harman and David Wong. Though purely philosophical, the arguments developed here, especially those relating to the foundations of morality, will certainly be of significance to those interested in Islamic Studies, and particularly, Islamic Ethics.

ICAS hopes that this book will prove an invaluable addition to this field of study.

ICAS Press

Mohammad A. Shomali

ETHICAL RELATIVISM
An Analysis of the Foundations of Morality

Preface by
A. Harry Lesser

Islamic College for Advanced Studies Press

British Library Cataloguing-in-Publication Data
A catalogue record for this book is available from the
British Library

ISBN 1 904063 00 4 (pb)

© Mohammad A. Shomali, 2001
This edition first published 2001

*The right of Mohammad A. Shomali to be identified as the author of this work has been
asserted by him in accordance with the Copyright, Designs and Patents Act of 1988*

Published by
Islamic College for Advanced Studies Press (ICAS)
133 High Road, Willesden, London NW10 2SW

Distributed by
Saqi Books
26 Westbourne Grove, London W2 5RH

Contents

Preface

There are two reasons why I have particular pleasure in writing a preface to Dr Shomali's book. The first is that, as the supervisor of the PhD thesis on which it is based, I have seen the growth and development of what is now an excellently argued and important contribution to contemporary ethical debate. The quality of the argument is something that the readers will be able to judge for themselves. The importance of the book lies firstly in the fact that the various kinds of ethical relativism are clearly distinguished, together with the arguments for and against them, so that they can be properly assessed. Secondly, the two authors singled out for special discussion, Harman and Wong, are the authors who present the most up-to-date and plausible versions of relativism, versions which avoid many of the objections that can be levelled at older presentations of a relativist theory. A skilful analysis of the types of ethical relativism and a critique of the two best versions is clearly something to be warmly welcomed. But I have another reason for welcoming this work. This is that, since I believe relativism to be a misguided ethical position, it is good to see the appearance of a work that argues against the relativist position in its most plausible form, and moreover does so, in my opinion, convincingly and conclusively – though that, as I have said, is for readers to judge for themselves.

But the main purpose of this introduction is to explain briefly the developments in philosophical ethics of which this book is part. Philosophical ethics in the English-speaking world may be divided, like mathematics, into "pure" and "applied". For most of the history of philosophy, these have been combined in the study of ethics, which has tried to understand the nature of morality, less for its own sake than in order that we may actually improve ourselves and our behaviour: thus Aristotle classifies ethics as practical, not theoretical, knowledge. But for much of the twentieth century ethics became a theoretical study of the nature of moral judgements and moral statements; the guiding of behaviour was seen as vitally important but not something to which philosophy could directly contribute. In the last quarter of the century, applied ethics has returned, and a great deal has now been written in this field. But I would like to begin by discussing "pure" ethics in the English-speaking world in the twentieth century.

"Pure" ethics has been mainly concerned with the nature and status of moral judgements and moral discourse, perhaps above all with whether moral judgements are objective or relative; whether they can be true or false and, if they can, what it is that makes them true or false; and what the connection is between empirical facts (e.g. that a course of action will probably cause only suffering) and moral conclusions (e.g. that this course of action would therefore be wrong). Indeed, one way of describing the progress of ethical theory during the twentieth century would be to describe the development of two forms of relativism, individual and cultural: individual relativism has, so to speak, risen and fallen while cultural relativism survives, though in a modified form.

The twentieth-century version of individual moral relativism has its origins (there are of course versions going back to the Greeks) in the work of philosophers who were not themselves relativists. The first stage on the road to modern relativism was Hume's observation in the *Treatise of Human Nature* that the passage from *is* statements to *ought* statements, the argument from the facts to what ought or ought not to be done (e.g. that because lying destroys trust between people one ought not to lie), has never properly been explained. Not only does Hume himself fail to draw any relativist conclusions from this but he seems also, in his philosophy as a whole, to accept inferences from facts to values as legitimate: but he has pointed out that these inferences have no obvious logical justification, even if they are psychologically necessary, and it is this that has been picked up and developed in the twentieth century.

The first development was the appearance in 1903 of G. E. Moore's *Principia Ethica*. This introduced the idea of the Naturalistic Fallacy, the idea that the inference from facts to values is a logical mistake – not merely unexplained but actually invalid. Moore, however, was not himself a relativist but an intuitionist: he held that, though it was a mistake to regard goodness as a "natural", empirically detectable property, nevertheless it was a "non-natural property", a genuine property of people and actions but known by intuition rather than perception. For a time many people agreed with Moore, but many others accepted the first part of his theory yet were unhappy with the second part. They accepted that moral judgements were not derivable from facts, but, largely because different people seem to have different moral intuitions, could not accept the role of intuition.

But if moral judgements are neither derivable logically from the facts nor knowable by intuition, how are they to be analysed? One answer, widely accepted in the middle of the twentieth century, was that they are not judgements at all, but expressions of emotion, and therefore necessarily subjective. This theory derived from the work of the group of Austrian philosophers known as the Vienna Circle, or more precisely from the interpretation of their work brought to the English-speaking world with the publication of *Language, Truth and Logic* by A. J. Ayer in 1936. Some have argued that Ayer oversimplified the ideas of the Vienna Circle, but it was this version of Logical Positivism, as the theory was known, that was initially influential.

According to Ayer's version of Logical Positivism, a statement has meaning only if it is possible to say how it can be verified: if you cannot say under what conditions a statement would be true, you cannot give it any meaning. But for Ayer the only possible ways of verifying a statement were either by showing that it is logically necessary or by showing that it is confirmed by observation or logically derivable from true observation-statements. Hume and Moore had shown (it was believed) that moral judgements were neither logically necessary nor logically derivable from anything observable: hence, if the Positivists (as interpreted by Ayer) were right, moral judgements could not be meaningful statements.

On the other hand, moral judgements are clearly important and influential: they cannot be dismissed as mere nonsense. Hence the proposed solution: that they are not in fact statements at all, not in any way "about" human beings and their actions, but expressing our feelings towards them. If we say that A took money away from B forcibly, we state a fact: if we add that this was wrong, we say nothing more about what happened, but express our disapproval or disgust at the action. We are not, it should be noted, describing our feelings (as we would be if we said, "We do not approve of stealing"), but giving vent to them. Hence, on this theory, the supposed statement "Stealing is wrong" is neither true nor false, any more than a cry of pain or pleasure is true or false (although it may be sincere or insincere).

The idea that "moral judgements" are not statements remained for many years; but this version of it soon came to be seen as far too crude and simple. Ayer himself modified his theory by recognizing that what moral statements expressed was not mere emotion but established attitudes. The American philosopher Stevenson added to this the element of guiding the attitudes and actions of others, so that on his view to call an action "good" or "right" is not only to express one's general approval of actions of this type but also to encourage others to have the same attitude of approval and to act in this kind of way. Then, in 1952, came Hare's *The Language of Morals*, which put forward the theory that moral statements are essentially action-guiding, and are not expressions of emotion but a type of command or imperative: "You ought not to steal" is not the same as "Do not steal", but belongs to the same general class of utterances.

Hare denied that his theory was subjectivist: and it does indeed make moral statements subject to objective logical inferences. This is in two ways. First, a more specific imperative may be derived from a more general imperative together with a factual premise: for example, from the imperative "One ought not to weaken trust between people" and the factual statement "Telling lies tends to weaken trust between people", one must infer "One ought not to tell lies". Also, "ought" imperatives are, in Hare's language, "universalizable"; if an action is right or wrong, or right or wrong under certain circumstances, it is always right, or always wrong, or always right or wrong under those circumstances. If, for example, it is wrong to tell lies, it follows that it would be wrong for Person X (e.g. oneself) to tell lies.

But, even if Hare wished to say that this theory was not subjectivist, it had the same problem as subjectivism. It is true that, on Hare's theory, once one accepts a basic imperative, for example, "One ought to obey God" or "One ought to promote human happiness", it is then possible, given that the facts are available, for ethics to become thereafter objective, the uncertainties remaining being all factual uncertainties, concerning for example what is required by the religious way of life or what in fact will promote happiness rather than suffering. But Hare is still forced to admit that logically any basic imperative is possible, and therefore, basic moral choices are, even if Hare objected to the word, "subjective" and relativist. Hare rightly points out in his second book, *Freedom and Reason* (1963), that adherence to his theory makes the adoption of some moral positions psychologically very difficult: a person can be a consistent racist only if he or she admits that, if it were to turn out that s/he belongs to the "inferior" racial group, it would be right to discriminate against him or her. Nevertheless, he has to concede that a "fanatic" could hold this position, and it would be logically consistent. One could say that, from one's own moral standpoint, racism is wicked; but one could not say it was objectively wicked.

Now this has always seemed to many to be an impossible conclusion: for many people, the certainty that some things (torture and mass murder, for example) are wrong and other things (mutual help, for example) are right is greater than the certainty that any overall moral theory is correct; and it is the theory that must fit these moral conclusions and not the other way round. Hence, if even the most sophisticated version of individual relativism cannot give us this, individual relativism must be incorrect as a moral theory. But there is a problem. If relativism is incorrect, objectivism must be correct, in some form. But on what is this objectivism to be based? The arguments of Hume and Moore give good grounds for saying it cannot be based on empirical facts. The attempt to base it on moral intuitions, which was popular at one time and adopted by Moore himself, seems to be defeated by the fact that moral intuitions are so different among different people and societies. And any attempt to base it on religion or metaphysics runs into the problem that there is no universal agreement on religious or metaphysical issues: indeed, if any philosophical justification of religion is possible, it looks as if it will itself have to be based on morality rather than being a basis for it.

This is the problem that faced philosophical ethics in the second half of the twentieth century: individual relativism cannot be right, but how can any objectivist position be justified? In the work of the ethicists of this period, it is possible to find three kinds of answers. They are not mutually exclusive, and are not always consciously put forward as answers to this problem, but they all derive fairly directly from the great classical works of ethics in the Western tradition, though they present the ideas based on these works in new, non-metaphysical terms. There is work deriving from Mill, from Kant and from Aristotle, all of which has in common that it seeks in different ways to find the foundation of ethics in the moral enterprise itself, and thus give it a grounding that is neither factual nor metaphysical but nevertheless objective.

We may first consider the revival of utilitarianism. Classical utilitarianism, as expressed by Bentham and Mill (if one ignores the complexity of Mill's theory), held that only pleasure (or happiness) was good and only suffering was bad, so that actions are right to the extent that they promote pleasure and wrong to the extent that they promote suffering. This ran into two major problems – that pleasure and the absence of pain are not the only things that people want, and that the fact that they are wanted does not make them good. Modern utilitarianism says in effect – not always explicitly – that, if ethics cannot be either empirically based or based on metaphysics, then the only alternative is to hold that whatever a person happens to want is good for that person. Moreover, there is no factual or metaphysical basis for deciding between wants; morally all are equal. From this it follows that the right thing to do is to satisfy as many wants as possible, each person regarding his or her own wants as no more and no less important than those of any other person. Hence, it will be wrong, for example, to commit murder, which, so to speak, thwarts every future satisfaction of wants for the victim and often many wants of the victim's family and friends; and it will be right to enhance the satisfaction of wants by, for example, relieving poverty and supporting or practising medical care. One place where this view can be found is in the later work of Hare himself (see *Moral Thinking*, 1981).

The Kantian justification of moral objectivity is found particularly in social and political philosophy, such as in the work of Rawls, Nozick and Dworkin, different as these are from each other. It is a theory that is not totally objectivist, and regards many moral issues as ones to be settled by the individual, but it is objectivist on certain very important points. The argument (again, it is often not explicit) is this: whatever else is held to be good, any morality must regard the existence of moral agents and the maintenance of their ability to act morally as being good. It must also regard all moral agents, *qua* moral agents, as being equal.

This has two consequences. The first is that there must be a set of moral obligations that all moral agents owe to all others and that are based on the obligation of mutual respect, the obligation to treat people "as ends in themselves", to use Kant's phrase. There are many questions to be settled here: what exactly these obligations are (do they go beyond not killing and not totally removing a person's freedom to act?); whether they are simply duties or based on "human" or "natural" rights; whether human rights, if they exist, can be forfeited (e.g. by threatening or taking the life of another); how much of the task of protecting these rights or enforcing these duties belongs to society as a whole and how much to individuals. But certainly a great deal of recent political and social philosophy has been about "human rights" – what they are; whether and how they can be justified; and how they can and should be guaranteed and protected.

Secondly, much work has been done, sometimes by the same philosophers who have worked on human rights issues, on the practical implications of the equality of moral agents. Again, there are very different opinions: there is a dispute as to whether this justifies only formal legal equality or whether it also justifies equality of opportunity or even some equality in the distribution of wealth. But the concern with equality, like the concern with human rights, has been a widespread common feature of recent political philosophy; and a widely shared (though not always explicitly recognized) assumption has been that, while no objective determination of moral ideals may be possible, it may nevertheless be possible to derive a conception of basic justice simply from considering what is involved in acting morally at all.

Both this tradition and the utilitarian tradition, in their modern versions, have a limited notion of moral objectivity. They both assume that no objective judgements can be made about the goals that people pursue or set themselves, but that it is nevertheless possible to work out principles governing the right way of co-operating in pursuit of these goals and dealing with situations in which they come into conflict. There is, however, a third, growing, tradition, that of virtue ethics, as it is commonly called.

More accurately, we may say that there is a neo-Aristotelian tradition, in which there are three elements, all stemming from Aristotle in the first instance: philosophers in this tradition broadly vary as to how many of these elements they incorporate in their work. The first element – a particular concern of political philosophers – is the stressing of the notion of community and of the fact that living in society is integral to humans and being part of society makes a person what s/he is, so that a concern only with individual rights misses some crucial moral issues: the debate between "liberals" and "communitarians" is another big current issue in social philosophy. It should be noted, however, that these positions are not necessarily opposed, and that there are philosophers such as Michael Walzer who consider themselves "liberal communitarians". The crucial point is that, once again, this is based on general features of morality: in this case, the fact that, though societies and cultures differ considerably from each other, the very fact that virtually all humans live in a society and are shaped by a culture has objective consequences for ethics.

But neo-Aristotelianism, for some writers, questions not only the individualism of some versions of the Kantian approach to ethics, but also the assumption of contemporary utilitarianism that whatever a person happens to want is a good for that person. Thus, John Finnis has argued in *Natural Law and Natural Rights* (1980) that the list of human goods is a limited one, and also open to rational discovery, and proposes a list of seven ultimate goods (though all seven can be achieved in many different ways). Since it must be the responsibility of any just society to make possible the attainment of these goods by all its members, it follows that everyone has a right to whatever is needed to allow their pursuit; and so from this Finnis develops a theory of natural rights.

Finally, there is the "virtue ethics" strand of neo-Aristotelianism, which is perhaps the most widespread. The basis of virtue ethics is that whatever purposes a person may have, in order to achieve them within society the person will need a specific range of qualities. No long-term goal can be achieved without self-control, industry and probably courage; no goal requiring co-operation can be achieved without justice, honesty and probably kindness. Hence, it becomes possible, if this is correct, to give an objective account of which qualities are good and which bad, without having to say that there is only one good way of using these qualities.

To summarize this, we may say that, as we enter the twenty-first century, philosophical ethics in the English-speaking world is growing, in both the extent and the importance of the work being done. Individual subjectivism has disappeared, as a serious philosophical position, although it survives, unfortunately, as an assumption often made unthinkingly by those who still believe that an objectivist position is somehow intolerant or arrogant. In general, many forms of objectivism are gaining ground: they are notably different from each other, but have in common that they take the classical works of ethics seriously and they look for the basis of ethics within ethics itself and not in empirical facts (though these are always relevant to the deriving of specific moral duties), metaphysics or intuition.

Parallel – in a way – to this work in ethical theory are two other kinds of work. One is meta-ethics, the study of moral language and the nature of moral utterances. Here a number of positions exist. There are still those who take a non-cognitivist position and regard moral judgements as neither true nor false; but contemporary non-cognitivists differ from the early non-cognitivists, such as Ayer, in that they try to avoid the subjectivist or emotivist conclusions with which non-cognitivism used to be associated. Hare (see above) is a good example of a philosopher who combines non-cognitivism with objectivism.

The alternative position, that moral judgements are true or false, which is probably by now the more common position, is generally called "moral realism". Moral realists divide into "naturalists", who hold, roughly, that moral discourse is not fundamentally different from talk about facts, and "non-naturalists", who hold that there is a real difference, but not one that prevents moral statements from having a truth value. Again, contemporary non-naturalists would, in many cases, resist the appeal to intuition or metaphysics, made by the older non-naturalists: in this way, meta-ethics and ethics have reached very similar positions and face the same problem – to produce a non-metaphysical version of moral realism or moral objectivism.

The other major area is, as I said at the beginning, applied or practical ethics. In the last thirty years, this has revived; and there is now a very large body of work, on a range of issues. The largest area is medical and health care ethics, but there is a great deal of work in environmental ethics; and on such questions as the responsibilities of the rich to the poor and when, if ever, the use of force or violence is justified. Most of this work uses either neo-utilitarianism or a broadly Kantian theory as a basis, sometimes trying to combine the two, or to consider a problem from both points of view in turn Some of the most recent work uses a virtue-ethics basis; and it looks as if this position is gaining ground. What does seem to be the case is that nearly all writers on applied ethics seem to find it necessary to assume or to argue for some kind of objectivist position.

However, though applied ethics tends to take its basic theoretical position from pure ethics, and to use one or more of these three currently most popular approaches, there are two theoretical issues that have in their turn emerged from applied ethics. The first is the issue of feminism, of the position of women. Two problems in particular have been discussed. The first is how to interpret the principle of equality between women and men: whether it should mean the giving of equal opportunities, e.g. in jobs, to women and men, or whether it should involve in addition, or instead, equality of respect, so that female occupations are treated as having the same importance as male ones. In other words, when does equality require the same treatment for all, and when does it require different but equally respectful treatment?

Second, there is the question of male and female values, the question of whether there are, if one generalizes, characteristic female and male approaches to ethics, women being particularly concerned with caring for individuals and men being particularly concerned with justice. Whether such differences exist is still uncertain; but if they do, then in order to have a properly human ethics we shall have to combine both viewpoints. The key question is whether what has been taken to be a fair and neutral approach to ethics is in fact one biased towards the male position.

The other theoretical issue "thrown up" by applied ethics is the question to whom or what moral duties are owed. Everyone agrees that they are owed to all self-conscious humans, and that every form of racism is wrong. But whether we have duties to infants, unborn children, animals and the environment in general has been much discussed. This also serves to illustrate the point – hardly a surprising one – that the relation between "pure" and "applied" ethics is two-way. Applied ethics is not only a matter of using the theories of pure ethics or even of testing them: it is also a source of problems that are theoretical as well as practical. But once again, the basic assumptions are objectivist and not relativist.

There is, however, one surviving relativist line of thought. Individual relativism is dead, but cultural relativism is still with us. There are various reasons for this. Cultural relativism is at least not as wildly implausible as individual relativism, and the idea that morality is essentially a matter of following the standards of one's own society, whatever these are, is not obviously wrong: it is, after all, exactly the view we take of customs, manners and etiquette. Moreover, the relativist view provides a way of doing justice to the differences in moral values that exist in different societies, and of avoiding the assumption, all too common in the past, that everything that is not Western must be inferior to what is Western. To this may be added the point, well shown by anthropologists and by philosophers such as Peter Winch, whose *The Idea of a Social Science* came out in 1958, that the practices and beliefs of other societies must be set in context even to be understood, which suggests that only in that context can they be seen as right or wrong, with the result that the outsider cannot pass judgement on them. So one may be led to the view that necessarily there can be no standard outside the standards of particular societies, by which these standards themselves can be judged.

But although there is something to be said in favour of cultural relativism, there is much to be said against it. Is it really the case, for example, that one cannot condemn a racist society, even if racism is a main part of its traditional values? And so, it is of great importance for philosophical ethics – which, except on this issue, has, as I hope I have shown, largely returned to objectivism – that cultural relativism, particularly in its most sophisticated, up-to-date and plausible versions, as found in the works discussed by Mohammad Ali Shomali, should be subjected to close investigation, and its errors, if they are errors, made clear. Only then can ethics proceed to consider what form an objective basis for morality should take: we have seen earlier that there has been progress, though no agreement, on this issue. In short, this book is appearing at exactly the right time: it forms part of the revival of philosophical ethics in general and of objectivist ethics in particular that we have seen in the last twenty to thirty years. In this book, Dr Shomali helps to demonstrate that no form of relativism is tenable, and therefore there must be an objective foundation for morality; and he takes the first steps towards working out what that foundation is. Some years ago, such a book would have been very much in opposition to current philosophical trends; but times have changed, and this book is very much part of a growing movement, and a movement – in my opinion – altogether in the right direction! I recommend it for the serious attention of anyone interested in philosophical ethics, in the hope that it will convert the relativists and provide some new arguments for the objectivists!

A. Harry Lesser
Manchester, February 2001

Introduction

The debate on ethical relativism and absolutism has been one of the most important and prolonged topics of philosophical reflection in ethics. The results of this debate, however, are not exclusive to ethics. The position one takes in this debate on the relativity or non-relativity of ethical values and standards certainly affects one's political, legal and social stances. The continuing strength of relativism has always been rooted in the impressiveness of the variation in ethical beliefs and the deep conflicts over ethical issues. In this regard, D. Wong says:

> Moral relativism is a common response to the deepest conflicts we face in our ethical lives. Some are quite public and political, such as the disagreement in the USA over moral and legal permissibility of abortion. Other conflicts inviting the relativistic response are of a less dramatic but more recurrent nature, such as the feelings of a first-generation Chinese American who faces conflicts between inherited values and the values of the adopted country (Wong, 1996, p. 442).

Yet although relativism has always had some adherents, the common-sense view has always been in favour of non-relativism. It has been even suggested that "there are virtually no relativists among significant figures in the history of philosophy. The principal exception is Protagoras" (Wood, 1995).

Despite the long history of this debate not much progress has been made. The main reason is that this debate involves some underlying issues in ethics that have to be settled before any proper decision can be made here. One has to define one's positions about the definition of ethics, the nature of truth and justifiability in ethics and in general, realism in ethics and semantic issues of meaning and interpretation. One has also to set up some framework to study empirical questions about what is really believed and practised in other groups and societies.

There are also three derivative reasons. One reason is that both advocates and opponents of relativism sometimes neglect to distinguish between different doctrines. Moral relativism is sometimes confused with *moral nihilism*, *moral scepticism* and the like. The second reason is that there are usually different definitions, different versions and several divisions of the same type of relativism and this makes the debate on moral relativism more complicated and confusing. The third is that each side sometimes tends to portray the opponent as holding the most extreme position, in order to make the debate easier.

In the first chapter of the present work, I shall try to clarify the conceptual context of the debate by projecting some light on relativism in general and then I shall focus on ethical relativism. In the second chapter, there will be a discussion of the history of ethical relativism, especially in the twentieth century and more especially in the 1980s and 1990s. The third chapter will study the various types of ethical relativism – the descriptive, the meta-ethical and the normative – and distinguish between different possible grounds for each. There will be also discussions on arguments for ethical absolutism and the absolutist account of moral diversity. I hope that clear descriptions and logical ordering of the subjects in these three chapters will help to put an end to some of the misunderstandings recurring in the discussion of ethical relativism.

In the fourth and fifth chapters, I shall study two of the most recent and important versions of ethical relativism, i.e. those developed by Gilbert Harman and David Wong. I shall explain the main features of their account of ethical relativism and then, in the light of comments made by others or myself, I shall try to assess the advantages and disadvantages of their views.

Finally, in the sixth chapter, I shall develop my theory about the foundations of morality. Since the topic of ethical relativism is closely related to that of moral objectivity or subjectivity, I think the most insightful way of studying ethical relativism and drawing clear and final conclusions is to explore the nature and origins of morality. I agree with many philosophers such as Thomas Scanlon that "the crucial question should not be whether a view is or is not properly called relativist, but, rather, what kind of foundation it takes moral standards to have and how much variation in such standards it allows for" (Scanlon, 1999, p. 335) Without being engaged in complicated discussions on the objectivity or subjectivity of morality, I shall try to develop my own view with special reference to the process of decision-making and different factors that bear on this process and might lead to different results.

In this work, I have tried my best not to ignore any important point in the vast literature on the topic. I will speak more about the difficulty of this task when discussing the history of ethical relativism. Further, I have tried to make everything as documented as possible. In respect to my own ideas, sometimes I found at a later stage that a similar point is asserted by other people. In these cases also, I have mentioned their names and works or at least one example, not only to support my view, but also to show my commitment to appreciating the efforts of other people who have contributed in the debate.

The present work was originally conceived as a PhD thesis and presented to the Faculty of Economic and Social Studies (now Social Studies and Law) of the University of Manchester in April 2000. In this edition the text has largely been left unaltered, with the exception of a few revisions and additions. This edition also contains a preface by Mr Harry Lesser, Chair of the Centre for Philosophy of the University of Manchester. I should like to take this opportunity to thank him. Not only has he written this preface, but he was also a good supervisor and Chair of the Centre for Philosophy. From the early stages of my study up to the end, he was always available, prepared to discuss and read every bit of my work, and encouraging.

My thanks are due to David Wong and Gilbert Harman for providing me with the information I required about their works. I wish to express my thanks to all who read and made comments on part of my work, such as Professor Thomas Scanlon (Harvard University) and Professor Jonathan Dancy (University of Reading), or who discussed the topic with me, such as Professor Peter Railton (University of Chicago) and Dr Mohammad (Garry) Legenhausen (Imam Khomeini Education and Research Institute).

Professor Robert Arrington, previous Chair of the Philosophy Department of Georgia State University, deserves a special mention. He too was very encouraging and he read every word of the draft of my thesis and made detailed and perceptive comments. I have also greatly benefited from his works on ethical relativism.

This book could not have been written without the generous support of Imam Khomeini Education and Research Institute, Qum, Iran. This institute sponsored my study and living costs during the period of my doctoral study. I should also thank the Islamic College for Advanced Studies in London for their encouragement and for publishing this book.

I am greatly indebted to my wife and two sons who have supported me with their love and encouragement throughout my study and tolerated all the difficulties of a student life abroad, in order to help me succeed. And, last but not least, I wish to express my feelings of deep gratitude to God for His every favour upon us and upon all His servants, past and still remaining.

Mohammad A. Shomali
London, February 2001

CHAPTER ONE

Relativism

Relativism in general may be defined as the denial of certain kinds of universal truth. By this definition there can be different types of relativism. Relativism can be and is discussed in different fields. What is common to all types and subtypes of relativism is that they all hold that one thing (e.g. knowledge or morality) is relative to a certain framework and that they all deny that any framework is uniquely true or most justified. The difference between these types and subtypes is due to the difference of objects (between types) and the difference of frameworks (between subtypes, such as the difference between individual ethical relativism, which takes ethical frameworks to be individually variant, and social ethical relativism, which takes ethical frameworks to be socially variant).[1]

In what follows, I shall try to explain two major types of relativism in philosophy: cognitive relativism and ethical relativism. Then I shall explain the subtypes of ethical relativism.

Cognitive relativism

Cognitive relativism is the view that asserts the relativity of truth in general.

---

1. The other way of treating the different types of relativism is to take them as varying according to the extent that one takes relativism to be true, i.e. as a claim about all types of *truth* (in the case of cognitive relativism) or about a specific type of *truth* (in the case of ethical relativism). A somewhat similar view is suggested by Blackburn (1994, p. 326). According to this, relativism may be taken as a global doctrine about all *knowledge* or as a local doctrine about some area, such as aesthetics and ethics. However, I think what I have suggested in the text above is more plausible, since some of those who believe, say, in ethical relativism (like some non-cognitivists) may not take morality as a matter of truth or as an area of knowledge.

It asserts that there are no universal truths or knowledge about the world. The world is just subject to different interpretations, since it lacks any intrinsic characteristics, and there is no one set of epistemic norms that is metaphysically privileged over any other.[1] On the history of cognitive relativism, L. P. Pojman writes:

> The Greek Sophist Protagoras, the first person on record to hold such a view, said, "*Man* is the measure of all things; of things that are that they are, and of things that are not that they are not." Nelson Goodman, Hilary Putnam, and Richard Rorty are contemporary philosophers who have held versions of relativism. Rorty says e.g. that "'objective truth' is no more and no less than the best idea we currently have about how to explain what is going on" (Pojman, 1996, p. 690)

An overview of the literature on the topic suggests that in the nineteenth century and more significantly in the twentieth century, there has been a growth in the number of those philosophers who adopted cognitive relativism. Better awareness of diversity of cultures, morals and world-views; taking Kant's "Copernican Revolution" in metaphysics more seriously (and drawing all its implications); and the criticism of the positivist philosophy of science are considered to be main factors that contributed to the development of cognitive relativism in contemporary philosophy. However, as I shall explain later in the discussion about the history of ethical relativism, the majority of philosophers have always seen serious problems in maintaining relativism. Especially in the second half of the twentieth century support for relativism has begun to decline.

Although the topic of this book is ethical relativism, cognitive relativism will be explored further within my discussion of the concept of relative truth. The typical criticism of cognitive relativism is that it is self-refuting, since it presents its statements as universally true, rather than simply relatively so.

Ethical relativism

There are different definitions of ethical relativism, presented by different writers. According to one common definition, ethical relativism is the view that there are no universally valid moral principles: the validity of all moral

---

1.   See, for example, Westacott, 1999a, p. 1.

principles is relative to culture or individual choice.[1] One problem with such definitions is that they are not comprehensive. There are different types and versions of ethical relativism, and this definition can be considered adequate just for one type of ethical relativism, that is, what we will call later "meta-ethical" relativism; it does not include "descriptive" or "normative" ethical relativism.

The other problem is that people with different positions often define relativism differently. This very problem has led people such as Mark P. Whitaker (1997, p. 478) to assert that to define relativism is, of necessity, to take a position in the controversy surrounding it.

A proper definition of ethical relativism has to give an account of ethical relativism that is more than a simple claim that people may have different moral judgements in different cases and less than the claim that contradictory moral views can be true.[2] A proper definition has to be also comprehensive and free from any dependence on a particular position in the debate on ethical relativism. Owing to the extraordinary difficulty (or perhaps impossibility) of presenting *a single comprehensive neutral faithful definition* of ethical relativism, I think that it would be better to content ourselves consciously with a rough general definition and then try to define every *substantially* different type separately.

Perhaps this is why Wong has preferred to describe ethical relativism as "a cluster of doctrines arising from reflection on differences in ethical belief across time and between individuals, groups, and societies" (Wong, 1992, p. 355). Elsewhere, Wong says, "Moral relativism is a cluster of doctrines concerning diversity of moral judgements across time, societies and individuals" (Wong, 1998, p. 539). Although this description seems to stem from the same concerns mentioned above, it obviously suffers from another problem. This description of relativism is too general in that it includes non-relativistic views as well, at least those non-relativistic views that are developed to explain moral diversity in a non-relativistic way.

---

1.   For example, see Pojman, 1996, p. 690.

2.   See Blackburn, 1994, p. 326, for a similar point about relativism in general. More recently, Blackburn refers to the difficulty of defining moral relativism and argues from that for the difficulty of defining moral objectivity and moral absolutism. He says: "It is notoriously hard to say what is intended by moral relativism. And I for one think it ought to be notoriously hard to say what is intended by moral objectivity, or moral absolutism" (Blackburn, 1998, p. 195).

Individual and social ethical relativism[1]

According to one classification, ethical relativism is divided into individual relativism and social relativism. Individual relativism is the theory that each individual justifiably determines his or her own moral code. Of course, as Hare (1993) believes, the moral codes of most individuals within a particular society are in practice likely to be similar, since they probably share a common cultural experience.

Social relativism is the view that each society justifiably determines its own moral standards. It has been suggested (Donaldson, 1989) that moral truth is simply internal cultural consensus. Ruth Benedict (1934) believes that morality is a convenient term for socially approved habits. This implies that there are no ethical rules that apply universally, and therefore what is considered morally right in one society is determined by that society's internalized beliefs, and another society with different cultural experiences may well hold a different, but equally valid, view of what constitutes right or wrong.

Social relativism is more common. Indeed, it has been suggested (Pojman, 1998) that this is the classic form of ethical relativism. Some writers only mention this when defining moral relativism. For example, Fieser writes, "Moral relativism is the view that moral standards are grounded in social approval, which varies from culture to culture" (Fieser, 1996, p. 1).

Here I have to note that different terms are sometimes applied to the notions of individual and social relativism. For example, Pojman (1996, p. 690, and 1998, pp. 16–8) uses the term *subjectivism* instead of *individual relativism* and *conventionalism* instead of *social relativism*. Conventionalism holds that moral principles are valid relative to the conventions of a given culture or society. Abortion, for example, can be right in society A and wrong in society B. Even in one society, abortion may have different status in different times, if people change their view about its permissibility. Subjectivism holds that individual choices are what determine the validity of a moral principle. Its motto is, "Morality lies in the eyes of the beholder."

However, I think it is clear, or at least I hope it will be clear after reading discussions about the subjectivist argument for meta-ethical relativism and about Harman's moral conventionalism in the present work, that

---

1. To prevent confusion, I suggest that it would be better to consider individual and social ethical relativism as two scales of relativism and what follows later, i.e. descriptive relativism, meta-ethical relativism and normative relativism, as three types, or more exactly levels, of ethical relativism.

conventionalism can be considered only as one of the various versions of social relativism, and that subjectivism cannot be identified with (individual) relativism, though they may overlap.[1]

Another example of varied terminology is that social relativism is sometimes called "cultural relativism", but cultural relativism may merely indicate the existence of moral diversity, which is a simple anthropological fact.[2] Because of this and because every group of people with some common objectives or commitments can make up a society, but not necessarily a culture, I prefer to use the expression "social relativism".

Note
There are other divisions within ethical relativism in different sources. In what follows, I refer to two important ones. Appreciating the points beyond these divisions, I reserve my right to have doubt about their necessity. I think the points beyond them will be better treated if we consider them as different reasons or arguments for meta-ethical relativism. This is exactly what I plan to do in the third chapter. For example, disbelief in the existence of a rational method in ethics can easily be taken as an argument for meta-ethical relativism, along with various separate and distinct ideas; otherwise any single argument could be taken as a basis for a further division.

Methodological and non-methodological ethical relativism
Basing his definition of ethical relativism on the view that there are conflicting ethical opinions that are equally valid, Brandt (1970, pp. 336–8) divides ethical relativism into two types. This division depends on taking one of two positions: either that there is no unique rational or justified method in ethics, or that there is such a method, but the use of the unique rational method in ethics, even in the presence of an ideally complete system of factual knowledge, would still not enable us to settle conflicting opinions.

He calls the radical relativist, who believes both that there are conflicting ethical opinions and that there is no unique rational method in ethics, a *"methodological relativist"* or an *"ethical sceptic"*. He calls a less radical relativist, who admits the existence of such a method, but still believes that there are

---

1. It is noteworthy that Pojman in both his earlier work (1996) and his later work (1998, p. 16) divides ethical relativism into two types only – conventionalism and subjectivism – but in the latter (1998, p. 18) he says that subjective universalism is another type of relativism that can be called *"universalizable relativism"*.

2. See my discussion of descriptive relativism and also Pojman, 1998, p. 16.

some instances of conflicting ethical opinions that are equally valid, a *"non-methodological relativist"*.

He adds that it would be better not to call the first group relativists at all, but rather "sceptics". However, he says that it is an established usage to define various writers, especially anthropologists, as "relativists".

Soft and hard ethical relativism

Matilal (1989, pp. 339–40) distinguishes between two types of ethical relativism: soft relativism and hard relativism. He means by "soft relativism" the view that there is no transcultural standard of evaluation, though moral norms available across cultures may be mutually comprehensible. Culture-bound norms are neither good nor bad. He means by "hard relativism" the view that culture-bound moral norms are both incommensurable and mutually incomprehensible; hence one may say that one norm is just as good or bad as the other.

Ethical absolutism

The opposite view to ethical relativism is *ethical absolutism,* which holds that there are universal moral truths, or at least there is one universal moral truth. It can also be defined as the view that there is only one single true morality or, as Wong puts it, the view "that both sides of a moral conflict cannot be equally right, that there can be only one truth about the matter at issue" (Wong, 1996, p. 442). Wong adds that this position is so common that William James (1984) called us "absolutists by instinct". Perhaps for the same reason many have viewed relativism as a temptation to be defeated, but the debate is a historical one and has to be taken seriously.

There are different views among moral philosophers on what to call the opposite view to ethical relativism. Like this writer, some call the opposite view "absolutism". For example, Unerman says, "The opposite view to ethical relativism is ethical absolutism, which holds that all moral statements are absolute, whether they be broad general moral principles or detailed moral codes of behaviour containing absolute moral rules" (Unerman, 1996, p. 14). Harre and Krausz also prefer absolutism as the term for the opposite view to relativism in its various forms including: the semantic, the epistemic, the ontological and the moral. They say, "As a general term for anti-relativism of all varieties we have chosen the term 'absolutism', and we would like it to be read always in this generic sense, as referring to any view which is anti-relativist" (Harre and Krausz, 1996, pp. 1 and 2).

Some people such as Wong prefer to call the anti-relativist view "universalism" Wong (1996, p. 442). believes that the term "absolutism" refers to something more than the denial of moral relativism, that is, to the view that moral rules or duties are absolutely binding without exception.

Others still prefer to use "objectivism" as a contrast to "relativism". For example, Pojman says:

> The opposite of ethical relativism is *ethical objectivism*, which asserts that although cultures may differ in their moral principles, some moral principles have universal validity. Even if, e.g., a culture does not recognize a duty to refrain from gratuitous harm, that principle is valid and the culture should adhere to it (Pojman, 1996, p. 690).

Pojman maintains that a valid ethical principle need not be absolute. In fact, Pojman (1996, p. 690) takes absolutism to be only one kind of objectivism, i.e. the stronger kind of objectivism, which holds that there is one true moral system with specific moral rules, such as the ethics of ancient Israel in the Old Testament with its hundreds of laws. Weak objectivism holds that there is a *core morality*, a determinate set of principles that are universally valid (usually including prohibitions against killing the innocent, stealing, breaking of promises and lying), but it also holds that there is an indeterminate area where relativism is legitimate, e.g. rules regarding sexual mores and regulations of property. In a recent work, Pojman (1998, pp. 16 and 17) defines an absolute ethical principle as one that may not be overridden by any other principle, i.e. has no exceptions, unlike some objective ethical principles. Therefore, absolutism is the view that there is one true morality with a consistent set of moral principles that never conflict and so need not be overridden. To me, Pojman's description of ethical absolutism has changed, but he still insists on using "objectivism" (instead of "absolutism") as the opposite to "relativism".

Among those who prefer "objectivism" as the opposite to "relativism" (in this case, instead of "universalism") is Bunting. He says:

> I use the term "objectivism" rather than "universalism" since the existence of principles applicable to all rational human agents is consistent with these principles not being recognized by some agents (Bunting, 1996, p. 73).

Although a name is in itself not very important in philosophical debates, it is highly desirable not to use equivocal, ambiguous and confusing terms. With regard to this, "objectivism" seems an inadequate expression, since its apparent meaning is the denial of subjectivism, but the refutation of relativism need not be anti-subjectivist. Some people may argue that ethics is rooted in human dispositions and still believe that ethical rules are universal, for example, because of the constancy of human nature. Therefore, there may be non-objectivists who are not relativist. On the other hand, there may be objectivists who are relativists, such as those who develop a semantic or functionalist argument for meta-ethical relativism. (We will discuss different non-subjectivist and objectivist arguments for meta-ethical relativism in the third chapter.)

Thus, non-relativism is different from objectivism and neither of them necessarily implies the other. In this work, the use of the term "absolutism" is preferred to denote the opposite of "relativism". The reason for such a preference is twofold. First, "absolutism" is semantically more suitable, because "absolute" literally means "non-relative" and "relative" means "non-absolute". Second, "absolutism" is technically less confusing, because "objectivism" or "universalism" usually are used in another sense so they can be *more easily* misunderstood, that is, they can be taken to mean respectively the denial of subjectivism and the denial of particularism and situationism in ethics.[1]

In the next chapter, we shall study the history of the debate on ethical relativism. This study will show the importance and status of the topic in the whole history of philosophical thought. It will also help to explain the historical development of arguments for and against ethical relativism.

---

1. I said "*more easily*", because even absolutism is sometimes misunderstood. For example, Renford Bambrough (1979) compares the belief in absolute values with belief in absolute time or space. He thinks that as soon as you suggest that there is a *right* answer to a moral problem you become accused of or credited with a belief in moral absolutes, but there is no necessary link between belief in moral objectivity and belief in moral absolutes. [See Bambrough Renford, *Moral Skepticism and Moral Knowledge* (Routledge and Kegan Paul, 1979), p. 33, as cited in Pojman, 1998, p.46.] I think what he asserts is an exaggeration of a real point: it is not appropriate to compare absolute values to absolute time or space. What I can accept is that the expression "moral absolutism" may have some connotations or apparent references to things that are not necessarily required to distinguish a given position from a relativist one. However, as discussed above, misunderstanding seems to be a common problem, to which other proposed expressions are still more prone.

CHAPTER TWO

The History of Ethical Relativism

The history of the debate between ethical relativism and ethical absolutism may be considered as equivalent to the history of ethical thought. The length and breadth of the debate make the historical review of the literature on the topic very difficult. Although unlike Harre and Krausz I have decided to undertake a survey of the literature as well as a study of the arguments, I have sympathy with them when they say, "The vast amount of writing on this topic by philosophers discourages one from undertaking anything like a 'literature survey'. Instead we shall set out what we take to be the range of possible arguments" (Harre and Krausz, 1996, p.160). Of course, if we add the literature provided by anthropologists to that provided by philosophers the literature survey becomes even more difficult.

In what follows, I shall try to focus on the turning points in the history of moral philosophy and the main figures whose works made major contributions to the debate.

Ancient times

There are historical records that in ancient times people were aware of the diversity of morals. For example, Hecataeus of Miletus (c. 550–480 BC) after his travels brought to Greece strange stories about the diversity of customs and described some of them in his *Travels around the World*. A generation or two later, Herodotus (485–430 BC), a Greek and the first Western historian, in his *History* (Book 3) describes how Darius, a king of ancient Persia, was surprised by the variety of customs in different cultures during his travels. For example, Darius noticed that the Callatians (a tribe of Indians) customarily ate the bodies of their dead fathers, while the Greeks instead burnt the bodies of their dead fathers. One day, Darius asked some Greeks who were at hand what he should pay them to eat the bodies of their fathers when they died. As

Darius expected, they were shocked and replied that no amount of money could persuade them to do such a terrible thing. Then Darius called in some Callatians and an interpreter so that the Greeks would understand what was said, and asked the Callatians what they would take to burn their dead fathers' bodies. This time the Callatians were horrified and told Darius not even to mention such a dreadful thing.

This story illustrates how different cultures may have radically different moral judgements or practices. Herodotus was completely aware that judgements on right and wrong differ from culture to culture. Having told the above story, Herodotus expresses his agreement with Pindar, who said, "Custom is the king o'er all". However, I think Herodotus wanted simply to illustrate the fact that in practice different nations have had confidence in their customs and have not been prepared to adopt any codes of practice other than their own. Of course, what their attitudes have been or should have been towards others who adopted different codes of practice is something else (on the relationship between relativism and tolerance see Chapter Three, Normative Relativism). So what Herodotus is suggesting cannot be understood to support the meta-ethical idea that different moral systems may be equally true. My reason for saying this is that Herodotus has narrated the story (and then expressed his agreement with Pindar) only as one of "very many proofs" for what he had argued earlier, namely that:

> if anyone, no matter who, were given the opportunity of choosing from amongst all the nations of the world the set of beliefs which he thought best, he would inevitably, after careful consideration of their relative merits, choose that of his own country. Everyone without exception believes his own native customs, and the religion he was brought up in, to be the best.[1]

Now let us see what reflections there were on moral diversity in ancient Greece. Of course, we have to remember that, as Henry Sidgwick suggested, in the pre-Socratic period of Greek philosophy philosophical inquiry was mainly concerned with the explanation of the external world; interest in human conduct occupied a secondary and subordinate place. Sidgwick writes:

---

1. The quotation and the story is from Herodotus, *The Histories*, III, Chapter 38, translated by Aubery de Selincourt, revised by A. R. Burn (Harmondsworth, Middlesex: Penguin Books, 1972). James Rachels in his *The Elements of Moral Philosophy*, pp. 15–7, David Wong (1996, pp. 443 and 444) and Pojman (1998, p. 20) have referred to this story.

It is in and through the teaching of Socrates that moral philosophy came to occupy in Greek thought the central position which it never afterwards lost: Socrates is the main starting-point from which all subsequent lines of Greek ethical thought diverge: speculations on conduct before Socrates are, to our apprehension, merely a kind of prelude to the real performance (Sidgwick, 1967, p. XVIII).

In any case, in ancient Greece, the Greeks, through trade, travel and war, were well acquainted with a wide variation in customs. At least some of the Sophists who were fully aware of disagreements in morals and customs among human beings developed a relativist view of morality. Wong describes their attention to the diversity of morals in this way:

In an ancient text (Dissoi Logoi or the Contrasting Arguments, Robinson, 1979) associated with the Sophists, it is pointed out that for the Lacedaemonians, it was fine for girls to exercise without tunics, and for children to learn music and letters, while for the Ionians, these things were foul (Wong, 1996, p. 443).

However, as far as I know this attention to cultural diversity was first philosophically formulated by Protagoras of Abdera (c. 490–c. 420 BC), a Greek sophist. Almost all books on relativism in general or on ethical relativism refer to him as a key figure standing at the beginning of the history of relativism. Even in encyclopaedias and textbooks we find that relativism is tied to his name. For example, in *Britannica* the history of ethical relativism is introduced in this way:

The view (ethical relativism) is as ancient as Protagoras, a leading Greek Sophist of the 5th century BC, and as modern as the scientific approaches of sociology and anthropology (*Britannica*, 1997).

Protagoras put forward a version of relativism in a treatise entitled *Truth*. None of Protagoras' writings have come down to us. There is an ancient report that the Athenians destroyed all the copies of Protagoras' book.[1] Protagoras' views are reported by others, chiefly by Plato in the dialogues *Theaetetus* and *Protagoras*. The most important source is *Theaetetus* (152a–179b and especially 170e–171c).

---

1.   See Margolis, 1989, p. 248.

Protagoras coined the phrase, "Man is the measure of all things". According to him, "the human being is the measure of all things, of those that are, that they are, and of those that are not, that they are not" (Plato, *Theaetetus*, 1973, 152a). He apparently meant that each individual person is the measure of how things are to that person: things are or are not (to me) as they appear to me to be or not be.[1] The question here is whether this was his view about all kinds of belief or understanding of the world or only about some special kind.

According to the *Theaetetus*, Protagoras was thinking of cases like this: to me the wind feels cold, while to you the wind feels warm.[2] For Protagoras the wind isn't (absolutely or in itself) either cold or warm; "cold" and "warm" are merely subjective states or feelings. To me the wind feels (or is) cold, and to you it feels (or is) warm, and beyond this there is no fact of the matter concerning the temperature of the wind.

Protagoras was apparently disputing the views of Parmenides (early fifth century BC) of Elea.[3] Parmenides' view was: what is, is; what is not, is not; and since the mere seeming of sense perception falls short of full being, it can have no reality at all. Against this, Protagoras wanted to defend the reality of sense perception. But according to Plato's account, Protagoras wanted to extend his defence of appearance beyond perceptual feelings to other kinds of appearance (seeming) such as beliefs about the world. If I believe that the world is a certain way, then that is how the world seems to me, and that is how the world is (to me). If you have a different belief, then that's how the world appears, and therefore how it is, to you. From this Protagoras concluded that error or false belief is absolutely impossible (ibid., 160c). Thus, presumably Protagoras wanted to defend the truth and the reality of perceptual understanding by considering appearance and seeming-to-human-beings as a sufficient ground for such a belief; then he generalized the point and considered the human being as the measure for all kinds of knowledge.

Thus, Protagoras' view also covers moral beliefs. The implication of his phrase "Man is the measure of all things" is that there are no universal standards of value, and all of our moral principles are created by us. Plato attributes to Protagoras the argument that human custom determines what is fine and ugly, just and unjust. Whatever is communally judged to be the case,

1. In my discussion about relativity of truth, Point a, I have explained why I believe that Protagoras' view was primarily individualistic, i.e. each individual person is the measure of all things.

2. *Theaetetus*, 152b.

3. See Wood, 1995, and Kahn, 1992, p. 459.

the argument goes, actually comes to be the case. Whereas the first part of *Theaetetus* was concerned with perceptions on an individual scale, the later part (*Theaetetus*, 172 a–b) presents a kind of ethical relativism on a social scale as well. What is just, courageous, and so on, is whatever conforms to public opinion in a given society.

In other words, Protagoras, as suggested by Richard Brandt, seems to have believed two things: a) moral views cannot be shown to be valid for everybody; b) people ought to follow the conventions of their own group. I think the most important aspect of Protagoras' position was the second and this suits better his phrase and arguments. The first position can act as a basis for the second. Protagoras, indeed, presented himself as a teacher of human virtue, which to him was an ability to reason consciously about practical matters, "beginning from and staying within the limits of the conventional norms of the particular city one lives in".[1] However, Brandt believes that the first part of Protagoras' view is theoretically more interesting and important than the second. So he applies the term "ethical relativism" to any theory that agrees with his sharpened form of the first part of Protagoras' view. Brandt restates the first part in this way: "There are conflicting ethical opinions that are equally valid".[2]

On the other hand, in ancient Greece, while many had been moved by diversity of customs and morals to adopt moral relativism, there were others who seriously doubted the soundness of the argument from diversity for relativism. As Socrates pointed out, we have reason to listen only to the wise among us (*Crito*, 44CD). Socrates actually tried to develop an ethical system that was based on reason itself, and not on what was traditionally approved of. It has been suggested (e.g. Cooper, 1992, pp. 464 and 465) that this rationalist theory of ethics became the dominant moral theory in the Greek tradition and was adopted later by Plato, Aristotle and the Stoics.

As I will explain later (first argument for meta-ethical relativism: the discussion about the relativity of truth), Plato himself attempted to refute

---

1. The quotation is taken from Cooper, 1992, p. 463.
2. Brandt, 1970, p. 336. Brandt also maintains that Protagoras' idea could not be completely new. He says: "Something like this combination of propositions probably had been thought of before his time. Primitive people are well aware that different social groups have different standards, and at least sometimes doubt whether their set of standards can really be shown to be superior to others. Moreover, probably in many groups it has been thought that a person who conforms conscientiously to the standards of his own group deserves respect" (ibid., p. 335).

relativism. Plato argued that Protagoras' relativism is necessarily false, because it refutes itself, since, according to Protagoras, those who deny relativism must also be right. But if the denial of relativism is true then relativism must be wrong (see *Theaetetus*, 161c–162a).

The modern age

Montaigne

Michel de Montaigne (1533–1592), the French philosopher, set forth the Renaissance version of Greek scepticism. Awareness of the variety of codes and practices throughout the world gave Montaigne doubts about the existence of universal or absolute moral values. As Schneewind (1996, p. 154) suggested, these doubts were debated during the seventeenth and eighteenth centuries and then revived "with great force and depth" by Nietzsche. It has been argued (Popkin, 1996, p. 506) that Montaigne's scepticism greatly influenced European thinkers by undermining their trust in previous theories and urged them to find new grounds for their ideas and that "his acceptance of religion based on custom and faith provided a way of life with total scepticism".

Montaigne believed that data from explorers about diversity of customs and morals reinforced the cultural and ethical relativism of the ancient sceptics. He prepared a list of strange customs, such as male prostitution, cannibalism, women combatants and the killing of one's father at a certain age as an act of piety, and quoted from Herodotus the story about Darius' experiment with the Greeks and Callatians. He also noted disagreements between Scholastics, Platonists and Renaissance Naturalists on almost everything, and between scientists such as Copernicus and Paracelsus. Montaigne said:

> Each man calls barbarism whatever is not his practice . . . for we have no other criterion of reason than the example and idea of the opinions and customs of the country we live in (Cited from Geertz, 1988, p. 14).

Like the sceptics, Montaigne believed that our perceptual and rational understandings are not reliable. Trying to know reality is like trying to clutch water. One has to suspend judgement on all theories that go beyond experience and follow the dictates of nature and the rules and customs of one's own society. Montaigne also insisted on the role of religion, advocating that one should keep the religion in which one was born and accept only the revealed principles.

In addition to his argument from the diversity of morals and customs, traces of a functionalist argument for relativism can be found in Montaigne's works. He sometimes makes the argument for relativism from the fact that customary ethical beliefs are functionally necessary for that society, so those beliefs are true for that society and not for others. This type of argument will be discussed in more detail later among arguments for meta-ethical relativism.

Hume

It has been suggested (Fieser, 1996) that in Hume's 1751 essay, "A Dialogue", the first systematic defence of moral relativism is presented. Of course, this does not mean that Hume himself was a relativist, but that Hume has expressed the relativist argument on behalf of one party of the dialogue. The fictitious dialogue is between the narrator and his friend, Palamedes. Palamedes has travelled everywhere and studied everything.

Palamedes begins the conversation by discussing several moral customs of a particular society (including infanticide and euthanasia) that are against the moral customs of his own day. Like Protagoras, Palamedes argues that fashion, custom and law are the chief foundation of all moral determinations. The narrator criticizes Palamedes by arguing that all moral behaviour is founded on four universal principles: (1) usefulness to society, (2) usefulness to the agent, (3) pleasantness to society and (4) pleasantness to the agent. For example, justice is socially useful, having good sense is useful to the agent, wit is pleasing to society and dignity is pleasing to the agent. If the conduct of a society is allowed to be natural and spontaneous, then moral considerations will be universally based on these four standards.

Thus, according to the narrator, morality is not as relative as Palamedes presumes. Palamedes agrees that these four principles are widely adopted in societies where value systems develop naturally. However, no universal standard of morality will apply to a vast number of cultures, which are developed artificially, that is, where value systems are imposed by religious or philosophical authorities. The narrator accepts Palamedes' point and the dialogue ends in agreement.

A study of "A Dialogue" shows, I think, that the narrator who presumably better represents Hume's position, denies relativism and furthermore emphasizes some actual common moral beliefs, and Palamedes presents merely *a diversity thesis* rather than relativism. For example the narrator says:

> I shall conclude this long discourse with observing that different customs and situations vary not the original ideas of merit however they may, some consequences in any very essential point, and prevail chiefly with regard to young men who can aspire to the agreeable qualities ... "What you insist on", replied Palamedes, "may have some foundation" (Hume, 1751, p. 172).

More clearly he later says:

> You see then, continued I, that the principles upon which men reason in morals are always the same; though the conclusions which they draw are often very different (ibid.., p. 167).

In general, Hume views morality as an entirely human affair founded on human nature and the circumstances of human life. Hume also believes that human nature is the same in all individuals and that human beings have the same feelings wherever they are. Therefore, he seems to believe in a kind of absolute moral values.[1]

Nietzsche

One of the important figures in the history of morality in general and moral relativism in particular is Nietzsche (1844–1900). Nietzsche believed that there is no "truth" in a correspondence sense, and indeed no "true world of being". We have no certain or absolute "knowledge" even of ourselves.[2] Nietzsche introduced truth as "a mobile army of metaphors, metonyms, and anthropomorphisms, in short a sum of human relations, which have been enhanced, transposed, and embellished poetically and rhetorically and which after long use seem firm, canonical, and obligatory to a people."[3]

Having mentioned that scepticism and relativism were revived with great force and depth by the brilliant and unsettling attacks of Nietzsche against any

---

1. For example, see Norton, 1996, pp. 342–7, and Schneewind, 1992, pp. 507 and 508.
2. For example, see Schacht, 1996, p. 534, and Schacht, 1992, pp. 520–2.
3. Nietzsche, "On Truth and Lie in an Extra-Moral Sense", in *The Viking Portable Nietzsche*, edited and translated by Walter Kaufmann, pp. 46–7, as cited in Rorty, p. 46.

kind of moral principles that could bind universally on human beings, Schneewind writes:

> In *The Genealogy of Morals* (1887) and other works Nietzsche did not try to refute Kantian and utilitarian theories. Instead he exposed what he took to be the psychological forces leading people to assert such views. In his view the struggle for mastery, and envy and resentment of those who achieved it, were the roots of modern morality. Not even abstract claims to rationality escaped Nietzsche's unmasking: they too, he held, are fronts behind which nothing but the struggle for power is hidden. There is no impersonal guide to action: all one can do is decide what sort of person one proposes to be, and strive to be so (Schneewind, 1996, p. 154).

Briefly, Nietzsche argued that there is nothing beyond this world or within ourselves from which we could drive universally valid moral principles. Instead, there are actual moralities that must be assessed in accordance with their functions and in terms of their "value of life". Every actual morality has emerged under various conditions and in response to specific psychological and social needs of human beings in the course of history.

Contemporary times

Like all other periods of human thought, absolutism has dominated this age. Bunting (1996) tells us that objectivism (for Bunting, objectivism is the opposite to relativism) is an influential tradition that covered most of the rationalist and naturalist standpoints, which, in turn, have dominated nineteenth- and twentieth-century moral philosophy. Even relativists themselves usually agree that objectivism is firmly rooted in common sense.[1]

In contemporary thought, moral relativism is notably founded on sociological observations of diversities and has been strongly defended by social scientists. The rise of modern anthropology encouraged people like William Graham Sumner, Ruth Benedict and Edward Westermarck to reopen the old relativistic question of whether there is some absolute or objective

---

1. I said "usually" because I take Gilbert Harman as an exception, since he holds that relativism is a common-sense view.

moral knowledge.[1] These three are the most important contemporary anthropologists who believed in a form of ethical relativism but the list does not stop here. I should like here to cite an informative passage from Whitaker in *Encyclopedia of Social and Cultural Anthropology* on the relationship between ethical relativism and anthropology:

> This kind of relativism was most popular, however, in the 1930s in both British social anthropology and American cultural anthropology. British anthropology's various forms of functionalism, for example, seemed to suggest that any given society's ethical practices were the result of long-standing structural or practical development, served complex and subtle purposes, and thus were not to be tampered with. Similarly, in the United States, Boas (1911), and his student Benedict (1934), and Herskovits (1972), held a diffusionist view of cultural development which tended to undercut universalist claims, and made ethical relativism seem empirically obvious, methodologically necessary (to avoid ethnocentrism), and obviously just (Whitaker, 1997, p. 479).

Kurt Vonnegut in his novel *Slaughterhouse Five* describes the relativistic atmosphere of teaching anthropology in the mid-twentieth century in an academic institute thus:

> I think of my education sometimes. I went to the University of Chicago for a while after the Second World War. I was a student in the department of anthropology. They taught me that nobody was ridiculous or bad or disgusting. Shortly before my father died he said to me, "You never wrote a story with a villain in it." I told him that was one of the things I learned in school after the war (cited in Schweder, 1989, p. 99).

The role of anthropology in promoting ethical relativism has been emphasized by Bernard Williams as well. He introduces ethical relativism as

---

1. Diversity of morals has always been a topic of profound interest to anthropologists. As Lukes's study shows, it was much discussed in the late nineteenth and early twentieth centuries by Wilhelm Wundt, Lucien Levy-Bruhl, W. G. Sumner, L. T. Hobhouse, Edward Westermarck and Morris Ginsberg, and it is still now and then addressed by social anthropologists and some sociologists. Lukes adds that this topic somehow has lost its central position in systematic social inquiry, see Lukes, 1991, p. 10.

"the anthropologist's heresy, possibly the most absurd view to have been advanced in moral philosophy" (Williams, 1972, p. 20).

On the other hand, Geertz, one of the great anthropologists, in his "Anti Anti Relativism", an essay written not to defend relativism, but to attack anti-relativism, rejects the idea that anthropology or anthropologists have promoted relativism. He writes:

The notion that it was Boas, Benedict and Melville Herskovits, with a European assist from Westermarck, who infected our field with the relativist virus, and Kroeber, Kluckhohn, and Redfield, with a similar assist from Lévi-Strauss, who have laboured to rid us of it, is but another of the myths that bedevil this whole discussion (Geertz, 1988, p. 14).

Geertz adds that Montaigne, for example, could draw relativistic conclusions from the information that he heard about diversity of ways of life; Montaigne did not have to read *Patterns of Culture* (by Benedict).

I believe it is true that relativism was not a necessary product of modern anthropology. There were in fact some anthropologists who were not relativists. There have always been anthropologists who have tried to look beyond the differences and search for significant or deeper or more abstract points of similarity. There have also been developmentalist anthropologists who have tried to find within the diversity a continuous process of growth. To them, diversity results from a battle between reason and superstition or between education and ignorance. I also believe that relativism did not depend on modern anthropology, since there were some relativists who were not anthropologists or whose relativism was not based on anthropological findings. However, it cannot be denied that the relativistic approach has been the popular current in modern anthropology, and that data collected by anthropologists *actually*, and not necessarily *justifiably*, served as a ground for many modern versions of ethical relativism. I trust that the present work supports both claims clearly.

William Graham Sumner, the early twentieth-century anthropologist wrote an influential book, *Folkways* (1906). Before I explain his position, we should first note that there are two ways to approach morality: as *de facto morality* (actual morality) or as *ideal morality*. Moral relativists and particularly social scientists and anthropologists usually consider only *de facto morality*. Of course, there is a wide range of diversity in *de facto morality*.

Sumner argued that the de facto morality is the only one that counts. When we look at how people actually behave, he continued, it is clear that morality is grounded in a culture's folk traditions; moral values are therefore relative, since folk traditions differ from culture to culture. Sumner writes:

The "right" way is the way which the ancestors used and which has been handed down. The tradition is its own warrant. It is not held subject to verification by experience. The notion of right is in the folkways. It is not outside of them, of independent origin, and brought to test them. In the folkways, whatever is, is right. This is because they are traditional, and therefore contain in themselves the authority of the ancestral ghosts. When we come to the folkways we are at the end of our analysis (Sumner, 1906, p. 28).

Sumner also developed a functionalist version of meta-ethical relativism. In general, functionalist argument has had its greatest acceptance among anthropologists of the twentieth century who have emphasized the importance of studying societies as organic wholes of which the parts are functionally interdependent.[1]

The American anthropologist Benedict (1887–1948), in her *Patterns of Culture* (1934), argued that different cultures are organized around different and incommensurable values, which depend on different histories and environments of different cultures. She suggested, for example, that the differing and even conflicting moral beliefs and behaviour of the North American Indian Kwakiutl, Pueblo and Dobu cultures provided sufficient standards for each culture so that their members could correctly evaluate their own deeds. Benedict and many other anthropologists were really against ethnocentrism and monopoly in cultural affairs. She wrote:

Most of the simpler cultures did not gain the wide currency of the one which, out of our experience, we identify with human nature, but this was for various historical reasons, and certainly not for any that gives us as its carriers a monopoly of social good or social sanity. Modern civilization, from this point of view, becomes not a necessary pinnacle of human achievement but one entry in a long series of possible adjustments (cited from Pojman, 1998, p. 34).

Benedict's *Patterns of Culture* and Sumner's *Folkways* are considered (e.g. in Rachels, 1993) as two important classic defences of Cultural Relativism. Rachels introduces Sumner as *the great pioneering sociologist*.

Edward Westermarck (1862–1939), the Finnish anthropologist and

---

1. As mentioned earlier, we will discuss this type of argument along with other arguments for meta-ethical relativism in the next chapter.

philosopher, spent his life studying the mores and moral beliefs of cultures. Westermarck was a professor of sociology in the University of London and a professor of philosophy at the Academy of Abo (Finland). Some writers, such as Bunting (1996), believe that twentieth-century interest in relativism can be traced to his impressive, though greatly neglected, empirical and philosophical work. His main works are *The Origin and Development of the Moral Ideas* (2 volumes, 1906–1908) and *Ethical Relativity* (1932).

We can somewhat understand the intellectual atmosphere of the twentieth century, at least in Finland after his first work, by reflecting on Westermarck's preface to *Ethical Relativity*. He writes:

> It appears to me that the present publication of a book in defence of ethical subjectivism and relativity is the more timely, as the large bulk of ethical literature which has been produced in this country [Finland] since the beginning of the century has championed the opposite cause (Westermarck, 1932, p. xviii).

Unlike Sumner, Westermarck admitted that cultural diversity in itself does not prove ethical relativism. He frequently asserted that it was not moral diversity that convinced him of the truth of relativism. However, he contended that there are so many comprehensive fundamental differences that they constitute a strong presumption in favour of relativism. Westermarck, indeed, justified his relativism mainly by his emphasis on the fundamental role of the emotions in moral life, which, in his view, undermines any belief in objective moral truth. Westermarck is an outstanding figure among those relativists who believed that moral expressions always describe the attitudes of the speaker himself or his group.[1]

In his works, Westermarck attacks the idea that moral principles express objective values. In defending moral relativism, he argues that moral judgements are based on emotional grounds and not intellectual ones. In his preface to *Ethical Relativity*, preserving mainly his ideas in *The Origins and*

---

1. Charles L. Stevenson describes different views among relativists and the position of Westermarck in this way: "one might expect them to conclude that the terms always describe the attitudes of the speaker or of some group by whom the speaker is influenced, and that is in fact the emphasis in Westermarck's relativism; but perhaps the other relativists consider such uses, though frequent, to be provincial, the provinciality being like that of a physicist who supposes that he must limit himself to frames of reference involving the earth or the sun." (Charles L. Stevenson, 1967, p. 77).

Development of the Moral Ideas, Westermarck explains his conclusion as follows:

> I arrived at the conclusion that moral judgments are ultimately based on emotions, the moral concepts being generalizations of emotional tendencies; although I recognize at the same time the enormous influence that intellectual considerations exercise upon those judgments, in the first place through the cognitions by which the moral emotions are determined (Westermarck, 1932, p. xvii).

As the above text indicates, this emotivist position of Westermarck does not mean that he did not consider any role for reason or rational method. Westermarck thought that in ethics, as in science, a rational method for answering questions is available.[1] On the other hand, he believed that "x is wrong" means "I have a tendency to feel impartial resentment towards people who do things like x". Thus, as Brandt (1970, p. 341) has suggested, given his premises, it is consistent for Westermarck to be a relativist, that is, to maintain that conflicting ethical statements are sometimes both "valid", because he thinks that, owing to different conditions in their lives, such as their upbringing and education, people may have different tendencies in their feelings towards those "who do things like x". Westermarck considers himself able to identify the relevant life conditions under which both statements can be "valid". Thus, a rational method can be applied to find out the validity of a given position, but the validity itself is not based on an independent reality.

To discover changes in the debate on moral relativism before and after Westermarck and to realize the role of Westermarck in the flourishing of moral relativism in the second half of the twentieth century, one has to consider that, as in Bunting's (1996, p. 73) formulation, traditional moral relativism normally involved these ideas:

1. different societies hold incompatible basic moral principles;
2. each of these incompatible principles is in some sense correct;
3. morality has its foundations in varying human affective dispositions;
4. therefore, there is no single true morality.

---

1. Unlike Brandt (1970, p. 341), which classifies Westermarck's position as a naturalistic one, I think the mere recognition of the role of rational method in morality does not make a position a naturalistic one. I will make it clearer in the following paragraphs.

Bunting adds that Westermarck drew the attention of moral philosophers to two important points: the role of truth for relativism and the role of emotions in morality. The central purpose of his moral theory was to undermine the various forms of objectivism, both naturalist and rationalist, that dominated late nineteenth-century ethics and to put in their place a descriptive-explanatory relativism that denied the relevance of truth to morality and stressed the role of the emotions in the moral life. In attempting this project, he sketched frameworks within which much recent relativist thought has operated.

In fact, there are two interpretations of Westermarck's opinion about the truth of moral statements. According to one interpretation, Westermarck held that all moral statements are false. Some recent moral philosophers have adopted the same view, which is now usually known as "error theory". For example, J. L. Mackie in *Ethics: Inventing Right and Wrong* (1977) argues for the subjectivity of values. He holds that moral judgements purport to be about objective matters, but they are really subjective. As we shall see later, this actually presents a subjectivist version of meta-ethical relativism.

According to the other interpretation which is inspired by his overemphasis on the role of emotions, Westermarck held that truth and falsity are inapplicable to moral statements. Bunting (1996, p. 75) calls the second view "irrealism". I personally think that "non-cognitivism" suits better. Indeed, it seems incomplete to define "irrealism" simply as a position that holds that moral statements have no truth value. (Both views will be studied later when I discuss the subjectivist and the non-cognitivist argument for meta-ethical relativism.)

In any case, Westermarck's view seems ambiguous. Nielson, a sympathetic commentator who has presented twelve sub-interpretations of Westermarck's view, says: "his account is just too indeterminate, too imprecise, and too subject to various readings to carry the day for ethical scepticism" (Nielson, 1982, p. 28, as cited in Bunting, 1996, p. 77).

After Westermarck some moral philosophers and particularly some moral relativists focused mainly on the issue of moral truth and some others focused on the issue of emotions. There will be a discussion of both issues later, but here, just to see the historical importance of the issues of truth and emotions for late twentieth-century moral philosophy, let us glance at these two trends.

Moral relativists such as P. Foot in "Moral Relativism" (1982) and R. Arrington in "A Defense of Ethical Relativism" (1983) and *Rationalism, Realism and Relativism* (1989) have tried to reintroduce the Protagorean idea of relative truth.[1] They think that Protagorean relativism has never been given a fair hearing. Right and wrong might be contradictory, but right for one society is not in contradiction with wrong for another one. They think that people like Socrates criticized relativism after adding some elements of absolutism to it. Foot says:

> If we are talking of the views of another society we shall speak of what is true by their standards, without the slightest thought that our standards are "correct". If the ancient Mexican admired the looks of someone whose head had been flattened, a proposition about this admiration may have been true as spoken by them, though it is false as spoken by us (Foot, 1982, p. 155).

Arrington says:

> The whole point of the relativist position is that we cannot assert that a moral judgment is true simpliciter; we can only assert that a judgment is true for a particular person or social group (Arrington, 1983, p. 228).

On the other hand, there have been some ethical relativists who focused on the role of emotions rather than on the role of truth in the debate on ethical relativism. These people were impressed by the claim that an adequate relativism has to be grounded in a theory of human dispositions. For example, G. Harman in "Moral Relativism Defended" (1975), *The Nature of Morality* (1977), "Relativistic Ethics: Morality as Politics" (1978), "What Is Moral Relativism?" (1978) and *Moral Relativism and Moral Objectivity* (1996) and B. Williams in "The Truth in Relativism" (1974–1975) have tried to provide an account of morality based on human emotions.

A central aspect of Harman's ethical theory is his internalism. Harman believes that moral requirements, unlike legal requirements, are binding only after the moral agent finds them acceptable. One is required to act according to moral rules only if one has compelling reasons for acting according to them. We can ask people to do something only if they have motivating attitudes towards that act that are the same as ours. Harman believes that this is why it is odd and "inappropriate" to say to Hitler, "You ought not to do that".

---

1. "Moral Relativism" by Foot has been considered as one of the most influential works on ethical relativism. For example, see Stewart and Thomson, 1991.

Harman also believes morality to be based on agreement, at least implicitly. Morality has no other ground according to which people can settle their moral debates. Harman combines internalism and conventionalism (or contractualism) to reconstruct a moderate version of ethical relativism that can avoid classic objections. (We will study Harman's view in detail later in Chapter Four, "Gilbert Harman and Ethical Relativism".)

The other theory in contemporary ethical philosophy that relates to our discussion about ethical relativism is "existentialism", developed by some Continental philosophers who believed that morality rests on nothing but the totally free decision of each individual. For example, Jean Paul-Sartre (1905–1980) – mainly in *Existentialism and Humanism* (1946) – maintained that nothing general could be said about morality.[1]

Sartre believes that there is no coherent reality outside. He speaks of "nausea", our anxiety about the *incoherence* of reality. For him, any belief in coherent reality such as the belief in the unity of God's creation and his lordship over history is wrong. Sartre does not admit any *generally* valid principles or any *universal* laws. Accordingly, every person must make a purely personal decision about morality and then live according to his decision. Every day or probably every moment we have to decide: we may reaffirm our previous choice or make a new decision. In other words, "we have no excuse behind us and no justification before us". Thus, in Sartre's view, to act morally simply means to have "good faith", that is, to act according to the morality one has adopted, to be far from hypocrisy.[2]

It seems clear how this kind of approach to ethics leads to ethical relativism. When morality is seen just as good faith in what one has freely chosen then one could justifiably perform various different actions, provided that one performs them in good faith. In fact, Sartre has offered another kind of relativism – later on modified by himself. In *Existentialism and Humanism,* Sartre refers to a dilemma mentioned by one of his pupils. Sartre was asked by his pupil to advise on what to do in respect of two conflicting obligations: his pupil wanted to know whether to join the Free French Forces or to stay near his mother and help her. Sartre's response was, "You are free, therefore choose – that is to say, invent. No rule of general morality can show you what to do" [Sartre, 1970 (1948), p. 38] Indeed, what Sartre suggested was that one

---

1. The French edition of this book was first published in 1946. The first English edition was published in 1948. This book is taken (McNaughton, 1998, p. 16) as a classic statement of existentialism.

2. See Schneewind, 1996, p. 155; McNaughton, 1998, p. 135; Schroder, 1992, pp. 532 and 533, and Fletcher, 1966, pp. 24 and 25.

should not look for universal principles in such dilemmas, since each case is unique.

Another important contemporary trend in ethics, which has to be noted in our discussion about the history of ethical relativism, is called "situation ethics". This view was very influential in the first half of the twentieth century. According to Kockelman (1992, p. 524), the origin of this view and even its name go back to Eberhard Grisebach's book *Gegenwart: eine kritische Ethik* (1928).[1] In this book he argued that a religious ethics cannot allow the existence of universally valid principles, laws, norms and rules. Most of the people who have supported situation ethics have been Christian philosophers.

The advocates of situation ethics believe that each moral problem is unique. Only the person who is engaged in the problem can solve the problem. Because of their religious background, situation ethicists allow formation of formal norms, such as "Love thy neighbour", but they believe that these formal norms do not have any real meaning until one becomes engaged in unique situations. Situation ethics is very well summed up by Billington. He writes:

> Situation ethics, then, means that the moral agent does not engage in debate on moral issues with his options already determined; it may be that these options are not available. He will instead approach these issues pragmatically, looking for the best option on the table. Faced with the same problem in different circumstances, he may well reach a different conclusion (Billington, 1993, p. 39).

It has been suggested (Unerman, 1996) that situation ethics is another form of ethical relativism, since it holds that even within one society at one point in time, there may be no absolute right or wrong behaviour, as the "rightness" or "wrongness" of a particular behaviour depends upon the particular circumstances (or situation) facing the person making the decision. Even if a person holds a belief in the absolute right or wrong of a particular action, the circumstances he is facing may, in practice, preclude the action he considers right or make the action he considers wrong unavoidable. We will see later

---

1. The title in Germany means: *The Present Time: A Critical Ethics*. For a fairly comprehensive list of those who have maintained a situationist approach to ethics, see Fletcher, 1966, pp. 34 and 35. Of course, since situation ethics is mainly a method (and not a substantive ethics) in ethical enquiry, they have not necessarily had similar theological or philosophical systems.

whether situation ethics has to be construed as a form of ethical relativism or not (the ninth argument for meta-ethical relativism).

Postmodernism

Postmodernism is not a single theory. It is, indeed, a cluster of reactions to modern philosophy and its presuppositions. It is difficult to find any agreement among postmodernists on any substantive doctrine. It has been suggested that the following elements are included in what is usually thought of as postmodernism: anti-essentialism, anti-foundationalism, anti-realism, rejection of the picture of knowledge as accurate representation, rejection of truth as correspondence to reality and rejection of principles, distinctions and categories that are thought to be unconditionally binding for all times, persons and places.[1]

Paul Healas, the editor of *Religion, Modernity and Postmodernity* (1998), draws our attention to James Beckford's characterization of postmodernism. Here, I mention two characteristics only, which are very relevant to our discussion: "a refusal to regard positivistic, rationalistic, instrumental criteria as the sole or exclusive standard of worthwhile knowledge" and "a willingness to abandon the search for overarching or triumphalist myths, narratives or frameworks of knowledge".[2]

Of course, these two characteristics do not necessarily lead to the denial of universal values, since they, indeed, focus on the process of discovering reality and not reality itself. In other words, these claims are compatible with the supposition that there are universal or absolute values that are not understandable and therefore there is no single method or standard for knowledge.

However, it seems that there is still more in the concept of postmodernism that suits relativism. I shall just mention one more aspect of postmodernist thought that supports relativism. From a postmodernist perspective, the characteristics required for something to be considered "good" are socially constructed and therefore what is considered good in one society may not be

---

1. See, for example, *The Cambridge Dictionary of Philosophy* edited by Robert Audi, p.634.

2. Healas, 1998, p. 23, cites from James Beckford, "Religion, Modernity and Postmodernity", *Religion: Contemporary Issues*, edited by B. R. Wilson (London: Bellew, 1992), pp. 11–27.

considered good in another society.[1] Similarly, Neimark argues that "what constitutes ethical behaviour at any point in time – like knowledge more generally – is socially constructed; it is a product of time and place". (Neimark,1995, p. 93). Thus, it seems that postmodernism has a close relationship to relativism and has to support it.

Regarding applied ethics, a postmodern position implies that the morality regarding items such as pollution, employee welfare and community involvement by business is socially constructed, and may be different in different societies and at different times. There will be a separate discussion of the social construction of morals later on.

Regarding religion, a postmodern position is suggested (Healas, 1998) to require that religion should be associated with forms of pragmatism and relativism. Healas says:

> Instead of authoritative narratives or other forms of knowledge providing truth, "truth" is seen in terms of "what works for me". People have what they *take* to be "spiritual" experiences without having to hold religious *beliefs* . . . And this results in a form of relativism: religion beyond belief is religion where "truth" is relative to what one takes to be involved in satisfying one's requirements (Healas, 1998, p. 5).

I think postmodernism has not yet found its way into moral philosophy. It seems that postmodernism is still in need of philosophical reflection to be in a position to be seen as a single consistent philosophical argument for any philosophical claim, such as ethical relativism. I have sympathy with Blackburn when he says, "Much postmodernist thought may be regarded as a somewhat abandoned celebration of relativism" (Blackburn, 1994, p. 326). It seems to me that postmodernism would be better treated if considered as a second-order theory about the socio-epistemological view of the world at the end of the second millennium. To be able to evaluate ethical implications of postmodernism and argue from it for ethical relativism, one has to evaluate separately those views that are incorporated in postmodernism, such as anti-realism.

But in general, an overall study of the literature on ethical relativism shows that, unlike in the late nineteenth century and the early twentieth, interest in

---

1. See Unerman, 1996, and Arrington & Francis, 1993. Blackburn says: "Much postmodernist thought may be regarded as a somewhat abandoned celebration of relativism." (Blackburn, 1994, p. 326).

ethical relativism has recently declined. Even the most important relativist thinkers of our time, such as Gilbert Harman and David Wong, who have tried to reconstruct ethical relativism, have developed subtle or moderate forms of relativism to meet standard objections to relativism. Their relativism strictly dismisses the idea that in morality *anything goes*. They both believe that morality is subject to some rational constraints; there are good and bad arguments for the moral positions people take. They both are also cognitivists, since they accept that moral claims have truth values. Even some of their critics (e.g. Arrington, 1989) have doubted whether their theories are really relativistic in a proper sense.

I think the rational explanation of this phenomenon would be found in the fact that none of the classic forms of ethical relativism has survived criticisms. I also think that the psychological explanation of this phenomenon could be that moral philosophers who were considerably shocked by mass information provided by anthropologists in the late nineteenth and early twentieth centuries gradually regained their confidence and once again realized that philosophical problems can be settled only with the application of the rational method. The social atmosphere of the mid-twentieth century onwards also has been influential.

A typical sociological approach to the above phenomenon can be found in *Encyclopedia of Social and Cultural Anthropology* (1997). Whitaker asserts there that support for ethical relativism began to fall during and after World War II for reasons such as: 1) the inadequacies of applying relativist tolerance to that period's bloodstained ideologies and 2) the realization that "ethical relativism, and the 'don't touch' approach to intercultural contact it seemed to approve, was merely a Western ideology that played into the hands of colonial masters by justifying their repressive status quo" (Whitaker, 1997, pp. 479 and 480).

In the next chapter, I will first explain different types of ethical relativism and then successively study the arguments and counter-arguments for each type. Then I shall try to explain the absolutist approach to the issue of ethical relativism; and since moral diversity and moral disagreements have always been seen as evidence, or for some relativists as a reason, for ethical relativism, there will be a discussion about how absolutists deal with the existence of moral diversity and disagreements.

CHAPTER THREE

Ethical Relativism Versus Ethical Absolutism

Types of ethical relativism and the arguments for and against

There are three types of moral relativism:[1]

1. The view that there are *substantially* (or *fundamentally*) different moral codes among societies or individuals, which cannot be explained by absolutists.[2] This is called *descriptive relativism*. In its strongest form it asserts that all basic moral values do vary from individual to individual, or from society to society. In its moderate form it asserts that at least some basic moral values vary. Descriptive relativists invoke different examples. Whether these examples really support their claim will be discussed later on. For example, Eskimos allow their old parents to die by starvation, whereas we believe that this is morally wrong. Similarly, there is a tribe in Melanesia, as described by Ruth Benedict in her *Patterns of Culture*, who believe in the wrongness of co-operation and kindness, whereas we see them as virtues. This diversity can also be found in a single society at different times. For example, as Pojman (1998, p. 40) suggested, one hundred years ago the majority of people in the southern United States viewed slavery as morally right, whereas they now take it to be wrong.

2. The view that among those substantially different moral codes there is no single true or most justified ethical code. All those substantially

---

1. I think that these three stand in a hierarchical order and, indeed, they are three stages or levels of ethical relativism. The first is the lowest or minimum.

2. Fundamental differences are those differences that are not results of different applications of common values or principles. In other words, "A fundamental difference of moralities is one in which two cultures accept two contrary principles of conduct." (Pojman, 1990, p. 24).

different moral codes are true (according to the stronger version) or at least there can be a plurality of true or best justified codes (according to the more moderate version). Wong writes:

> Radical relativists hold that any morality is as true or as justified as any other. Moderate relativists, such as Foot (1978), Walzer and Wong (1984), deny that there is any single true morality but also hold that some moralities are truer or more justified than others (Wong, 1998, p. 541).

This is called "meta-ethical relativism".[1]

3. The view that it is morally wrong to pass ethical judgement on the behaviour and practices of another individual, group or society with a substantially different moral code that is, or can be, as true or justified as one's own, let alone to try to make that other individual, group or society conform to one's code or intervene in their affairs on the basis of such ethical judgements. This is called "normative relativism".

As described above, descriptive relativism means that there are *substantially* (or *fundamentally*) different moral codes among societies or individuals. Some people call this view "cultural relativism", but I think the expression

---

1. David Wong in his "Moral Relativism" (in *An Encyclopaedia of Ethics*, 1992) uses the term "epistemological relativism", but elsewhere he says: "Moral relativism often takes the form of a denial that any single moral code has universal validity, and an assertion that moral justifiability and truth, if there are any, are in some way relative to factors that are culturally and historically contingent. This is called *meta-ethical relativism*, because it is about the relativity of moral truth and justifiability."(Wong, 1996, p. 442).

    It seems to me that in "Moral Relativism" (in *Routledge Encyclopedia of Philosophy*, 1998), Wong distinguishes between meta-ethical relativism and epistemological relativism. He seems to take the latter as one of the proposed bases or foundations of meta-ethical relativism. Having spoken about those relativists who are unimpressed with the analogy of moral disagreements with disagreements in sciences and who reject absolute truth, Wong says: "This defence of meta-ethical relativism amounts to founding it upon a comprehensive *epistemological relativism* that expresses scepticism about the meaningfulness of talking about truth defined independently of the theories and justificatory practices of particular communities of discourse." (1998, p. 540). Therefore, since there are some people who believe that there is no single true morality but are not sceptical about moral truths, I think it is better to call the second type of ethical relativism meta-ethical relativism and not epistemological relativism.

"descriptive relativism" is more suitable, since it can more appropriately include both individual and social scales (i.e. cultural relativism is better used only for descriptive relativism on a social scale) and that it clearly indicates that there is nothing evaluative or normative in this view (i.e. the term "descriptive" clearly and more easily indicates that this view is just a report about *de facto* morality and has nothing to do with the nature of morality).

In contrast, Rachels (1993, p. 18) takes *cultural relativism* as a meta-ethical theory which challenges the objectivity and universality of moral truth: there are only various cultural codes and our own code is merely one among many. He tries to analyse cultural relativism in order to assess its constituents. He argues that, on analysis, some parts of the theory turn out to be correct, whereas others seem to be mistaken. Rachels mentions six propositions that clearly, as I said earlier, include all three types of moral relativism.[1]

On the other hand, Pojman identifies *cultural relativism* with the mere diversity thesis that moral rules differ from society to society, an idea that both ethical relativists and non-relativists typically accept.[2] In this way, unlike "descriptive relativism", "cultural relativism" does not depend on the belief in the existence of *fundamental* differences. Further, Pojman distinguishes between cultural relativism and ethical relativism.[3] He takes cultural relativism as a descriptive thesis, whereas ethical relativism is a *normative* thesis that grants ultimate validity to diverse ethical codes or rules.

I suggest that both Rachels's and Pojman's descriptions are confusing. To have a clear understanding of different positions and concepts, we have to distinguish between four positions:

---

1. Those six propositions are:
   a) Different societies have different moral codes.
   b) There is no objective standard that can be used to judge one societal code better than another.
   c) The moral code of our own society has no special status; it is merely one among many.
   d) There is no "universal truth" in ethics, that is, there are no moral truths that hold for all peoples at all times.
   e) The moral code of a society determines what is right within that society; that is, if the moral code of a society says that a certain action is right, then that action *is* right, at least within that society.
   f) It is mere arrogance for us to try to judge the conduct of other peoples. We should adopt an attitude of tolerance toward the practices of other cultures.
2. See Pojman, 1996, p. 690.
3. See Pojman, 1996 and 1998, pp. 16, 38 and 39.

1. The belief in the mere existence of moral differences, which is acceptable to both relativists and non-relativists. This is not a kind of relativism at all and I see no need to give it a certain name here. However, it can be called "moral diversity", if necessary.

2. The belief in the existence of *fundamentally* different moral rules, which may presumably be accepted by all relativists and possibly even by some non-relativists. This view can be called "descriptive (ethical) relativism" or "anthropological ethical relativism". This view comes in two versions: first, that fundamentally different moral rules are found among individuals and, second, that fundamentally different moral reasons are found among groups, societies and cultures. As I described in the first chapter, I prefer to call the former "individual (descriptive ethical) relativism" and the latter "social (descriptive ethical) relativism".

3. The view that there is no single true morality. This view can be called "meta-ethical relativism" (or "philosophical ethical relativism").

4. The view that one ought not to pass judgement on others' moral positions or to interfere in their moral behaviour. This view can be called "normative relativism".

Descriptive relativism

The strongest form of descriptive relativism is clearly better for further relativistic argumentation because it can, alone or combined with another premise, better serve as an apparently plausible ground for meta-ethical relativism. If one grants that *all* basic moral values are different one may more easily argue that there is no single true morality. Certainly, many customs and at least some moral values vary from culture to culture or individual to individual, such as wearing clothes, child marriages and eating the bodies of dead relatives.

But to hold the strongest version is very difficult, since it is really dubious that all moral values, or even the most important moral values, vary. In any case, those who maintain descriptive relativism, before showing any case of fundamental difference, must first of all make clear what they mean by the ethical (compared to the non-ethical, such as customs or simple social contracts) and by expressions such as the "basic", "substantial" or the like.[1] Second, they must make sure that they understand, interpret and translate the moralities of others truly; otherwise out of misunderstanding they may take cases of agreements as cases of disagreements.

Many relativists adopt Quine's thesis about the indeterminacy of translation and the impossibility of determining how people of a radically different language understand and view objects. These relativists mainly take it as an argument for ethical relativism and as a ground for asking people not to pass any judgement on the behaviour and moralities of others. I shall consider this argument later (the fourth argument for meta-ethical relativism) but here I should like merely to say that Quine's thesis actually can be used against relativism: If we cannot really understand what other people do or say, how can the relativist be sure that, in spite of different appearances, there is no common moral principle? For example, even if some people eat the bodies of their dead relatives, is it not possible that they have also the same value of respect for the dead, especially relatives, as ours? So, even in cases in which the actions of others seem to us completely strange and irrational, there may be many things they share with us.

In any case, those who hold the stronger form have to undertake a further task, that is, to show that all basic moral principles or values have always and everywhere been varying. This is an empirical job, which is practically impossible. Although the burden of argument is on the relativist side, some absolutists have gone further and tried to show some articles of agreement among all rational and reasonable individuals or societies or across time. We will discuss this later. Thus it is better to consider the moderate version. But it has to be noted that, even if we accept the strongest form, it will not lead to meta-ethical or normative relativism and will not have any significance for moral philosophy. I shall argue for this later.

Those who support a moderate version of descriptive relativism have put forward some candidates for substantial differences. We have mentioned some of them before, but it is better now to examine a new one. David Wong in *Moral Relativity* (1984), "Moral Relativism" (1992), "Relativism" (1996) and "Moral Relativism" (1998) puts emphasis on this example and takes it to be explicable only through relativism. As we shall see later, he in fact believes that the best way to argue for ethical relativism is to point to such differences in moral belief. The example is the contrast between those ethical codes that

---

1. For my account of customs and morals, see the final chapter. It will make it clear that many examples of differences are irrelevant to ethics.

emphasize individual rights to liberty and well-being and those that emphasize the community life and the capacity for the individual to flourish within it. Wong says:

> One apparent and striking ethical difference that would be a good candidate for this sort of argument concerns the emphasis on individual rights that is embodied in the ethical culture of the modern West and that seems absent in traditional cultures found in Africa, China, Japan and India. The content of duties in such traditional cultures instead seems organized around the central value of a common good that consists in a certain sort of ideal community life, a network of relationships, partially defined by social roles, again, ideal, but imperfectly embodied in ongoing existing practice. The ideal for members is composed of various virtues that enable them, given their place in the network of relationships, to promote and sustain the common good (Wong, 1996, p. 445).

Unfortunately, I cannot agree with Wong. I think rights-centred moralities and common good-centred ones are not radically or fundamentally different. Indeed, they share common values and rely on some common grounds. They really differ only on where to put the emphasis. My argument is that an ideal moral system should accommodate both sets of values, i.e. the individual values and the common-good values. For example, there seems to be no doubt that helping others is one of the key elements in human understanding of morality, to the extent that some view altruism as the essence of morality.[1] This is underlined by the fact that, when human beings live in the same society, the very fact of deciding to live collectively implies that a better life for individuals is seen in the life of society. In other words, from a moral

---

1.　It has sometimes been claimed that human beings out of their nature just look after their own interests (*psychological egoism*), so morally they should be advised to look after their own interests only, because no moral system can recommend something against human nature.

　　In response, I have to say that even advocates of psychological egoism do not agree on its scope and interpretation. A more sophisticated egoism may allow that part of the process of securing one's interests is to care for others or that by helping others one gains more than one can gain from selfishness. Moreover, there is a real doubt about the natural and therefore necessary status of egoism. There will be a discussion about self-love and self-interest in the final chapter of this work. I shall also study Wong's supplementary argument when discussing the eleventh argument for meta-ethical relativism.

point of view the individual first of all considers kindness, benevolence and helping others both obligatory and, in fact, ultimately to his or her own benefit, and then, when it comes to members of one's own society, feels more responsible because of the closer relationship that strengthens the sense of responsibility, and because of the necessity to reciprocate benefits and services that are received from them. Of course, from a *legal* point of view only the minimum might be required, i.e. the obligation not to harm others.

Thus, it can be claimed that there is a harmony between the common good and an individual's real and long-term interest. Even if this involves sacrificing some of one's derivative or short-term interests, one can finally get more benefits and be more content and feel more satisfied at heart. Of course, there may be different perspectives on what the most important good for society is and on how to achieve it. Affected by the metaphysical or religious or mystical or folk views of the society, and by variations in circumstances, different societies may come to different judgements. Some may consider welfare as the most important good and see protecting human rights and liberty as the best policy for encouraging people to work for the good of themselves and their society. Others may put emphasis on the role of benevolence and the dangers of self-interest and consider welfare and self-denial as the best policy.

Therefore, I think the relativist explanation is not the only possible account of such cases. The relativist explanation of such cases is based on what can be called "social choice" or more exactly "arbitrary social choice" in adoption of moral norms. In the relativist account, moralities of different societies have to be recognized just as they stand, since they are *facts* that happened to be there; those *de facto* moralities or at least their adoption of differing values may remain rationally *untouched*. But a non-relativist explanation is also possible, which is based on what can be called "moral prioritization". This explanation justifies the existence of different moral systems or traditions without holding them to be equally true or justifiable. This explanation still has some advantages. It is compatible with common sense and can explain all aspects of our moral experiences, such as why and how members of these two types of systems can argue with each other for the correctness of their own system as if they do not believe in the so-called *right* of each society to choose its moral system by itself.

It is interesting that Wong himself clearly seems to believe in the truth of a range of human goods and sees the problem in our inability to reconcile them in a single moral system and the possibility of setting priorities in different ways. He says, "It should not be surprising, after all, if the range of human good is simply too rich and diverse to be reconciled in just a single moral ideal" (Wong, 1996, p. 446). In other words, he himself seems to believe in the absolute truth of both the good of belonging and contributing to a community and the good of respect for the individual, and assume that there is implicit agreement that both are good. However, since usually human beings cannot acquire all types of goods and they face practical conflicts among themselves, they have to make a system of rules, in which every single good has a certain position and certain degree of priority. Some individuals or societies may assume that individual good and right are prior to the good and welfare of the community and others may assume vice versa.

Summary
Descriptive relativism in its strongest form suffers from lack of evidence. There is not enough evidence provided by relativists to support the claim that all basic moral values vary from individual to individual or from society to society. In fact it is practically impossible to investigate the truth of such a claim inductively, since such an investigation demands knowledge about *all* individuals and societies across ages and across cultures. The strongest form is also contradictory to the fact that many moral principles and values have been common among the majority of people and in some cases among all reasonable human beings and typical civilized societies.

Descriptive relativism in its moderate form is more tenable, but it still suffers from the fact that many examples that are mentioned by relativists are either irrelevant to morality or do not show fundamental differences.

In any case, descriptive relativism as such in either of its forms can be accepted by objectivists or absolutists, because their belief in a single true or most justified morality does not require any level of agreement, just as physical facts may be both true and disputed. (There will be a separate discussion on the extent of diversity in morality and on how it is treated by non-relativists later in the discussion: Ethical Absolutism and Diversity of Morals.)

Meta-ethical relativism

There have been different ways to argue for meta-ethical relativism. In what follows, I will do my best to explain distinctly whatever arguments are or can be developed to support meta-ethical relativism. Of course, every argument is studied only insofar as the discussion about ethical relativism is concerned. In many cases, to come to a final judgement needs some independent research.

I believe that, despite the huge literature on ethical relativism, the topic still needs such attention. Readers on ethical relativism can hardly find a single work that covers all types of ethical relativism and the different sorts of arguments for them, together with a well-explained terminology and both standard and original comments.

1. Relativity of truth in general or in morality alone

Those who hold that truth and justifiability are defined through a person's or a group's knowledge-seeking practices and who doubt the value of seeking independently definable truth would simply apply this view to ethics to get meta-ethical relativism. To be able to assess this kind of argument, one has to settle the debate about the truth or objectivity of knowledge in general. There are also some people who hold that there is no absolute truth in morality, though they may believe in absolute truth in other fields. Equally, to assess this view, one has to study the issue of relative moral truth.

In what follows, I examine the concept of relative truth in general, and then the concept of relative moral truth in particular. I also consider some other aspects of the problem of objectivity (and also rationality) of moral knowledge throughout this work, especially in the final chapter. There I shall give some clues to the issue by showing that our moral understanding in principle does not depend on external knowledge of the world and can be saved from scepticism.

One of the most controversial topics in the history of philosophy is that of "truth". The common-sense view that has been accepted by most philosophers is that our ideas somehow "model" reality, and are true when they do so correctly. The correspondence theory holds that a true idea is what corresponds to reality. Naturally the question arises, "How can we know what the world is really like in order to judge?" The correspondence theory and this question presuppose that there is an external world existing independently of us, whether we know it or ignore it, whether we agree on what it looks like or disagree.

Among different attitudes towards the issue, there is the relativistic attitude, which denies either the existence of an independent universe or the necessity of correspondence and conformity to it for truth. The notion of truth is crucial for relativists. They deny absolute truth on the one hand but argue for the truth of relativism on the other. Plato and many others through the history of philosophy believed that the issue of truth is fatal for relativism. As Siegel and many others have put it, the notion of truth can be understood only non-relativistically. The relativist argues that relativism is right or true or cognitively superior to non-relativism, but the counter-argument is that, if the relativist makes this claim non-relativistically, he has given up relativism and, if he makes this claim only relatively, he has not made it at all.[1] Let us look at this idea more elaborately and then see whether it makes any difference to hold a global relativism about truth or a local one, say, just in morality.

We will begin with the idea of "global relativism" or "relative truth" in general and then consider "relativity of moral truth" in particular. The idea of "relative truth" is traced back to Protagoras. (I have already studied some aspects of this subject in Chapter Two, which deals with the history of ethical relativism.) Plato in the *Theaetetus* explains Protagoras' argument in this way:

> Socrates: Therefore, since each perception is peculiar to my being, my perception is true for me and, as Protagoras says, I am the judge of the things that are for me, that they are, and of the things that are not, that they are not (Plato, *Theaetetus*, 160c).

Thus everyone is right in his belief about the world and furthermore no one can be wrong in his belief. For Protagoras false belief is not possible.

It may seem at first that there is little to criticize in this view. It is clearly fallacious to argue from *seeming* to *being*. There is no direct or indirect implication there. One cannot justifiably conclude from what something seems that its being is relational, that is, relative to one. The only way is to conclude from seeming "being, in my view" and then consciously or unconsciously neglect "in my view". However, there are still some philosophers who more or less take the same path. Therefore it is worthwhile to examine Protagoras' view in detail.

Let us go back to the argument. When I believe that the world is in a certain way it means that I believe that the world as a subject has some quality as its predicate. So my belief is about the relationship between the subject and its predicate. For example, through my visual perception. I believe that the tree before me is tall. In other words, the tree seems or appears tall to me, so I believe that it is tall. If an outsider wants to report my situation he will say that "It *seemed* to him that the real tree had the quality of tallness and then he came to believe that the real tree *had* that quality". It is noteworthy that my belief comes necessarily after the appearance and that the object of my belief is the relationship between the tree and tallness in reality. (I mean by the

---

1. For example, see Siegel, p. 4.

object of the belief its content, that is, what is believed.) By no means could my belief or opinion or anything like that be part of its own object. Obviously the belief logically comes in order after the appearance of what is believed. So its inclusion in its object would imply that it has preceded itself in order, which is a clear contradiction.

Accordingly, when another person also believes that the tree is tall, his belief is not included in what is believed: so what is believed is exactly the same. If that person believes that the tree is not tall, what is believed is contradictory, but not the beliefs themselves. Indeed there can never be any contradiction between two beliefs, because they are two existential mental states of people or of a single person and there can be no contradiction between two beings. For the same reason there can be no unity in its proper sense between the beliefs of two persons or even between beliefs of a single person, even when the objects are the same. My belief that today is Sunday is numerically different from my belief one hour later that today is Sunday.

Therefore, when there is agreement or disagreement among people on beliefs, the objects of the beliefs are concerned, that is, the objects of the beliefs must be exactly the same. When I say that today is hot and you say that tomorrow will not be hot we are not disagreeing with each other, or if I say that this place is hot and you say that another place is cold we are not disagreeing with each other. Even if I say that it is hot for me here at this second and you say that it is not hot for you at the same time and at the same place, we are not disagreeing because there is no unity between the two objects of the beliefs.

Thus, in my view there is no place to claim relative truth in the way that Protagoras does. What Protagoras does is to insert a psycho-epistemic element in the object of belief to make it personal, subjective and relative. Every person, in his view, speaks only about his own universe. In other words, every person speaks about the universe as he himself believes, so there will be no place for error and no sense for disagreement. The only thing that there can be is lying. Since Protagoras identifies how the universe appears to someone with what someone believes the world to be in reality, the result is that one cannot make any mistake in his belief about the world, but one can express his belief in words in a way other than he believes. If I believe that the tree is tall this cannot be false, but if I say at the same time that the tree is not tall I have just lied.

By the way, it is noteworthy that we have different types of understanding. Our mind is so capable that it can observe the external subject and come to some belief about that, and then, at a higher level, it may observe its previous observation of the external subject as a second-order subject. In this case, the object is an internal one in which a psycho-epistemic element is included. For example, I believe that the tree is tall, then I can consider my belief that the tree is tall and have some judgements about that belief. I am certain about my belief (that is, I am certain that I have such a belief), but I might still have some doubt about what is believed. I can say that I am certain that I believe that the tree is tall, but I am not certain that the tree is tall. Likewise, I can say certainly I believe that the tree is tall or certainly the tree is tall to me, but there should be a belief, whether true or false, about the real tallness before that, or, more exactly, about the factual relationship between the subject and the predicate. Therefore, I think that there is no place for "relative truth."[1]

According to Protagoras, there can be no common experience. Everyone in fact lives in his own world. There is no objective world in which all can share or at least there is no access to that world, if there exists such a world. There is no place for *falsity* in Protagoras' world and therefore there is no proper sense in which *truth* can be applied, since falsity and truth are contradictory and without understanding one side the other cannot be understood. So, if falsity does not make any sense in one theory, the truth would not make any sense either. Unfortunately, Protagoras does not locate or observe the two sides of the correspondence properly. There is a real need for the notions of truth and correspondence in Protagoras' theory. Therefore, there is a real need for the notion of falsity as well. It cannot be claimed that there is no need for the possibility of *falsity* for a proper usage of its contradiction, i.e. *truth,* and for the correspondence of our belief to external facts in order to have a true belief about what the world is like. For according to Protagoras' account, truth means the correspondence of our belief to the

---

1. I hope it is now clear that one should not say (on behalf of Protagoras): "Wouldn't Protagoras say that if I believe the tree is tall, then the tree is tall *for me*? So, what I believe is something about the tree, but the only thing I apprehend is a truth for me." As I explained above, when I believe that the tree is tall I believe the tree is tall in reality, that is, the tallness of the tree is a reality existing independently of me. However, the only way for me to grasp this reality is through my apprehension of the notions of the tree and the tallness that exist in my mind, but are meant to act just like a mirror to look *through* them and not *at* them. Of course, in another sort of reflection (a second-order one) we may take these mental notions as some second-order objects to reflect on them. In this case, we look *at* them just as we do when we want to buy a mirror and we want to test, say, its material.

    In addition to the problem that "X is Y" cannot be taken to mean "X is Y for me", another problem arises here that if "X is Y" meant "X is Y for me", then after all the statement "X is Y" would become an absolute truth or falsity.

appearances and this finally means the correspondence of our belief to our belief.

In Protagoras' world "doubt" also is meaningless, because I cannot have any doubt about the way in which the world seems to me. When I see a glass in the distance and I do not know whether that is cold or warm I *can* doubt, because I believe that there is a real thing there and I do not know its qualities, so I should make an inquiry to realize its qualities. But for Protagoras there is only an appearance of that glass that includes nothing about its temperature. It seems neither cold nor hot to me, so why should I have any doubt? Why cannot I say that it is neither cold nor hot?[1] To defend the Protagorean position, and not necessarily Protagoras' view itself, it might be said that through our experiences it seems to us that all materials have a certain temperature, so when we do not know the temperature of that glass we find that something is just missing in our apprehension of that glass. To reply, one can say this is one way that the world can seem to people. It is equally well conceivable that to some others nothing is missing, because they have no reason for themselves, for example, to generalize their previous experiences.

Furthermore, the concept of scientific investigation becomes very ambiguous. Indeed, for Protagoras, it is doubtful that there can be any such thing. If the world is just as it seems to people and there is no external or objective world or at least there is no access to that, how can we distinguish between scientific investigation and fictitious investigation, or between empirical study and building castles in the air? How can we explain the huge convergence between scientific ideas? Therefore, one has to admit that there are universal laws that apply to all human beings by which we can distinguish between reality and fiction, between scientific study and making a fictitious story. By means of those absolute universal laws, we can argue with each other and try to convince others to make their ideas conform with ours or refute them. The very fact that we can conceive Protagoras' world and examine it to come to a shared idea shows that, in contrast to his belief, we do

---

1. It should be clear that it does not solve the problem if one says, "Why not? It may appear neither cold nor hot". Indeed, the real problem lies in the fact that in this case the glass has appeared to me neither cold nor hot, but in other cases it may appear either cold or hot and I know that in reality the glass cannot be neither cold nor hot. (It must be noticed that "cold" and "hot" are meant here to be the only possible variables; there are no middle positions. For example, "cold" means "not hot" and vice versa; below a certain degree is to be called "coldness" and from that degree upwards is to be called "hotness".) This shows that *appearance to me* is different from *being in reality*. Thus, what I believe, for example about the tree, is being tall in reality.

not live in separate worlds, each of which has no "windows" to the others.

There is also a historical response to general relativism. Plato maintains that relativism is self-refuting. If the relativist asserts that the relativism is true for all people, so he has admitted at least one absolute truth. Even if he treats this as an exception or *ad hoc*, the result will be that there is no problem in the concept of absolute truth and therefore we have a right to ask for the reason that has led to this discrimination. If the relativist says that relativism is true only for those who accept it, then those like Plato who reject it are also right. But if the rejection of relativism is true, relativism itself must be false.[1]

Moreover, if Protagoras asserts that relativism is true for those who believe it, the question arises whether for him this final idea is absolutely true or not! If the answer is negative, he has to admit Plato's refutation, and if the answer is positive he has admitted an absolute truth.

Alasdair MacIntyre (1989, p. 183) holds that relativists can learn from what he calls "the purported refutations of relativism" (which to him have largely missed its point) how to formulate relativism in such a way as not to be subject to those refutations. It is interesting that he gives the example of Socrates' encounter with the formulations of Protagoras in *Theaetetus* and then says that relativists must be careful not to "allow themselves to be trapped into making some type of universal self-referential claim". But he also adds that if one denies to all doctrines, whatsoever the predicates, "is true" and "is false", except when they are taken to mean just "seems true to such-and-such a person" and "seems false to such-and-such a person", the result will be that the assertion that relativism is true turns to the uninteresting assertion that relativism seems true to relativists.

Before I study the idea of relativity of moral truth, I would like to make some points:

a. The Protagorean conception of relativism is individualistic. Copleston (1970) reports that some people have taken his famous statement "Man

---

1. Indeed, in the last part of the argument I am invoking the common-sense conceptions of falsity and rejection, which seem to be less affected by the relativistic approach. One has heard the phrases such as "true for me" and "true for you" so much that one may see nothing strange in them before philosophical reflection. But I think this has not been the case with the negative side of the problem. It seems still strange to say that Plato is right in rejecting relativism and believing in its falsity, but that relativism still can be valid for someone else.

    If someone does not agree with me about what I have said here, then he or she may say in response to my argument above, "Yes, relativism is false, false *for Plato*, but true *for Protagoras*".

is the measure of all things" to mean man as a species and not as an individual. However, I personally think that Plato's account of Protagoras' idea in the *Theaetetus* leaves no doubt that Protagoras just meant that every individual is the sole judgement.[1] For example, Socrates says:

> For if truth is only sensation, and no man can discern another's feelings to determine whether his opinion is true or false, but each, as we have several times repeated, is to be himself the sole judge, and everything that he judges is true and right, why, my friend, should Protagoras be preferred to the place of wisdom and instruction, and deserve to be well paid, and we poor ignoramuses have to go to him, if each one is the measure of his own wisdom? (Plato, *Theaetetus*, 161).

b. In my discussion about relative truth, I have mainly focused on the Protagorean version of relative truth. The reason lies in its absolute importance. Actually it is the standard and classic form of the theory of relative truth. And since my discussion is mainly concerned with morality-specific relativism, I will study more than one view there. Of course, it is clear that a comprehensive discussion about the problem of truth is out of the limits of this book.

c. Although my critiques of the notion of relative truth were directed towards Protagorean individualistic relativism, they are more general and farther-reaching in their nature. It is my argument that all theories of relative truth, or at least all that I know of, fail to distinguish between belief and what is believed (the object), or between the context of judgement and the context of what is judged, no matter whether it is individual judgement or collective judgement.

Similarly, I would like to say that my argument above against relative

---

1. As we know the *Theaetetus* is a very good source to understand Protagoras' view, since its principal subject is the nature of knowledge and the way we receive it through perception. Alain de Botton in his introduction to the *Theaetetus* says, "It takes the form chiefly of a criticism of the doctrine of Protagoras that 'man is the measure of all things', which is identified with the Heracleitean theory that 'all is in a flux' and is explained by Socrates to mean that all knowledge is relative, both in the intellectual and the moral sphere" (Botton, 1999, p. 1168).

truth addresses Protagoras' idea that whatever seems to one is true for one, or is what is there. (See my discussion about Protagoras' view on perception in contrast to Parmenides' view in the discussion about the history of ethical relativism!) Of course, it is possible to hold a relativist view about truth and at the same time to distinguish between what appears to me to be the case (say, visually) and what is the case for me. But again this does not affect my argument in its essence. What really matters is the relativist's failure to distinguish between what is perceived or known and perception or knowledge themselves. In this way, recognition or non-recognition of the difference between perception and knowledge, or between what seems, say, visually to be the case for me and what is the case for me is irrelevant to my argument.[1]

Now let us consider the "relativity of moral truth". In this case certainly we will no longer have any problem like those mentioned above about non-moral beliefs, such as scientific ones. Also it may seem that we shall not need to discuss whether ethical relativism is self-refuting or not, since ethical relativism itself is not an ethical belief. But there are two doubts in my mind. First, it is not clear for me why ethical relativism cannot be considered as an ethical belief, given that relativists mostly treat it as an ethical position, encouraging tolerance of people with different beliefs. Second, even if ethical relativism is not treated as an ethical belief, this does not explain why it does not share the features of ethical beliefs that make them only relatively true. The moral relativist has to show why he has limited relativity to ethical truth. As we know, the main argument for ethical relativism has been the claim that moral debates are interminable and endlessly controversial. Why cannot the same thing be claimed for ethical relativism? We know that the debate on ethical relativism has been endless, just as debates on some moral issues have been endless. Therefore, it seems to me that ethical relativism must share the same problem of moral claims and, accordingly, it too has to be relative. But to suppose that all moral claims are relative means that ethical relativism must be absolute. Thus, ethical relativism is inconsistent and self-refuting.

---

1. Indeed, what I have suggested in the above three points: a, b and c, is to make clear that I accept the possibility of having a collective version of relative truth and the difference between what appears to me to be the case and what is the case for me. However, I pointed out that my argument primarily has been concerned with Protagoras' version, which is the standard form. First, I tried to show that his version of relativism should be taken as an individualist version, and then, second, I tried to show that even if a collective version was concerned it would make no difference to my argument. I also showed that my argument against relative truth works, even though I admit that one (presumably not Protagoras himself) may distinguish between what appears to be the case for me and what is the case for me.

There is another problem with the relativity of moral truth that arises from the ambiguity of its meaning. J. Meiland is one of the few philosophers who have tried to describe this concept. He believes that there is a substantial difference between absolute truth and relative truth. Absolute truth, he says, involves a two-term relation between the statement and the state of affairs, while relative truth involves a three-term correspondence relation between the statement, the state of affairs and the person (or the world-view or the cultural situation). Meiland says:

> Thus one can no more reasonably ask what "true" means in the expression "true-for-W" than one can ask what "cat" means in the word "cattle". True-for-W denotes a special three-term relation which does not include the two-term relation of absolute truth as a distinct part (Meiland, 1977, p. 574, as cited in Bunting, 1996, p. 79).

Bunting (1996, p. 79) at first reports Harvey Siegel's criticism of this view and then he tries to defend Meiland, although he believes that Meiland is not clear enough in explaining what he means. Siegel (1987) points out that the analogy with "cat" and "cattle" does nothing to help explain the meaning of relative truth. The word "cattle" is made up of the letters c-a-t-t-l-e; "cat" is no more independently meaningful than are "att" or "ttle". "True-for-W", on the other hand, is made up of the hyphenization of distinct concepts, each of which is independently meaningful. Defending Meiland, Bunting says:

> What Meiland is arguing in the (admittedly strange) passage quoted above is that relative truth is a primitive term and that it is not reducible to or analysable in terms of anything else. The concept of relative truth may fail for other reasons but it does not fail because it is unanalysable in terms of other things (Bunting, 1996, p. 79).

It seems to me that Meiland's analysis is based on a mistreatment of the concept of truth. I can see no difference between relative truth and absolute truth in their nature. I think that it is inappropriate to suppose that absolute truth is a two-term relation between a state of affairs and a statement (e.g. telling lies is wrong), while relative truth is a three-term relation between a state of affairs, a statement and the person (or the world-view or the cultural situation) involved. Truth is neither a relationship between the statement and the state of affairs nor a relation between the statement, the state of affairs and the person. Truth (in moral matters) involves a correspondence between the relationship in the statement (between the subject and the predicate) and the external relationship between the state of affairs and its moral status. The meaning of relative truth, if there is any, has to reside in the role that the particularities of the person, which for absolutists are morally irrelevant, can have in the moral status of the state of affairs in reality (that is, in the external relationship). So there is no difference between absolute truth and relative truth in their nature, which is the correspondence of the internal relation, i.e. the relation within the statement, to the external one. I should note that my argument here does not depend on assuming the objectivity of morality. Whatever is held to determine moral status, even if it is simply agreement or affective dispositions, makes no difference.

Moreover, if the particularities of the person or the world-view or the cultural situation bear on the moral status of the state of affairs, as claimed by the relativist, it will be the same in all similar cases for that person (or according to that world-view or in that cultural situation) and if not it will again be the same in all similar cases. In other words, if those features are morally relevant, they are so absolutely, and, if they are morally irrelevant, they are so absolutely. The relativist cannot make the case a unique one to which nothing can be similar. For this leads, not to cultural relativism or individual relativism, but to what might be called "this individual-in this culture-in this place-at this time" relativism, which seems unpleasant to relativists, though it may be the real implication of a consistent relativism.

There is a further point that I should like to mention here, namely, that adding concepts to a universal concept may narrow its extent but never makes it particular. For example, the concept of man becomes narrower and more confined by adding to it extra concepts, such as being in this room at this moment and sitting on this chair, to the extent that it becomes applicable to one person only at a given time. However, it still remains universal and can be applied to different individuals. Even if we make it so narrow that there could be only one person in the world fulfilling all the required conditions, it will not become particular. What really matters in being universal is the possibility of applicability to more than one instance, not that there be actual instances, so there might be some universal concepts without any instances at all. Accordingly, the case that one agent or observer considers to decide its rightness or wrongness can never be a unique case in the proper sense. Moreover, the relativist has to show the relevance of whatever he claims to bear on the moral judgement.

The other view about relative truth is presented by F. C. White (1986). He believes that "P" in society S1 is different from "P" in society S2 and gets different meanings. Therefore, "P" can be true in one society and false in the other without commitment to any contradiction. It seems to me that obviously there are some terms that have more or less different meanings in different contexts. The meaning of modesty, for example, in a Western country may be considered radically different from that in an Eastern country. However, it is obviously groundless to claim that in all cases of various moral evaluations there are different meanings. This view leads to the denial of the possibility of moral dialogues and debates. Even more, this view finally leads to a strong form of absolutism. For according to this view there is no reason for disagreement among people on any topic, provided that they consider the same thing, because this view suggests that whenever there are different moral evaluations there are different meanings involved, that is, different subjects are concerned. This means that there is no way to conceive of any disagreement between two societies; whatever seems to be a case of disagreement finally turns into a case of misunderstanding. However, there should be no doubt that different societies could and actually do disagree over whether P, given its meaning, is true or false.[1]

There is still another view presented by Harry Bunting. He calls it a "minimalist account". According to this account, "P is true for S1" merely means that P is believed by that society. He tries to enrich this account with appeal to the *coherence theory* of truth. He says:

> However, in addition to asking if a belief is justified within a total belief-system S1 we can also ask if a belief coheres and is justified within a specified sub-system of beliefs S2. If a belief displays maximum coherence within such a sub-system then we may express this by saying that it is justified-in-S2. The purpose of the hyphens in this context is to indicate a qualified form of justification: the belief is justified, but it is justified only in relation to a limited class of beliefs. A similar point might be made in connection with truth. (Bunting, 1996, pp. 80 and 81).

Bunting thinks that this is the most plausible way to construe Protagoras' idea of relative truth. However, he admits that this conception of moral truth does not undermine absolutism. He admits that "the fact that relative truth

---

1. See also my discussion about the semantic argument and about the argument from indeterminacy of translation in this chapter, arguments 3a and 4 for meta-ethical relativism.

can be predicated on sub-systems of belief is wholly consistent with the absolute truth of those beliefs which display maximum explanatory coherence within a comprehensive belief-system."

I think what Bunting really means is that the "truth" of those relatively true beliefs is just provisional and temporary. They are taken as true as long as they are not intentionally compared with absolute truths or as long as absolute truths are neglected or unknown. Act A that seems good to someone is good for *him* (i.e. relatively good) before he considers his world-view or comprehensive framework of beliefs. Having considered his world-view or comprehensive system of beliefs, A either becomes *absolutely* right, if it is in maximum harmony with the comprehensive moral system, or becomes *absolutely* wrong, if it is not compatible with the comprehensive moral system. Other people might have different *absolute* truths. I do not think that Protagoras or any other person who believes in relative truth has had this kind of distinction between absolute truth and relative truth in mind. In the end, I endorse Bunting's statement that truth is "a fundamental obstacle to the development of a relativist ethics, rendering relativism incoherent if construed in absolute form, and failing to undermine objectivism if construed in relative form" (ibid., p. 81).

Summary

One way of arguing for meta-ethical relativism has been to adopt the Protagorean idea of the relativity of truth and then simply apply it to ethics. If there is no absolute truth at all, there can be no absolute truth in morality.

My study of this approach has shown that it was based on a confusion between "belief" and "what is believed". Every belief is a state of mind and as such depends on the person who has the belief. However, the object of belief is independent and free from any particularity and subjectivity of the belief as a mental state. This is just like a mirror, which reflects, for example, a flower. What the mirror itself is has nothing to do with what is shown, i.e. the flower. When we observe "what is shown" we are not concerned with the material or the owner of the mirror. Nor are we *primarily* concerned with the picture of the flower in the mirror itself. Our concern is the real flower outside: this is why the question of accuracy and certainty of our conception of the real object remains crucial, even if we may know exactly what the mirror is made from or what picture is visible on the surface of the mirror.

In addition to this problem, there are some other problems in the Protagorean idea. I have argued that according to this idea everyone, in fact, lives in his own world and there remains no chance for common experience.

I also argued that the Protagorean idea of global relative truth leaves no place for the concept of "falsity" and, in turn, makes even the concept of "truth" meaningless. Moreover, I argued that in the Protagorean world there is no place for "doubt". Finally, I argued that this idea makes the concept of "scientific investigation" ambiguous. Besides my own objections, I also referred to the historical objection to the Protagorean idea that it is either self-refuting or does no harm to absolutists who believe that it is false.

Having argued that there is no good argument for global relative truth, I looked at the idea of relativity of *moral* truth. I argued that, although the previous problems of global relative truth do not apply here, this view still suffers from some difficulties. One problem is to show what is the substantial difference between individual moral truths and the truth of moral relativism that causes the former to be relative and the latter to be absolute. Unless this is explained, the theory is once again self-refuting.

The other difficulty is the ambiguity of the very concept of *relativity* of moral truth. In this respect, we studied the suggestions made by J. Meiland, F. C. White and H. Bunting to clarify this concept.

Meiland holds that there is a substantial difference between absolute truth and relative truth. Absolute truth involves a two-term relation between a statement and a state of affairs, while relative truth involves a three-term relation between the statement, the state of affairs and the person. I argued that his analysis is based on a mistreatment of the concept of "truth". I argued that there is no difference between absolute truth and relative truth in their nature, that is, the correspondence of the internal relation between the subject and the predicate with the external one, i.e. the actual relation between what subject and predicate refer to. The truth of the proposition "this flower is red" depends on the correspondence of the internal relation between concepts of "this flower" and "red" to the external relation between the real flower and the real redness. In this case, if both relations are the same, i.e. positive, the proposition "this flower is red" is true. The meaning of relative truth, if there is any, has to reside in the assumption that the particularities of the person may affect the moral status of the given states of affairs in reality. I further argued that this assumption could fit in with moral absolutism.

The other view about relative truth belongs to F. C. White. He believes that "P" in society S1 is different from "P" in society S2, so that "modesty is good" in S1 may be as true as "modesty is bad" in S2. In response, I have argued that it seems obvious that no one can claim that in all cases of different moral evaluations there are different meanings for the similar terms involved. If it were the case we could not have moral dialogues and debates. It may also be argued that this view is, indeed, in favour of ethical absolutism. For it presupposes that people never disagree on any subject, provided that they understand it in the same way, while relativists need to show that people may have justifiably different ethical positions about the same subject, understood by all parties in the same way.

The last suggestion discussed above is that of H. Bunting. He suggests that "P is true for S1" can be taken to mean that P is true only in relation to a limited class of beliefs, while absolute truth means that P is true in relation to a total belief system. Bunting himself expressly asserts that this view is wholly consistent with absolutism. Therefore, there is no need to disprove this idea to support absolutism. However, I have argued that Bunting's view implies that relative truths are just provisional and temporary and, as soon as they are compared with the total belief system, they become either absolutely true or absolutely false, depending on their coherence with that belief system.

All in all, no strong argument from the relativity of truth in general or of truth in morality was found for meta-ethical relativism. In the following pages we shall study other sorts of argument for this theory.

2. The argument from descriptive relativism

Here, I discuss different attempts to argue from descriptive relativism, or the existence of fundamental differences in the moralities of individuals or societies, for meta-ethical relativism. (Of course, the discussion here is better understood if the reader keeps in mind my earlier comments on descriptive relativism.) Actually, as Wong (1998, p. 539) suggested, the most heated debate about relativism concerns whether descriptive relativism supports *meta-ethical relativism* or not. I think that we can classify those attempts as follows:

a. The argument is sometimes simply based on descriptive relativism. Some people may take the fact of *diversity* (i.e. what is considered morally right and wrong varies from society to society or from individual to individual) as their single premise to conclude that there is no single true or most justified morality.

   One of the most comprehensive and clear accounts of this kind of argument for meta-ethical relativism (along with its criticism) is given by Rachels (1993, pp. 18 and 19). He asserts that at the heart of meta-ethical relativism – in his words, Cultural Relativism – there is a certain form of argument that he calls the *Cultural Difference Argument*.[1] The *strategy* in this kind of argument is to argue from facts about the differences between cultural outlooks to a conclusion about the status of morality. He articulates the general argument as follows:

- Different cultures have different moral codes.
- Therefore, there is no objective "truth" in morality. Right and wrong are only matters of opinion and opinions vary from culture to culture.

The standard objection to this argument is that there is no direct path from descriptive ethical relativism to meta-ethical relativism. The mere fact of difference in ethical codes does not imply that the codes are equally true or justified. Such variation is in itself merely a truth of descriptive morality, a fact of anthropology, which entails no meta-ethical view.[2] There is no way to go from *what people believe* to *what really is the case*. There is no logical implication here.

Diversity in belief may result from varying degrees of wisdom. As the Socrates of Plato's dialogues observed, we have reason to listen only to the wise among us *(Crito,* 44cd);[3] or it may be that different people

1. Please remember that Rachels means by cultural relativism a full-fledged ethical relativism. Refer to my comment on his account of cultural relativism at the beginning of this chapter.

2. This is why Mackie (1977) tries to supplement this diversity with his famous argument from queerness to arrive at subjectivism.

3. "Socrates: No, a clear one, at any rate, I think, Crito.

   Crito: Too clear, apparently. But, my dear Socrates, even now listen to me and save yourself. Since, if you die, it will be no mere single misfortune to me, but I shall lose a friend such as I can never find again, and besides, many persons who do not know you and me well [44c] will think I could have saved you if I had been willing to spend money, but that I would not take the trouble. And yet what reputation could be more disgraceful than that of considering one's money of more importance than one's friends? For most people will not believe that we were eager to help you to go away from here, but you refused.

   Socrates: But, my dear Crito, why do we care so much for what most people think? For the most reasonable men, whose opinion is more worth considering, will think that things were done as they really will be done. [44d]

   Crito: But you see it is necessary, Socrates, to care for the opinion of the public, for this very trouble we are in now shows that the public is able to accomplish not by any means the least, but almost the greatest of evils, if one has a bad reputation with it.

(continued...)

have their own limited perspectives of the truth, each perspective being distorted in its own way; or that differences in moral beliefs between societies may be caused by differences in basic moral values and such differences in values could be caused by religious beliefs (which differ between societies). Because of the importance of this issue for both relativists and non- relativists, there will be a specific discussion in the next part, Ethical Absolutism and Diversity of Morals, in which I will discuss how to explain moral differences from an absolutist perspective.

In any case, the simple fact of diversity in belief does not disprove the possibility that there are some beliefs better to have than others, because they are truer or more justified. If half the world still believed that the sun and the planets revolved around the earth, that would be no disproof of the possibility of a unique truth about the structure of the universe. Similarly, if half the world still believed that slavery is right, it would be no disproof of the possibility of a unique truth about the structure of the morality. In science, it is accepted that disagreement is consistent with the existence of an independent reality. Rachels has a very insightful saying here. He says that, just as there is no reason to think that if the world is round everyone must know it, there is also no reason to think that if there is moral truth everyone must know it.[1]

Relativists often attempt to counter this by arguing that ethical belief is not about an independent reality in the way scientific belief is.[2] Thus, this argument (a) changes in its nature and reduces to one of the following arguments, such as the non-cognitive argument or the subjectivist argument (see below).

b. The argument is sometimes supplemented by another claim, so that it consists of two premises. The first is descriptive relativism or a *diversity thesis*, but the second premise can be articulated in more than one way. There are two different articulations:

(...continued)

Socrates: I only wish, Crito, the people could accomplish the greatest evils, that they might be able to accomplish also the greatest good things. Then all would be well. But now they can do neither of the two; for they are not able to make a man wise or foolish, but they do whatever occurs to them" (*Crito*)

1. See Rachels, 1993, p. 19.

2. Wong calls the view that takes morality to be relativistic and science to be non-relativistic a *morality-specific meta-ethical relativism*. (Wong, 1998, p. 540).

- "There is nothing in morality beyond actual morality." In other words: *de facto* morality is all that counts. According to this view, we should not bother ourselves to find some ideal morality in which people should believe. Social scientists are most likely to accept this as true. By definition, social sciences deal only with perceivable or *de facto* behaviour, and the question of ideal morality falls outside these boundaries. A sociologist as such may have no way to define which culture or which moral code is right and which one is wrong. However, unfortunately, many social scientists and social anthropologists have tried to draw evaluative or meta-ethical conclusions from data available to them and denied the possibility of a single true morality. We saw in the discussion about the history of ethical relativism how, for example, Sumner asserted that the "right" way is the way the ancestors used and that has been handed down, and that "when we come to the folkways we are at the end of our analysis" (Sumner, 1906, p. 28).

  But neither philosophers nor ordinary people are bound by the rules of social sciences. Philosophers address this issue directly in the dispute between moral realism and moral scepticism. A philosopher may start his analysis just where a social scientist or anthropologist stops – or, more precisely, *should* stop. It should also be noted that "true morality" or "ideal morality" is a normative matter, while scientists, such as anthropologists are concerned only with factual descriptive matters. Of course, as I explained earlier, it cannot be denied that the above line of thought has persuaded many people to be sceptical about the existence of universally binding values.

- "All moral principles derive their validity from cultural acceptance." Pojman calls this the *dependency thesis*.[1] According to this thesis, the rightness and wrongness of individual acts depend on the nature of the society. Morality does not happen in a vacuum; every action must be seen in a context of goals, wants, beliefs, history and environment of the society. The complete argument is that there are different moral

---

1. See Pojman, 1996, p. 690, and 1998, pp. 39, 40 and 45. Pojman (1990, p. 24) introduces an idea similar to the dependency thesis as a second premise for such argument for ethical relativism, i.e. the *normalcy thesis*. He defines it as "the claim that each of the different moral systems can be thoroughly rational despite the differences, and that there are no overriding moral grounds for accepting one and condemning the others."

principles from culture to culture and that morality is rooted in culture, therefore, there are no universal moral principles for all cultures at all times.

Again, this issue in fact rests on the whole issue of the objectivity or subjectivity of moral ideals. I have already studied some of its aspects and shall consider some more aspects of that later. However, there are some specific problems that I should like to raise here. Briefly, the problem with the dependency thesis is that it makes the process of adopting or changing moral principles by a society unintelligible and significantly ambiguous. Before adopting any moral principle, a society has either its opposite or nothing. In both cases it is not clear why people should come to believe in some new (and therefore invalid) principle and try to apply it. If they believe in the opposite principle, it will not be reasonable to put the valid moral principle (which simply means the "believed moral principle") aside and adopt its opposite, given that nothing really changes except people's decision. (This is because this view is against objectivity of morality and assumes that morality just follows people's choice.) If they have no belief in advance it may be because of the newness of the subject or because of their adoption of a neutral and indifferent position. The latter finally leads to the above problem, since having a neutral position means that they have adopted the opposite of belief in P. (In the first case the transition was from P to *its opposite*, i.e. *not P* or from *not P* to *P*, but here the transition is from *no belief in P* to *belief in P*.) So in both cases the transition is from one side of a contradiction to the other side and there must be an explanation for this radical change.

Finally, even in cases in which the subject is new and therefore the problem of radical change does not exist, there are still some other problems. Why should a society adopt any moral position knowing that without its acceptance no moral stance is broken and no moral stance is morally valid or obligatory? How does a morality whose validity is based only on a people's decision become authoritative for them?[1] People may, for good reasons, assume a special way of conduct, such as following an ascetic diet, or adopt certain laws, such as traffic laws, and find themselves guilty if they disobey them. But if there is no real ground, no real difference, and it is just a matter of taste or whim,

---

1.   For a somewhat similar objection, aimed against Kierkegaard, see MacIntyre, 1984, Chapter 4.

why should not they easily ignore the code when it is not compatible with their desires? How can both sides of an opposition be invalid? How does society come to adopt a moral code? How can the society get a unique voice (or at least a prevailing one)? What is the role of individuals, especially when there is no established social view? What is the status of individual ethics?[1]

3. The semantic argument

There are different versions of this type of argument:

a. Logically inherent relativity

Some relativists have argued that the meaning of ethical statements contains a logically inherent relativity to the ethical code adopted by the society in question. Therefore, when we reflect on the analysis of their meaning, we find that this logically inherent relativity prevents us from applying them to any group other than the group that has adopted the relevant code.[2]

The standard objection to this argument is that the scope of ethical judgement is not limited by the allegedly particular reference of ethical terms. This can be shown by considering the fact that members of every society are willing to pass ethical judgements on behaviour in other societies, even in societies with a substantially different ethical code. Therefore, there is nothing in the meaning of the ethical statements that prevents people from applying them interculturally.

In addition to the standard objection, I think that there are other problems with this view. As mentioned above, this view holds that in each society meanings of ethical statements are inherently relative to the ethical code adopted by that society. Now, my first concern is that this theory has to make clear the status of that ethical code, before one may draw any relativistic conclusions. If that ethical code in itself is absolute another question arises, that is, why moral statements that are based upon it must count as relative (and not simply relational, i.e. to be in relation with that ethical code). Indeed, implications of an absolute moral code should themselves be seen as absolute, and not as relative, if they are logically derived from it. And if that ethical code in itself is relative it means that there must be an underlying explanation as to why this is the case, since obviously this view (the logically inherent relativity of the meanings of ethical statements to the adopted ethical code).

---

1. See also my criticisms of Hare's view in this chapter.
2. See Wong, 1992.

cannot account for the relativity of the ethical code itself. If that explanation is one of many explanations discussed here, it will be subject to the relevant criticism made in this work; otherwise a new explanation will have to be formed.

My second concern is related to the second part of the argument, i.e. that the meaning of ethical statements contains a *logically inherent* relativity to a particular ethical code. It implies that if a society believes that abortion is good and another society believes that abortion is bad, the badness of abortion is a meaningless notion to the first society, just as the goodness is to the second. This follows because, say, the badness of abortion in the second society loses its meaning (or at least part of its meaning) when taken apart from the adopted ethical code of the second society. My objection is that, if the statement "abortion is good" is meaningful and acceptable to a particular society, its opposite, "abortion is bad", which is believed by the other society, also must be meaningful; otherwise there can be no real dialogue and mutual understanding among members of the society and outsiders, and there can be no place for anthropological studies.[1]

My third concern is that this argument makes no harm to ethical absolutism, since what it at most suggests is that a single phrase such as "modesty is good" has different meanings in different societies and, therefore, may be judged differently. In this way, that phrase indeed refers to two ideas and each idea is judged independently. However, what a relativist needs to show is that a *single* idea or concept may justifiably be judged differently in different societies.

Let me note that this argument can be interpreted in another way that seems better and that is to focus on the meaning of ethical *terms*, instead of focusing on the meaning of ethical *statements*. According to this version, one may hold that there is a logically inherent relativity in the meaning of ethical *terms*, rather than ethical *statements* as a whole. When we consider the statement "honesty is good" it makes sense to say that the meaning of "honesty" as the subject or "good" as the predicate is relevant to the ethical code of the society in question. In my opinion, the claim that there is an inherent relativity in the meaning of the statement as a whole, independent

---

1. Of course, a moderate version of this argument might suggest that to be able to understand ethical statements one does not need to be a participant of the society in question. In this way, moral dialogue and communication become possible, but difficult, since it requires full information of the moral code of the society in question in order to make sure that one has fully grasped the meaning of that ethical statement.

from the terms, makes no sense and, as far as I know, no one has held such a view.[1]

Of course, from a grammatical or logical point of view it makes sense to distinguish between the qualities of a statement as a whole and the qualities of its terms. However, in this debate it seems that advocates of this argument have just meant (and could just have meant) one thing, i.e. the logically inherent relativity of the meaning of ethical terms, either as subjects, such as "honesty", "modesty", "respect", or as predicates, such as "good" and "bad", "right" and "wrong", "ought" and "ought not".

In any case, this argument in its second form also suffers from the same problems as the first form. The first problem is that members of every society are willing to pass ethical judgements on behaviour in other societies, even in societies with a substantially different ethical code, and there seems to be nothing in the meaning of the ethical terms that prevents people from applying them interculturally.

The second problem is that this argument overlooks the status of the ethical code, to which the meanings of ethical terms are claimed to be inherently relevant. If that ethical code itself has absolute truth, its derivative concepts that get their status from it have to be absolute as well and if not, advocates of this argument have to go back and appeal to one of the other arguments mentioned in this chapter for meta-ethical relativism. Thus, this argument is either weak or reducible to other arguments.

The third problem is that this argument closes the door to anthropology and moral dialogue and communication between members of different cultures, since ethical terms become ambiguous and lose part of their meaning when they are isolated from their cultural context. Of course, a moderate version of this argument might suggest that to be able to understand ethical terms one does not need to be a participant of the society in question but only to know the way the culture functions. In this way, moral dialogue and communication become possible, but will be difficult, since they require full information about the moral code of the society in question.

The fourth problem is that this argument makes no harm to ethical relativism, since what it suggests at most is that a single term such as "modesty" or "good" has different meaning in different societies and, therefore, may be judged differently. In this way, "modesty" or "good" indeed

---

1. Perhaps this is why Wong (1992), who has mentioned this argument (the logically inherent relativity of the meaning of ethical *statements*) in the same place and in respect to the same argument, speaks of a logically inherent relativity of the meaning of ethical *terms*.

become two concepts. However, what a relativist needs to show is that a *single* concept may justifiably be judged differently in different societies.

b. Conceptual relativity

According to this view, the meaning of ethical terms, either as subjects like *modesty* and *respect* or as predicates like *good* and *right*, varies across time, individuals, groups or societies, so that there might be two fundamentally different and at the same time true ethical beliefs about what is good or right. This view, which is called "conceptual" meta-ethical relativism (Wong, 1992), differs from the previous version of the semantic argument in that it does not hold that if we analyse the meaning of ethical terms we shall find a logically inherent relativity and, therefore, this view does not ban the transcultural application of ethical terms.

Advocates of conceptual meta-ethical relativism need to discuss every particular case that is presented as evidence for variations in meaning. Part of this task is to show that they have followed the best way to analyse ethical meanings and that the cases really manifest a fundamental difference. As far as I know, it seems that no relativist theory has ever fulfilled this task.

Apart from this, there are two other problems. The first problem is that this claim has nothing to do with relativism. For if one claims that, for example, the meaning of *modesty* or *respect* varies from society to society one means that *modesty* or *respect* is not one term. How can an ethical term be in some sense the same term if its meaning or conditions for correct application vary? They, indeed, split into different separate subjects, and each receives its own judgement in the relevant society. What a relativist needs to show is that a *single* subject is evaluated differently in different societies.[1]

The second problem is that whoever holds this view has to admit that in some way or another he or she has been able to find out the difference between two usages or two meanings of, at least, a few terms in two different societies, even though s/he may not necessarily belong to either of those societies and has not grasped in full their ethical codes; otherwise, the argument for the relativity of the meaning of ethical terms would not have been possible. Now, if we go beyond *terms* such as "m-o-d-e-s-t-y" and consider just the notion of the term when used in S1 we will see a *notion*, which is understandable for the members of S2 as well, whatever they call it. This is so, regardless of the fact that people in the two societies may have a

---

1. See my discussion about F. C. White's view on the concept of relative moral truth, when discussing the first argument for meta-ethical relativism.

different colour or race or religion or the like. Now, it is not enough that people in one society say "modesty is good" and the people in the other society say "modesty is bad". What the semantic relativist has to show is that there are necessarily different judgements in those societies about *the same notion*.

It should be noted that in his latest work (1998, p. 540) Wong introduces a type of meta-ethical relativism as "standards relativism". He asserts that some cognitive relativists tie the cognitive content of moral terms to certain standards and rules. These relativists agree with Mackie that there are no moral properties. However, unlike Mackie, they think that there is no need to take moral terms as if they refer to non-existent properties. Wong writes:

> According to such a standards relativism, moral language is used to judge and to prescribe in accordance with a set of standards and rules. Different sets of standards and rules get encoded into the meaning of ethical terms such as "good", "right" and "ought" over time, and into individuals, groups, or societies in such a way that two apparently conflicting moral beliefs can both be true (1998, p. 540).

Accordingly, ethical beliefs of different cultures do not contradict each other, since different standards are incorporated in them. Ethical beliefs conflict in practice, since they prescribe different actions. Therefore, the disagreement is only in practice, though parties to the disagreement may not realize that, if they wrongly think that they share the same standards. As we shall see later in the discussion about Harman, one problem with this version of moral relativism is that, on the one hand, it is at least partly based on the existence of moral disagreements, but on the other hand, it interprets moral phenomena in the way that it makes real moral disagreement *impossible*.

As I mentioned at the beginning, this version of the semantic argument (unlike the previous version, 3a) allows transcultural judgements. However, one controversial and crucial question for this view is *whose* standards and rules apply when someone wants to make a moral judgement about others. Harman believes that one should judge others by standards one shares with them, but other proponents of this view, as described by Wong (1998, p. 540), believe that people should use their own standards, whether or not they believe that others may share them.[1]

1.　One of the commentators on the draft of this work here ventured the addition, "Surely, the ones that define one's own terms." I agree with him that this seems to

(continued...)

In any case, I think it is now clear that standards relativism is a form of conceptual relativism, since it holds that the meaning of ethical terms is different from culture to culture. Therefore, it is subject to the same objections. (Perhaps, Wong himself did not intend to distinguish completely between standards relativism and conceptual relativism.)

4. Indeterminacy of translation

As I mentioned earlier (in the discussion about descriptive relativism), some relativists have adopted W. V. Quine's (and also B. L. Whorf's) theory of *indeterminacy of translation* to argue for meta-ethical relativism and probably, furthermore, for asking people not to pass judgement on the behaviour and moralities of others. According to this theory, languages are so fundamentally different that it is impossible to determine how the people of a radically different language from ours understand and indoctrinate objects and, therefore, one cannot translate concepts from one language to another. Like Pojman, I think this argument can be counted as a form of the conceptualist argument for meta-ethical relativism.[1] However, I think it is important enough to be discussed separately.

The standard objection to the theory of the indeterminacy of translation is that it is against our undeniable experience of learning foreign languages and communicating with people from other cultures. Actually communications between languages enrich the languages. Also, general moral principles, such as the obligations of parents towards children and a no-unnecessary-harm principle, clearly can be communicated transculturally. Besides standard objections to this theory and my objections above to any type of conceptual argument for relativism, I should like to remind the reader that, in my view, this argument actually works against relativism. Without being able to understand properly what the other people say, how can the relativist assure us that, in spite of different appearances, there are no common moral principles? Indeed, this theory teaches us not to be hasty in inferring

---

(...continued)

be the natural or logical implication of this view, but we have to note that this implies the possibility of passing judgements on others who do not share our standards, an idea that is extremely hard for many ethical relativists to accept. Perhaps it is in order to avoid this that Harman says that one has to apply the common standards. As I mentioned above, the question is a controversial and crucial one for advocates of this view.

1. Of course, the semantic argument is more general, since it applies even when there are two different cultures with the same language, as in some British colonies where the inhabitants speak English.

fundamental differences from mere different appearances. For example, if some people ate the body of their dead relatives, this does not mean that they had no respect for their dead relatives. Indeed, as we saw earlier in the story of Herodotus, they took it as an exercise of respect to eat the bodies of their dead relatives. So, even in cases in which the actions of others seem to us completely strange and irrational, there may be many things that they share with us.

5. Functionalism

We saw earlier in the discussion about the history of ethical relativism that Michel de Montaigne made this type of argument, but it has had its greatest acceptance among contemporary anthropologists who emphasize the need to study societies as organic wholes, of which the parts are functionally interdependent.[1] For example, we saw that Sumner developed a functionalist version of meta-ethical relativism. We also saw that in the 1930s functionalism was the dominant view among British anthropologists, who held that "any given society's ethical practices were the result of long-standing structural or practical development, which served complex and subtle purposes, and thus were not to be tampered with" (Whitaker, 1997, p. 479).

To have a better understanding of the principle of functional necessity, it would be appropriate to consider Radcliff-Brown's account of functionalism. He was an anthropologist who maintained that institutions, including moral systems, are responses to permanent needs or local necessities. Instead of some vague notion of "rightness", he uses the concept of *necessary for social/biological survival*. Cultural practices "exist and persist because they are part of the mechanism by which an orderly society maintains itself in existence" (Radcliff-Brown, 1952, p. 152). Accordingly, those practices that result in the long-term survival of the society are good. For example, the Yunamuno, with their culturally embedded violence and cruelty, are to disappear since their persistent warfare is harmful to the long-term survival of their moral order.

Thus, according to functionalism, ethical codes or customary ethical beliefs play an essential role in and are functionally necessary for the maintenance of the societies in which they are accepted. Therefore, the functionalist goes on,

---

1. Two important discussions of the idea that the word "good" might be considered in functional terms are to be found in Philippa Foot, "Goodness and Choice", *Proceedings of the Aristotelian Society*, Supplementary, Vol. 25 (1961), and Jerrold J. Katz, "Semantic Theory and the Meaning of 'Good'", *Journal of Philosophy*, Vol. 61 (1964).

those ethical codes and beliefs are true for that society, but not necessarily in another. In this way, what is morally good in one society may not be good in another society. Unerman (1996) gives the actual example of capitalism and social corporate responsibility. In a capitalist society, if corporate social responsibility is seen as a challenge to capitalism, corporate social responsibility is likely to be regarded as morally wrong in that society.

It is noteworthy that Williams maintains that relativism in its vulgar and unregenerate form, which, to him, is both the most distinctive and the most influential form, involves functionalism. He articulates the relativism as follows:

- "right" means "right for a given society";
- "right for a given society" is to be understood in a functionalist way;
- therefore, it is wrong for people in one society to condemn and interfere with the values of another society.

Williams adds that this view has a long history. It was also popular among "some liberal colonialists, notably British administrators in places (such as West Africa) in which white men had no land" (Williams, 1972, p. 20).

I think it is clear that functionalism is a teleological theory that tries to justify morality by the means of its results. The end of morality is to maintain or stabilize a social order or system. In different conditions, different regulations are required. Therefore, if there are any differences between moralities, they will be only because of different conditions. By implication, in all the same conditions there will be the same morality with the same functions. But this is simply what absolutists believe. There will be shortly a discussion about the various kinds of differences that are explicable according to absolutism. Thus there seems to be a gap between functionalism and ethical relativism.

Another difficulty with the functionalism and therefore with the functionalist argument for ethical relativism concerns the identification of a "society". If we consider society as a cultural unit that includes moral values, its maintenance will obviously imply the preservation of those values, but then this view turns out to be circular. It will not bear any empirical or synthetic claim about the world; necessarily survival of a group-with-certain-values depends on preserving those values. On the other hand, if we consider society just as a number of people, its survival will just depend on the survival of those people even through the following generations. The result, then, would be that the maintenance of moral values would not be necessary for the survival of that society.[1]

Between these two poles, there is a place for the fair contribution of values to the maintenance of a society. There may be institutions or values or beliefs or even practices that play a crucial role in a society to the extent that their change or absence may lead to unpredictable events in that society. People may physically survive, but they will lose their peace of mind and will be in a hopeless condition. Such social phenomena are, in a sense, functionally necessary for the society (or, in other words, for its stability). These phenomena must be considered in deciding what to do, but the problem is that they cannot decide for us and tell us what to do. In our assessment of morality of any society we go beyond the question of what that society needs in order to sustain itself, and face the question of whether it is right for that society to maintain its current form. We cannot justify our moral beliefs just by arguing that they are necessary for preserving our society in its present condition. For example, the fact that racist beliefs were necessary to sustain the former apartheid society in South Africa does not make such racist beliefs morally acceptable.

Another objection to the functionalist argument (Harre and Krausz, 1996) is that it has two absurd implications: first, that we must consider a code of practice in a culture as morally acceptable simply because it has happened that the given culture still exists and, second, that we must consider another code of practice as morally unacceptable simply because that culture has ceased to exist, such as Hellenistic Greece or classical China.

I personally think that a better policy is to base the argument only on the implausibility of the first implication of the functionalism, i.e. the implausibility of approving whatever happens to survive. For there is a potential response on behalf of the functionalists in respect to the second implication, and that is to say that extrinsic circumstances can destroy morally better cultures or civilizations and leave others. What is essential for the functionalist argument is the claim that if a moral system has persisted for a long time it should be considered as good. Of course, functionalism requires that a moral system would be bad if it is *shown* to have ceased to exist owing to internal factors. In any case, it does not seem sound to praise cow worship in a given society on the prudential grounds that it is beneficial for the ecological conditions of that society. Nor does it seem sound to blame the Nazis only because their actions were in the long term bad for business. It

---

1. For this kind of objection, see Williams (1972) and Wong (1992 and 1996).

seems that this kind of praise or blame is irrelevant to our moral assessment of the practices.

Another difficulty of this view is that people, because of their nationality, race, religion, profession and the like, usually belong simultaneously to different groups or societies. In many cases, there is no uniformity between the functionally necessary requirements of these groups or societies. As a citizen one may be required to do a certain act for the security and welfare of the state, which is strictly against the basic norms of racial or religious culture. My question is: should an African American or a Native American do what is functionally necessary for the survival or stability of the African American or Native American community or of the American society in general? It does not solve the problem to suggest, as does Harman (1977, p. 113), that one can act according to the conventions of the society, which is more important to the individual, since they may have equal importance for that person and since it makes morality dependent on arbitrary choices. We normally do not take moral rules to depend on our own choice. Moreover, we sometimes feel morally compelled and responsible to change or reform the very group which is most important to us.

6. Non-cognitivism

One potential ground for meta-ethical relativism is (claimed to be) non-cognitivism. For example, on an emotivist ground one may argue for ethical relativism by saying that all moral values are simply statements of emotional reactions; therefore, owing to variation of emotional reactions among individuals or groups and to changes in emotional reactions of one individual or group over time, moral values also change and there can be no standard moral values. Wong (1998) speaks of a non-cognitive version of morally specific relativism and Billington (1993) even argues that this leads to an *extreme* form of relativism.[1] To evaluate this claim, I shall try first to explain the idea of non-cognitivism in morality and then consider whether it really leads to ethical relativism or not. Of course, our main concern is to explore

---

1. Wong (1998, p. 540) divides "morality-specific relativism" into *cognitive* and *non-cognitive* versions. Cognitive relativists, such as Mackie, Harman and Wong, interpret moral judgements as expressing beliefs, on the grounds that moral judgements are often argued or judged true or false on the basis of reason. Some cognitive relativists such as Wong and Harman believe that there is no single true morality because more than one morality is true, and some others like Mackie believe that there is no single true morality because all are false.

    Since cognitive relativists have different arguments for ethical relativism, I have discussed them separately.

the relation between ethical relativism and non-cognitivism. Therefore, we shall mention non-cognitivism only as much as needed. To make a final decision about non-cognitivism needs an independent study.

It is difficult to present a single short and clear definition that can include all various non-cognitive theories of morality. Simon Blackburn explains non-cognitivism in this way: "A common but potentially misleading title for projectivist, expressivist, emotive, or prescriptive theories of ethics. A state of mind is non-cognitive if it involves no cognition or knowledge of any kind."[1] To have a better understanding of non-cognitivism, let us first consider it in general and then look at some of the non-cognitive ethical theories in particular.

Non-cognitivists believe that moral utterances are not cognitive statements, verifiable as true or false. According to non-cognitivism, moral judgements are simply not judgements about facts. Moral utterances assert nothing true or false about the world; they simply express our own reactions to certain facts and happenings. Some important sources of non-cognitivism are *Ethics and Language* (1944) and *Facts and Values* (1963) by C. L. Stevenson; *Language, Truth and Logic*, 2nd edition (1950) by A. J. Ayer, and *The Language of Morals* (1952) and *Freedom and Reason* (1963) by R. M. Hare.

There are different views among non-cognitivists themselves. Stevenson (1967) admits that no one continues to hold this view just as it stands. In the following pages, we shall study two of most important versions of non-cognitivism, i.e. *emotivism* and *universal prescriptivism,* to see whether they can support ethical relativism or not.

a. Emotivism
C. L. Stevenson and the logical positivist A. J. Ayer developed a special form of non-cognitivism, which is called "emotivism". It has been suggested (e.g. Rachels, 1998, p. 5) that emotivism was the most influential theory of ethics in the mid-twentieth century. Stevenson and Ayer hold that moral utterances express the emotions, feelings or attitudes of the speaker.[2] They believe that

---

1. Simon Blackburn, *The Dictionary of Philosophy* (Oxford and New York: Oxford University Press, 1994), p. 264.

2. Ayer, after the appearance of *Ethics and Language*, uses the term "attitude" instead of "feeling". Stevenson always uses the term "attitude". Although this may be seen as a modification of emotivism, we have to note that they both still take moral attitudes to be non-cognitive and to be feelings or emotions. For example, Stevenson clearly says that the term "attitude" means "any psychological (continued...)

we use moral utterances to express our feeling of approval or disapproval. Of course, Stevenson believes that moral utterances are also used to influence the behaviour of the hearer and to persuade him or her to act in a certain way. Stevenson asserts that his view in *Ethics and Language* can conveniently be referred to as "the so-called non-cognitive view". He writes:

> According to this view, "a speaker normally uses 'X is yellow' to express his belief about X, he normally uses 'X is good' to express something else, mainly his approval of X." It adds that "good," being a term of praise, usually commends X to others and thus tends to evoke their approval as well (Stevenson, 1967, p. 79).

This is the case also with "right", "duty" and so on. As we can see, emotivism offers *easy* solutions for historical problems of ethics. It suggests that there is no need to discuss how we can know moral truths, since there are no moral truths at all. It also suggests that there is an obvious relation between moral beliefs and motivation. Indeed, a moral belief is a certain sort of attitude, i.e. a certain disposition to act. Therefore, there remains no need to discuss how we get motivated to act according to our moral beliefs. There would be also no need to discuss the ontological problem of moral facts.[1]

It is noteworthy that, having denied moral truths, Stevenson (1967) clearly points out that *moral* disagreements are not due to disagreements about facts of the case; moral disagreements are disagreements in attitude, even though people may have the same beliefs about the facts of the case.

Thus, it seems obvious that emotivists such as Stevenson leave no ground for regarding either side of a moral disagreement, that is, the disagreement in

---

(...continued)

disposition of being *for* or *against* something. Hence love and hate are relatively specific kinds of attitudes, as are approved and disapproved, and so on. (Stevenson, 1967, p. 1) Perhaps he takes moral attitudes as a non-cognitive state that has a *minor* judgemental aspect as well. My reason is the existence of passages like this:

> Doubtless there is always *some* element of description in ethical judgments, but this is by no means all. Their major use is not to indicate facts, but to *create an influence.* Instead of merely describing people's interests, they *change* or *intensify* them (Cahn and Markie, 1998, p. 497, cited from Stevenson, "The Emotive Meaning of Ethical Terms", *Mind*, Vol. 46, 1937).

1. On non-cognitivism see, for example, Rachels, 1998, pp. 437–9, Rachels, 1996, pp. 5–7, and Donagan, 1992, p. 539. For a comparison between Stevenson and Ayer, see McNaughton, 1998, pp. 24 and 25, and Rachels, 1998, pp. 5–7.

attitude, as more or less reasonable. As I mentioned earlier, Billington (1993) believes that this leads to an extreme form of relativism. If we take our moral stances just as emotional reactions, the results will be that moral judgements can neither be right nor wrong and that our moral judgements will resemble strong emotional reactions that are just transitory reactions against whatever disaster or distasteful incident is currently, say, headline news. When the headlines change our emotional feelings also change.

Emotivism as an ethical theory should be examined separately. However, for the sake of our study of ethical relativism I have to say briefly that emotional functions of our moral utterances form an undeniable part of our moral experience. No moral theory can be faithful to morality while ignoring this aspect of moral experience. Yet, as I shall assert in the final chapter on the foundations of morality, it seems implausible to reduce morality to expressions of emotions. It would be appropriate here to refer to what Hume has argued about the balance between reason and emotion. In his *Enquiry Concerning the Principles of Morals*, Section I, Hume argues that the role of reason and the importance of reasoning are undeniable, just as the role of emotions is undeniable. He mentions modern enquirers who "talk much of the beauty of virtue, and deformity of vice, yet have commonly endeavoured to account for these distinctions by metaphysical reasoning, and by deductions from the most abstract principles of the understanding."

Our moral experience shows that morality cannot be taken just as another form of emotional behaviour or reactions. Unlike emotional behaviour or reactions, it does seem that in practice many people hold long-term and deeply rooted moral values, such as beliefs for or against racial equality, capital punishment, slavery, environmental protection, capitalism, private health, sexual equality and animal rights. These values can hardly be explained by transitory and unstable emotional reactions. If there were no such stable values that were likely to be more powerful in achieving a change in society, then society would be less likely to strive for social reforms, since such changes are in need of some goalposts that are not constantly changing.

Emotivism is also in conflict with our moral language, that is, with ways in which people use and treat ethical statements as stating cognitive attitudes: the application of the words "true" and "false" to ethical statements, for instance. Therefore, until there is no forcing argument for non-cognitivism one is justified in preferring the common-sense view.

Emotivism is not compatible with the fact that people argue for and against ethical positions. To express our emotions we do not need to argue. People would not challenge us if, for example, we say, "I like or dislike some kind of food or game". However, if we want to explain what we judge about a certain action or if we want to persuade our hearer to act in a certain way we do need to support what we say with good reasons. To repeat Hume's words, "No man reasons concerning another's beauty; but frequently concerning the justice or injustice of his actions" (ibid). A failure to appreciate this point may reduce moral dialogue and education to some sort of propaganda or advertisement; or, as Rachels puts it, "the business of giving reasons turns out to be an exercise in psychological manipulation" (Rachels, 1998, p. 8). Again, as Stevenson himself puts it, "any statement about any fact which any speaker considers likely to alter attitudes may be adduced as a reason for or against an ethical judgement" (Stevenson, 1944, p. 114, cited from Rachels, 1998, p. 8).

I think a consistent emotivist has to rephrase Stevenson's statement into: "Anything, such as statements and actions, that is likely to alter attitudes may be adduced as reason for or against an ethical judgement, even if the speaker or the agent fails to notice that his statement or his act or the like could lead to such alteration." This implies that in ethical reasoning neither the person who argues nor the hearer needs to be conscious.

Thus, emotivism is not a tenable meta-ethical theory and cannot be taken as a good basis for meta-ethical relativism. Further, it may be added that even if one accepts emotivism it does not mean that one has to be a relativist. In other words, there is no necessary implication between emotivism and meta-ethical relativism. The reason is that, even if we take moral utterances to be non-cognitive and emotional, this does not mean that they have to be changing from one person to another or from one group to another. Human emotional reactions, or at least some of them, may be related to common desires, needs and wants that are essential to human nature, and therefore the same everywhere and in every age.

Now, it becomes clear that, to be able to draw a relativistic position from emotivism, one has to supplement emotivism with the argument either that human nature has no such common, enduring desires, needs and wants or that, if it does, they cannot be discovered. Also, as Wong (1992) suggested, non-cognitivists can avoid accepting meta-ethical relativism, if they stick to justifiability, rather than truth, and admit that ethical statements can be evaluated along some epistemic dimension of justifiability that does not involve truth, and that there is a single most justifiable ethical code.

It should be noted that our discussion here concerns a view of emotion that takes it to be a feeling or reactionary type of mental states that are transitory, approximately equal to what was called "passion" by Descartes and

Hume. Typical examples are fear, anger, sadness and joy. In a psychological analysis, an emotional state can be defined as "a disposition to act in particular ways, produced by exposure to stimuli the subject wants to experience or avoid, or by exposure to signals predict the imminent occurrence of such stimuli. Such states are, of course, accompanied by changes in neural and hormonal processes" (Jeffery A. Gray and Roy Porter, 1999, p. 267).[1] Of course, if one means by "emotion" any mental state (other than belief) the case will be different. For example, in a virtue-centred morality, there can be stable states that characterize the virtuous person and thus act as the basis of morality. For example, Aristotle defined virtue as *hexis*, a stable state of character (which is *not* belief). This view of emotion is not subject to my objections on emotivism, but it better serves my general argument here that the belief in the centrality of the role of emotions in ethics does not grant ethical relativism. As Aristotle himself believed, human virtues can be the same for every human being (and human beings should do the same thing in similar circumstances).

Finally, I should like here to refer to what Stevenson himself has mentioned in this regard. He admits that it may at first seem that there is no distinction between "the so-called non-cognitive view" and moral relativism or that the distinction depends on a technicality, but he thinks that this is not true. For example, one difference is that, according to relativism, there can be no real disagreement because different parties have different issues about which to make judgements, but in Stevenson's view both are praising and condemning the same thing. He says, "In an important sense of words, then, the so-called non-cognitive view defends neither an ordinary relativism nor a methodological relativism. It is an *answer* to relativism" (Stevenson, 1967, pp. 81–93). Now, it is clear that even an emotivist like Stevenson is not happy to let his view be identified with ethical relativism and tries to show some differences.[2]

---

1. As I mentioned in an earlier footnote, Ayer in *Ethics and Language* and Stevenson use the term "attitude" instead of "feeling" or "emotion". This can be seen as an improvement for the emotivist theory, but we have to note that they are still non-cognitivists and still want to reduce ethics to the *expression* of feelings or psychological dispositions. It should be noted that this modification (that is, speaking of attitudes and dispositions which are more stable compared to transitory emotions) better suits my general argument here that emotivism as such cannot be taken as a proof for ethical relativism. In similar circumstances, there can be similar attitudes among people.

2. Of course, this does not mean that I am happy with *the way* Stevenson distinguishes

(continued...)

b. Universal prescriptivism

According to Hare, moral judgements are "universal prescriptions", not felt attitudes or emotions; but he believed in the logical gap between "is" and "ought" or between "fact" and "value", and therefore between describing and recommending. For Hare the primary role of evaluative language is not to describe, but to prescribe. Hare points out that the chief difference between moral prescriptions and straightforward commands lies in the fact that acceptance of a moral judgement implies commanding consistently in relation to everything that is similar in morally relevant respects.[1]

One of the main differences between Hare's position and emotivism is that Hare emphasizes the possibility, and indeed the necessity, of logical reasoning in ethics. Therefore, for Hare morality is objective in the sense that moral problems can be solved by the application of rational methods and by showing that some moral positions are true and some are false. Hare, as he himself expressed, was greatly influenced by Kant. However, he did not agree with Kant about the power of reason. Unlike Kant, he thought that the only requirement of rationality is consistency.

In *The Language of Morals*, Hare accepted that different people could adopt different principles as their moral principles without any irrationality. Someone might consistently associate murder with wrongness and another person might decide not to do so; but neither of them is guilty of any logical error.

In *Freedom and Reason*, Hare claimed that a racist who is prepared to agree that, if he or she belongs to the "inferior" group, s/he should be discriminated against, is not illogical, although Hare seems to regard that person as psychologically disturbed, and calls such a person a "fanatic". Such a person is as justified and logical as a person who consistently believes in equal treatment of human beings and better justified than such a person, if he is not consistent.

(...continued)

between his theory and ethical relativism. For example, I think that emotivism leaves no place for a real moral disagreement. According to emotivism, when A says "X is good" and B says "X is bad" they are not really disagreeing. What A is saying is just *A's approval of X* and what B is saying is just *B's disapproval of X* and there is no conflict between these two. Indeed, Stevenson has first represented ethical relativism as a simple form of subjectivism and then has tried to make some distinctions between relativism and emotivism.

1. See Hare, 1952, 1963, 1981 and 1993. See also *Hare and Critics: Essays on Moral Thinking* edited by Douglas Seanor and N. Fotion (1990), Sayre-McCord, 1996, and Bunting, 1996.

If, like Hare, we accept that the only rational requirement for morality is consistency, it will lead us to ethical relativism, since there can be various consistent ethical systems at the same time. A consistent racist is as right as a consistent non-racist. Of course, Hare himself was not prepared to be charged with relativism. Again, like Stevenson, Hare rejected ethical relativism. However, I agree with Bunting (1996, p. 82) that Stevenson and Hare rejected relativism by misrepresenting it and by neglecting important relativist features of their theory; they identified "relativism" with a naïve subjectivist view that moral predicates describe subjective states of mind and then they said that their views are different from "relativism".

Hare's theory of ethics is not our main subject here and it should be examined separately, but as far as our study of ethical relativism is concerned, I have to say here briefly that the fundamental problem with Hare's view, which also underlies his charge with relativism, is that it makes morality a voluntary business or, more precisely, a *consistent* voluntary business. Consistency does not seem to be able to provide Hare with sufficient ground for objectivity of morals. If morality derives its validity and strength from individual adoption, it cannot have any sanction. Also, any principle can logically be a moral one, as long as it is universalized, e.g. "everyone should lie, if it suits him". The third problem is that we normally suppose morality to transcend the principles that we ourselves have adopted; otherwise we should have to conclude that there are no moral constraints of the sort we ordinarily believe to exist. In Harman's words, "If externalism is dead, everything is permitted" (Harman, 1977, p. 93). To repeat Benn's words, "Our best moral responses are guided by considerations external to us, which dictate what moral commitments we should form" (Benn, 1998, p. 50).

Of course, Hare himself has later modified this position by adopting a utilitarian approach to ethics. He claimed that moral consistency could be developed in the way that it yields utilitarianism.[1] In his *Moral Thinking*, Hare says:

> For now all the preferences for what should happen to us in hypothetical situations in which we were in the other's roles have acquired the same weight as they would have if we were actually going to be in those roles and were perfectly prudent. This, indeed, is what makes utilitarians of us (p. 226).

---

1. See Hare, 1981. See also Donagan, 1992, p. 539, and McNaughton, 1998, pp. 168–71.

More precisely, Hare's argument for utilitarianism can be put in this way:

To make honest universal prescription one must investigate, as thoroughly as is practicable, how those affected by the various ways in which the agent might act would be benefited and harmed, imagine each such way of acting from the point of view of each such person, and calculate which would produce the greatest net benefit or the least net harm (Donagan, 1992, p. 539).

Despite this modification, Hare's view has always been very influential. W. D. Hudson, in his " Development of Hare's Moral Philosophy" in *Hare and Critics: Essays on Moral Thinking* (1990, p. 22), maintains that Hare is still at the centre of critical attention. What is important for us here is that Hare still defends the twin foundations of his universal prescriptivism: that "the freedom which we have as moral thinkers is a freedom to reason" (*Moral Thinking*, pp. 6, 7). and that "we remain free to prefer what we prefer" (ibid., p. 225).

Regardless of the fact that it is not clear how consistency alone can lead to utilitarianism, nor why a consistent prescriptivist has to count himself "just as one", and regardless also of the fact that utilitarianism seems to be in conflict with our freedom "to prefer what we prefer", I would say that Hare's embrace of utilitarianism is in favour of the general argument in this work against ethical relativism. To the extent that Hare moves towards utilitarianism, he gets farther from relativism, since in addition to consistency he has to observe another objective standard, that is, the maximum good for the maximum number of people.

To conclude, I should like to emphasize again that even if we take moral utterances to be non-cognitive, this does not mean that they are relative to changeable elements. At least some of them might be related to common individual or social needs and wants that are essential to human nature and, therefore, the same everywhere and in every age. Thus, a non-cognitivist, to be able to support relativism, needs to supplement non-cognitivism with other arguments. We saw problems with both emotivism and universal prescriptivism, which make them not strong enough to support ethical relativism. Also, as mentioned earlier, although non-cognitivism is not compatible with the recognition of moral truth, it can avoid accepting meta-ethical relativism by sticking to justifiability, rather than truth, and admitting that ethical statements can be evaluated along some epistemic dimension of justifiability that does not involve truth, and that there is a single most justifiable ethical code.

7. The subjectivist approach

Ethical subjectivism is a theory that holds that there are no "moral" facts, although ethical judgements at first might seem to be objectively true or false, i.e. true or false independent of what people believe or want. Here we shall look at two versions of ethical subjectivism to see whether they can be taken as good arguments for ethical relativism or not. Of course, we are not going to discuss the whole issue of subjectivism here. Our main concern here is the relation between subjectivism and ethical relativism.

a. Simple subjectivist theory

Simple subjectivism holds that moral judgements are propositions about feelings, beliefs or attitudes of individuals or groups. According to this view, " X is good" is true if and only if some individual or group approves of X, or has some other appropriate belief or attitude towards X. It is called "simple subjectivism" (Rachels, 1996, p. 433), since it holds the basic idea of subjectivism in an uncomplicated form.

On a subjectivist theory of ethics, one may argue for ethical relativism by saying that moral propositions are expressions of what people feel or believe about moral subjects, therefore, anyone's moral proposition can be as true as any other's. Moral judgements are like judgements about what people like, such as their favourite colour or taste. Again, the problem of moral relativism is tied in with the debate on the origins or foundations of morality. Apart from my discussion about the foundations of morality in the final chapter of this work, I should like here to refer to some problems with this approach to morality.

One important problem with simple subjectivism is that it renders morality and moral praise or blame completely useless. If morality were subjective, as taste or aesthetic judgements are, little or no moral interpersonal criticism would be possible. This view allows that Hitler or a serial murderer such as Ted Bundy could be as moral as Gandhi, provided that each lives by his own standards. In other words, subjectivism implies that we are morally infallible. As long as we do what we approve of, we can do no wrong.

The other problem is that simple subjectivism makes moral disagreements impossible, because if every person is reporting his own subjective attitude or position, he or she is not making a judgement about the same thing. When A says "X is good", it means that A approves of X and when B says "X is bad" it means that B disapproves of X. Obviously there is no conflict between saying that A approves of X and saying that B disapproves of X.

Moreover, the subjectivist view makes moral argumentation and communication pointless or impossible, since it holds that in ethics everybody expresses only his or her personal attitude, something that is not questionable. To repeat Pojman's words, "Subjectivism treats individuals like billiard balls on a societal pool table where they meet only in radical collisions, each aimed at his or her own goal and striving to do in others before they themselves are done in" (Pojman, 1998, p. 41). However, it is part of our moral experience that we get seriously involved in moral debates and reflect on both sides and finally may make a judgement that we are prepared to defend.

One way of having a better understanding of the above point and in fact of our moral experience is to think about the following questions. Do we not take the moral badness of racism, infanticide and indifference to the starving poor to be a perfectly intelligible notion? Don't we, including subjectivists, take morality seriously? Don't we in fact have moral beliefs, rather than just moral taste or feeling? Don't moral beliefs require being in some relation to moral facts? Don't we argue with each other on moral issues in order to come to some agreement? As Benn puts it, "There is such a thing as persuasion and the emergence of a consensus, and this is not merely a matter of mesmerizing opponents into acquiring new feelings about moral issues" (Benn, 1998, p. 56).

Here I should like to reiterate what I said earlier in this work: one may be a subjectivist and still not believe in relativism. The refutation of relativism need not be anti-subjectivist. Some people may argue that ethics is rooted in human dispositions and still believe that ethical rules are universal, for example, because of the uniformity of human nature. Therefore, there may be non-objectivists who are absolutist. On the other hand, there may be objectivists who are relativist, such as those who develop a semantic or functionalist argument for meta-ethical relativism. Therefore, even if we suppose that subjectivism is true it does not prove the truth of ethical relativism.

b. The error theory

John L. Mackie in *Ethics: Inventing Right* and *Wrong* (1977) has developed a form of ethical subjectivism, which is known as the error theory. According to this theory, moral judgements have truth value and contain referring expressions. However, these referring expressions are empty, since there are no moral facts.

Mackie is in favour of ethical relativism. He believes that there is no single true morality because *morality* is completely a fiction, and so all moral claims are false. Of course, Mackie does not deny that common-sense morality presupposes objectivity of morality, but he takes that to be a systematic error. Mackie argues that ethical statements involve mistaken assumptions about the existence of objective values in the world. They purport to report objective matters of fact, but there are no such matters of fact. Mackie points out that since the times of Plato, the objectivity of moral values has been an underlying assumption of much Western moral philosophy. He believes that morality actually arises out of custom and convention, but the meanings of moral terms presuppose a mistaken reference to real properties that provide everyone with a reason for acting accordingly.

Mackie's famous argument from *queerness* against objectivity is, basically, that if ethical terms such as "right" and "wrong" had an objective meaning, we would need sensory perception quite different from the ordinary sensory perception that informs us about other objective phenomena. However, we do not have any such sensory perception or faculty. Mackie writes:

> If there were objective values, then they would be entities or qualities or relations of a very strange sort, utterly different to anything else in the universe. Correspondingly, if we were aware of them, it would have to be by some special faculty of moral perception or intuition, utterly different from our ordinary ways of knowing everything else (Mackie, 1977, p. 38).

An important problem with the view that all moral statements are false (the error theory) seems to be that it does not fit in with our moral experience. In other words, the error theory does not present a coherent picture of our moral experience. Reflection on the process of moral reasoning shows that we discuss with each other and argue for or against moral positions and believe in a moral position, if there are good reasons for that. How can we take all moral judgements to be false and still seriously engage in moral discourse and practice? How can we coherently believe in the error theory and still hold beliefs about moral goodness or badness and practise accordingly, or as Darwall (1998, p. 64) puts it, "How can we coherently believe both that deliberate killing is vicious and that it is false that deliberate killing is vicious?" Is it rational to hold both these two beliefs together?

Therefore, error theory is not compatible with common-sense morality and our moral experience, and unless there are overriding reasons we have to rely on them. Of course, this type of argument does not prove that the error theory is mistaken.

It should also be noted that Mackie's proposal is to some extent ambiguous.[1] Presumably, he believes that morality as normally conceived should be replaced with something else, but he does not indicate exactly what sort of replacement he has in mind. For example, do we need to establish a certain institution?

Someone who has developed an error theory need not necessarily be a relativist as well. It is possible to believe that morality is a fiction and moral judgements are false, but still believe that all human beings make similar *wrong assumptions* and project them to the world. Therefore, although all moral systems are false, there may be one system that is most justified and best fits into the picture.[2] It should also be noted that most of the recent ethical relativists such as Harman and Wong have developed forms of ethical relativism that are neither simple subjectivism nor error theory. They believe that moral judgements depend for their truth or justifiability on social institutions or practices that do not necessarily depend on the taste or feeling of the individuals who take part in them. Often such relativists agree with non-relativists that the truth or justifiability of moral claims is independent of the current beliefs, attitudes and feelings of those to whom they apply.

8. Existentialism

As we saw earlier in our discussion about the history of ethical relativism, existentialists such as Sartre believe that there are no general principles or universal laws at all. Every person has to make his or her personal decision in each case and follow it. To act morally simply means to have "good faith", that is, to act according to the morality one has adopted. In this way, morality becomes relativist, since every case is unique and there is "no justification before us". When morality is seen just as good faith in what one has freely chosen, then the existence of different sorts of actions that one could justifiably perform becomes possible, provided that one performs them in good faith. As Sartre responded to his pupil, "You are free, therefore choose – that is to say, invent. No rule of general morality can show you what to do" (Sartre, 1970 (1948), p. 38).

The problem with Sartre's view is that morality, as we shall see in the final

---

1. See for a similar point Harman (1989, p. 366).

2. It should be noted that Mackie himself was a cognitivist and therefore he must have believed in a type of justifiability that is not based on truth.

chapter, seems to be more than just good faith. Moral maxims such as "Do not murder", "Help those in need" and the like require more than simply being true to yourself. It has also to be noted that Sartre's view is in a sense an absolutist view, since it takes "good faith" as a universally valid value, which all have to grasp.

9. Situation ethics

As I mentioned earlier in the discussion about the history of ethical relativism, one important contemporary trend in ethics is called "situation ethics". The advocates of situation ethics believe that each moral problem is unique.[1] Only the person who is engaged in the problem can solve the problem. It has been suggested (Unerman, 1996) that situation ethics is another form of ethical relativism, since it holds that even within one society there may be no absolute right or wrong behaviour, as the "rightness" or "wrongness" of particular behaviour depends upon the particular situation of the agent. Along similar lines, Billington (1993) points out that even if detailed moral rules were absolute, there are likely to be situations in which one absolute rule gives conflicting guidance to that given by another absolute rule.

The first problem with the argument from situation ethics is that it would be consistent to believe in situation ethics and still reject ethical relativism. We know that each situation is, indeed, built up by a set of parameters or factors. People can have absolute principles, in which every parameter may have a special role and, owing to the changes of those parameters, different principles become applicable. Therefore, one may believe in the uniqueness of situations but still believe that one has to observe absolute and general principles that define the status of the involved parameters. For example, one can articulate a general rule for dealing with special cases such as Sartre's student who sought his advice on whether to join the Free French Forces or to stay near to his mother. As Hare (1996, p. 457) suggested, the student ought to have been able to articulate a specific principle for situations *just* like this, even if such situations never happen.

A second problem is that, according to situation ethics, we cannot judge anyone's action, even our own actions in the past, because we are not engaged any more in that situation. However, it is part of our ordinary moral life that

---

1.   Fletcher (1966, p. 32) distinguishes between the antinomians' position, which holds similarity of moral cases altogether, and the situationists' position, which holds that there are similarities, but these similarities are not enough to "validate a law or to support anything more than a cautious generalization". In Edmund Cahn's phrase, "Every case is like every other case, and no two cases are alike" (ibid.).

we make judgements about actions of others and about our actions in the past.

The third problem is that, according to situation ethics, we must not be able to speak about any moral values, because this will make them universal and not relative to a unique situation, just as we cannot describe moral situations, because whatever is described cannot be unique.[1]

To sum up, I should like to mention that even situationists themselves admit the existence of some moral principle/s. For example, Christian situation ethicists believe that there is only one norm or principle (or whatsoever called), which is always good and right regardless of the circumstances. That norm or principle is "love" or *agape*. All other norms or principles or laws are valid, *if and only if they happen* to serve love in a given situation. Christian ethics is defined as "an effort to relate love to a world of relativities through a casuistry obedient to love".[2] Thanks to this acceptance of the existence of a general norm or principle, it has been suggested (ibid.) that situation ethics can be called "principled relativism," a type of relativism that admits the existence of principles or maxims or general rules as *illuminators* (and not as *directors*).

10. Social construction of "good" and "bad"
There are various theories that hold that reality or part of it is socially constructed. These theories may be taken as a ground for ethical relativism. According to a general sociological theory, which is called "the social construction of reality", the world is constructed through collective human affairs. Peter Berger and Thomas Luckmann, who advanced this theory, say:

> Everyday life presents itself as a reality interpreted by men and subjectively meaningful to them as a coherent world . . . The world of everyday life is not only taken for granted as reality by the ordinary members of society in the subjectively meaningful conduct of their lives. It is a world that *originates in their thoughts and actions*, and is

---

1. I have argued earlier for the fact that adding concepts to a universal concept may narrow its extent but never makes it particular.

2. Fletcher, 1966, pp. 30 and 31. Borrowing Tillich's terminology, Fletcher later elaborates on this point by saying that "the Christian situationism is a method that proceeds, so to speak, from (1) its one and only law, *agape* (love), to the *sophia* (wisdom) of the church and culture, containing many "general rules" of more or less reliability, to (3) the *kairos* (moment of decision, the fullness of time) in which *the responsible self in the situation* decides whether the *sophia* can serve love there, or not (ibid., p. 33).

maintained as real by these (*The Social Construction of Reality: A Treatise in the Sociology of Knowledge*, 1971, p. 33, cited in Watt, 1983, p. 7; italics are from Watt).

In a later work, *The Social Reality of Religion,* Berger writes:

Man's world-building activity is always a collective enterprise. Man's internal appropriation of a world must also take place in a collectivity (*The Social Reality of Religion*, 1973, p. 25, cited in Watt, 1983, p. 8).

More particularly about ethics, I explained earlier (in the discussion about the history of ethical relativism) how postmodernism is thought to support ethical relativism. From a postmodernist perspective, the characteristics required for something to be considered as "good" are socially constructed and therefore what is considered good in one society may be considered bad in another society that has a different socially constructed notion of the characteristics of "goodness" (Arrington and Francis, 1993). Postmodernism therefore seems to argue in favour of ethical relativism.

Similarly, as we saw earlier, Neimark (1995, p. 93) argues that "what constitutes ethical behaviour at any point in time – like knowledge more generally – is socially constructed; it is a product of time and place". This, as I mentioned earlier, implies that the morality regarding items such as pollution, employee welfare and community involvement by business is socially constructed, and may *happen to* be different in different societies and at different times.

This view was partly examined before when discussing the analysis of right-centred morality and common good-centred morality, and some aspect of that will be studied more in the discussions about the social custom theory (Chapter Four) and about the foundation of morality (Chapter Six). However, I should like to mention briefly some problems inherent in this view.

One is that this view makes societies morally infallible. If societies make moral standards there remains nothing to judge about the rightness or wrongness of norms or values of one society. If one society holds that slavery is good, then slavery must be good. This is contrary to what we usually believe, i.e. that societies may make wrong decisions or may have wrong standards and that they are constantly in need of improving their standards.

Another difficulty is that, according to this view, people may disagree only when they have different ideas about conventions of their society. For example, people may have disagreement about the permissibility of abortion, but only in the sense that they disagree about what the people or the majority of people in society actually believe. Therefore, the only way to settle moral problems is to have an opinion survey. This in turn means that moral inquiry can never be normative and turns out to be only descriptive.

A further problem, common both to this view and functionalism, arises from the fact that people usually belong to different groups and societies, which may have conflicting demands. A person may have to choose between these. It does not solve the problem to say that one can act according to conventions of whichever society is more important to him or her, since they may be of equal importance and since this suggestion makes morality arbitrary. We normally do not take moral rules to depend on our own choice. Moreover, we sometimes feel morally compelled and responsible to change or reform the very group that is most important to us.

11. Inference to the best explanation of moral fundamental differences
Gilbert Harman argues that moral relativism is "a reasonable inference from the most plausible explanation of moral diversity" (Harman, 1996, p. 8). David Wong in *Moral Relativity* (1984), "Moral Relativism" (1992), "Relativism" (1996) and "Moral Relativism" (1998) argues that the relativist argument is best conducted by pointing to particular kinds of differences in moral belief, and then by claiming that these particular differences are best explained under a theory that denies the existence of a single true morality. Because of the importance of Wong's theory of relativism in general and in the present work in particular, I shall try first to explain his argument in detail and then evaluate it. For Wong, one good example of radical difference is to be found between rights-centred and common good-centred cultures. He says:

> If the contrast between the two types of morality is real, it raises the question of whether one or the other type is truer or more justified than the other. The argument for a relativistic answer may start with the claim that each type focuses on a good that may reasonably occupy the centre of an ethical ideal for human life. On the one hand, there is the good of belonging to and contributing to a community: on the other, there is the good of respect for the individual apart from any potential contribution to community. It would be surprising, the argument goes, if there were just one justifiable way of setting a priority with respect to the two goods. It should not be surprising, after all, if the range of human good is simply too rich and diverse to be reconciled in just a single moral ideal (Wong, 1996, p. 446).

What was said before (when I discussed descriptive relativism) in objection to Wong's account of those two types of morality seems to me to leave no doubt that the above two moral systems are not radically different; one can, as I have argued above, locate them in a single comprehensive moral outlook with some underlying principles. Therefore, there remain no grounds for claiming that the best explanation of this *radical* difference is ethical relativism. However, Wong has tried to supplement his argument by a teleological account of morality that allows the existence of different moralities provided that they all bring about the intended result.

Wong's supplementary argument can be summarized as follows. Morality is a social creation that serves two universal human needs. It helps us to regulate *personal* and *interpersonal* conflicts of interests. Although any enduring and stable moral system, for instance, will not permit the torture of persons at whim, it is quite possible that different moralities perform the practical functions, i.e. to regulate personal and inter-personal conflicts of interest equally well, at least according to common standards. Of course, needs and human nature place conditions on what could be adequate morality, but our nature is so plastic and complex that we may have a variety of goods and we can put them in different orders. This is the very point that opens the way for relativism.

The idea that morality is created to resolve conflicts of interests thus has a central position in Wong's view on morality. However, this view has been expressed by previous ethicists as well. For example, Kart Baier in his book *The Moral Point of View* (1958) argues that we need moral rules "only because our interests sometimes come into conflict".[1] Accordingly, if there were no conflicts of interest there would be no need for the kind of guidance with which morality can provide us.

The final chapter of the present book deals with the question whether ethics is a social creation or not. This particular idea – that ethics exists in other than individual contexts only to regulate conflicts of interests between people – I regard as very dubious. The aim of morality is to create an atmosphere in which there are no conflicts of interests between people.[2] In fact, it is only the lowest level of morality to respect others' rights and

---

1. The quotation is taken from James Rachels, 1993, p. 83.

2. H. L. A. Hart believes that there are four factors that distinguish morality from law itself; namely, importance, immunity from deliberate change, the voluntary character of moral offences and the distinctive form of moral pressure (Lukes, "Taking Morality Seriously", *Moral Conflict and Politics*, 1991, p. 22, from H. L. A. Hart, *The Concept of Law* (Oxford: Clarendon Press, 1961).

interests. This is obligatory for all people and functionally necessary to sustain society and secure the benefits of social life. Legal systems usually undertake no more than this, but in many moral systems one is encouraged to consider others prior to oneself and to sacrifice personal interests for the interests of others. This is clear in altruistic views of morality. It is also a tenet of utilitarianism, which holds that everyone counts only as one and therefore it is morally good that a person should sacrifice his or her interests to the interests of society as a whole or of a number of people.

Further, it may be well argued that if every member of the society considers the interests of any other member of the society before his own this will bring greater happiness for society, in the form of kindness, trustworthiness, peacefulness, honesty and so on, which obviously outweighs the short-term interests of that individual. This fact has been noted by different thinkers. For example, Robert G. Olson in his book *The Morality of Self-Interest* (1965) writes, "The individual is most likely to contribute to social betterment by rationally pursuing his own best long-range interest." Rachels (1993, p. 79) reports that Alexander Pope said, more poetically:

> Thus God and nature formed the general frame
> And bade self-love and social be the same.

Moreover, I would argue that this is even explicable through egoism, granted that we consider the long-term interests of the individual and do not restrict interests to the immediate ones or materialistic ones. Even an egoistic mother, for example, may justifiably consider the happiness and pleasure of her child prior to her own. She may not sleep at times her child needs care. She may feed her child and herself go hungry when food is in short supply. In all such cases she gets more pleasure, more satisfaction, than if she were putting herself first, and indeed if she is not allowed to do those things she will feel deprived and in loss. To be egoistic does not necessarily mean to be selfish. One may believe in a harmony between one's real interests and others' or society's interests, as is believed in many religious or Eastern ethical systems. Rachels (1993) makes a different objection. He points out that an ethical egoist might say that life is essentially a long series of conflicts in which each person is struggling to come out on top. On this view, morality is needed to show how people can secure their *genuine* interests in conflicts and not to resolve conflicts. Rachels says, "The moralist is not like a courtroom judge, who resolves disputes. Instead, he is like the Commissioner of Boxing, who urges each fighter to do his best."

Thus, morality may start with respect for the interests of others and go on towards ideas such as human happiness or self-realization or acquiring divine pleasure or the like. So Wong's picture of morality and its function is not compatible with many moral systems and does not explain all aspects of the moral experience.

Even if we accept Wong's picture it is not clear why there cannot be a moral system that regulates conflicts perfectly or at least better than any other. Here we can notice an important aspect of today's moral experience. There are very deep or, as Wong says, "deepest" conflicts in contemporary ethical lives, some of which "are quite public and political, such as the disagreement in the USA over moral and legal permissibility of abortion." None of the parties of these debates is prepared to admit that the other party's morality is as valid or functionally capable as its own. The very fact of commitment to a moral system implies a strong sense of preference for the system at issue. Rarely we can find among morally committed people (even if they are pluralists) any who are prepared to consider another moral system as capable and faithful as their own, and thus to discard their own and adopt another one. There will be a separate discussion of how relativism leads to lack of confidence (at the end of next section), but confidence is a general feature of moral experience.

In conclusion, I would say that Wong's argument has the advantage that it does not consider all moralities acceptable and justified. Although he is a relativist, he does not deny that some moralities may be false and inadequate, owing to their malfunctions. Besides ruling out moralities that would provoke interpersonal conflicts, he also recognizes that adequate moralities must aim at producing persons capable of considering the interests of others. Therefore, another test of an adequate morality is to see whether it prescribes and promotes the sorts of upbringing and continuing interpersonal relationships that produce such persons. Wong admits that this kind of ethical relativism, which allows for such constraints on what a true or most justified morality could be, may not fit the stereotype of relativism, but he insists that it is a reasonable position to hold.

Summary
In this section I have tried to explain carefully the various grounds on which an argument for meta-ethical relativism has been or may be developed. I believe that, despite the huge body of work that exists on ethical relativism, it has not been treated like this before. Altogether, eleven arguments or, more exactly, eleven grounds for relativist positions are studied. In each case, I have

aired my own objections and comments. I have also tried to adduce standard objections to those positions or some of the objections made by others. In some cases, further assessment of arguments for meta-ethical relativism was shown to depend on other discussions in the present work, such as the discussion about descriptive relativism and the discussion about foundations of morality. There were also cases that deserved some independent studies, such as in the areas of objectivity of morality, the possibility of knowledge and Quine's theory of translation. In such cases references to further works have been given.

In general, I think it is now clear that none of the above arguments for meta-ethical relativism works. In the next two chapters, we shall see whether the modifications or supplementations made by Harman and Wong make any crucial change in the situation or not. For example, we shall see whether Harman's combination of internalism with conventionalism, which avoids some of the standard objections to ethical relativism, is able to meet other objections or not. In fact, in the next two chapters we shall have more focus on the last two arguments along with modifications and supplementations developed successively by Harman and Wong.

Finally, I should like to emphasize that there is no reason to think that an absolutist must refute all the arguments for meta-ethical relativism before he can construct an alternative. In my discussion about ethical absolutism and diversity of morals, I shall show how an absolutist account of morality can explain different aspects of our moral experiences, especially the existence of substantial differences. In the final chapter on the foundations of morality, I will try to show how an absolutist account of morality can be constructed.

Normative relativism

Normative relativism is usually defined as the view that it is ethically wrong to pass ethical judgement on the behaviour and practices of another individual, group or society with a substantially different ethical code; and that it is wrong to intervene in the affairs of that other individual, group or society on the basis of such ethical judgements. We saw earlier in the discussion about the functionalist argument for ethical relativism that Bernard Williams (1972) after the articulation of (normative) relativism asserted that this view had a long history. He added that it was popular among some liberal colonialists, especially among British administrators in West Africa and the like. Williams admits that despite inconsistency of this view it may have had a beneficent influence at that time.

I think Wong is also right in saying that normative relativism "is often defended by anthropologists, perhaps in reaction to those Western conceptions of the inferiority of other cultures that played a role in colonialism" (Wong, 1998, p. 541).

As we know, Boas, Benedict and Herskovits are among those outstanding anthropologists who defended relativism. Boas (1928) and Benedict (1934) claimed that there is a great variety of moral systems. The same action may be morally assessed in different ways. Boasians believe that "Every human society everywhere has made . . . [a] selection in its cultural institutions" (Benedict, 1934, p.24). One society may select one aspect of life to be morally central and another society may take another aspect to be morally central. One society may select the military virtues and the other may select the arts of peace. In the absence of an overall and comprehensive view about human nature that can define the overarching criterion of moral worth, the Principle of Tolerance might be supported, according to which each culture's moral system is right for it and therefore no culture can be condemned for practising its own moral values, although it may radically differ from one's own.

The Boasians have two arguments for the Principle of Tolerance. First, they argue that, because there are differing moralities about the same practice, we must accept the Principle of Tolerance. The second argument is that if a moral system is right for a culture it must be tolerated. For the Boasians the practical value of a custom in the life of the tribe shows whether a moral maxim is right for that tribe or not. For example, polygamy may be morally right in an agricultural society and wrong in an industrial one.[1]

Pojman (1998, p. 42) introduces Melville Herskovits as the most famous anthropologist who holds (normative) relativism. Herskovits in his *Cultural Relativism* (1972) argues that meta-ethical relativism entails intercultural tolerance. Taking as his premise that morality is relative to its culture, he argues that there is no independent basis for evaluating the morality of other cultures and then he argues that in the absence of such an independent basis for evaluation we ought to be tolerant of the moralities of other cultures.

In general, adherents of normative relativism, including anthropologists and non-anthropologists, argue for it, or for the principle of tolerance, from descriptive or meta-ethical relativism. I have not yet observed any other argument.

The problem with the former, i.e. the argument for the normative relativism from descriptive relativism (other than the problems with

---

1. See Harre and Krausz, 1996.

descriptive relativism itself), is that it ignores the logical gap between the empirical fact of the diversity of morals and the non-empirical normative claim of the necessity of non-interference with behaviours of others. In other words, there is no way to go from the *a posteriori* fact of the diversity of morals to the *a priori* claim of normative relativism that defines, for example, the position one society has to take towards another. Actually, the relativist has to agree that whether to judge others or not (or whether to be tolerant of others or not) can be one of the things on which societies may disagree with each other. The problem with the latter, i.e. the argument for the normative relativism from meta-ethical relativism (other than the problems with meta-ethical relativism itself), is that in no clear way do any of the previous meta-ethical doctrines imply normative relativism. One can consistently maintain that there is no single true morality and still judge, and interfere with, others on the basis of one's own morality.

Moreover, I think that normative relativism lacks universalizability. To explicate what I mean by "universalizability" I have to point out that there are two rules of reason that logically we have to observe in developing any theory, including moral ones. One is *internal consistency*, which means that the theory in question should not contradict itself. The other is *external consistency* or *universalizability*. This principle means that numerical differences are irrelevant and whatever applies in one case should apply in all similar cases. Therefore, in morality, when one makes a judgement about one situation, this judgement has, on pain of logical inconsistency, to be true of any similar situation or, more precisely, "any situation which is exactly similar in its universal non-moral properties".[1] What universalizability really demands is that there must be morally relevant differences between those groups if they are to be right to judge the acts of their own group and refrain from judging or make different judgements about the same acts if they happen to be performed by the other group. Of course, it is possible that there are conditions under which some moral rules apply to a certain group and not to another. For example, rules that apply to parents as such do not apply to children as such, or moral rules that apply to employers as such do not apply to employees as such. However, regardless of the non-relevant factors such as shape, name, colour, race, job and the like, whoever becomes a parent or an employer has to observe those rules.

Now, my argument is that one cannot ignore one's own moral code

---

1. Hare, 1990, p. 268. On the concept of universalizability introduced above, see Hare, 1990, and Hare, 1963 (pp. 7–50), Singer, 1990 (esp. pp. 147–9), and Fletcher, 1966 (esp. p. 32).

simply because one has come to encounter people from another group or society with a different moral code. One cannot refrain from condemning a young boy in another group or society who bites his old mother just because he has no value of respect for human beings in general and for parents in particular in his own moral code or in that group's or society's moral code. In such cases, people pass judgements even before they make inquiry about the moral code of that person or group or society. Suppose that you go to another country and see that someone is endangered and is going to die, but his son can save his life. Would you base your judgement about the necessity of helping on the condition that people there have made the same decision in advance for issues like this in their moral code? What will be your own duties in that country with respect to treating those people? Would you leave your morality aside and just say, "When in Rome do as the Romans do", which is at best only a principle of etiquette, or would you try to make an agreement with them by showing some compromise from your side and asking some from them? I trust that you agree that we stick to our morality as much as possible. We do not feel that our morality depends on others' approval and is thus limited in its scope. The reason for that lies in the fact that people do not believe that moral rules are contractual, like traffic rules. This is why they do not see any limit in their moral scope and why they can have confidence about their moral positions.

Of course, an adequate moral system certainly sets up some practical rules as how to behave in a multicultural world or society. There is a great difference between practical compromise and doctrinal compromise. Moral compromises are forced on people by circumstances and we should not think that they change the moral quality of actions. When we are forced to compromise practically what we need to have is an excuse (to show that it is wrong but circumstances forced us to compromise), but when theoretically we change our idea or compromise we need a justification (to show that it is really right to do so). Those forcing circumstances support excuses and do not serve as justifications.

Furthermore, normative relativism is standardly criticized as incoherent and self-refuting. It seems to prescribe for all individuals, groups and societies an ethics of non-judgemental tolerance and non-intervention, but such a universal prescription would turn incoherent. If I pass judgement on those who pass judgement on the behaviours of others with different morality and condemn them, I must condemn myself, since I have tried to impose a value of tolerance on everyone, even if they had no such value. But this is not what I am supposed to do under the normative version of ethical relativism.

There is still one more problem in the second argument of the Boasians. In my view, when the Boasians say that polygamy works in one society and not in another and therefore it is right for the former and not for the other, their claim shows that they have adopted a universal teleological principle, which they think ought to be adopted by those societies as well. Moreover, this account also implies some universal ideals, according to which customs and practices have to be measured to see whether they work (if they conduce to those ideals) or not (if they fail). Furthermore, this account leaves some place for an external or independent judgement about the set of moral maxims in each society based on whether they *really* work or not. Finally, the Boasian account asserts that it is not arbitrary that polygamy is right for one society and wrong for the other; it is a matter of practical value. Therefore, some factors of efficiency that are involved in the polygamy make it good or bad. If the relevant factors that produce a good result instead produced a bad one, the judgement would be just the opposite. This is perfectly compatible with moral absolutism.

Some philosophers have tried to present a more modest version, that might be more tenable.[1] They believe that normative relativism is not just a philosophical doctrine but also a stance adopted towards morally troubling situations. This more modest version of normative relativism arises from combining meta-ethical relativism and a kind of liberal, contractualist ethics requiring that individuals justify and consent to the principles that govern them or apply to them. Accordingly, one has to justify one's treatment of others in a way that they could accept it were they fully rational and informed of all relevant facts. The result of this combination is a version of normative relativism. Wong believes that the source of reluctance of many of his readers to intervene in the affairs of others with substantially different values is that "a liberal, contractualist outlook is very much part of our ethical life in the postmodern West" (Wong, 1996).

However, I have several reservations about this version of normative relativism. First of all, it is obvious that this version of normative relativism does not apply to all persons or all cultures. It can be applied only to those who acknowledge both meta-ethical relativism and the liberal contractualist approach to ethics.

Secondly, passing judgements on practices of others is different from

---

1. See Wong (1992, 1996 and 1998). Many people such as Harman have suggested that this idea was proposed by Wong. Fortunately, Wong in his last work clarified that he himself proposed this view to supplement meta-ethical relativism with a liberal, contractualist ethics to imply an ethic of non-intervention (see Wong, 1998, p. 541).

enforcing one's moral values. The normative relativist certainly accepts that one is entitled to pass judgements on the practices of people with the same values, but can he assure us that one is always entitled to enforce those moral values on them, even though they have the same morality? Clearly, the wrongness of enforcing one's values on others who have different moralities does not entail wrongness in passing judgement on them. An absolutist also may be reluctant to enforce moral rules on people with substantially different values and sometimes even on people with the same values.

Thirdly, commitment to tolerance is different from normative relativism or from contractual liberalism. An absolutist may subscribe to tolerance, either because he thinks that interference would do more harm or because he thinks that one should properly understand others' practices before passing judgements – lack of tolerance may be a strong obstacle to understanding.

Fourthly, there are cases in which no one, including ordinary relativists or liberal relativists, hesitates to pass judgements on, or even interfere with, practices of people from substantially different cultures. Wong (1996 and 1998) himself believes that a more reasonable version of normative relativism has to permit one to pass a limited range of judgements on others with substantially different values when their values contradict our most important values or when the requirement of non-interference comes into conflict with our other moral requirements, such as prohibition against torture or the killing of the innocent. Of course, as Wong himself has admitted (1996), what one is entitled to do in the light of such judgements is something else and needs to be studied independently.

Finally, it must be said that advocates of normative relativism have to admit that it is wrong to hold that people in other societies can be treated in ways that we do not accept, simply because they do not share our values, such as privacy, individual liberty or even life. As Scanlon (1999, p. 340) puts it, "t often seems evident that, whatever 'they', or some of them, may actually think (they may have become accustomed to harsh treatment, for example, and think it inevitable), they in fact have the same reasons that we do for wanting not to be treated in these ways."

What is crucial is not what people *actually* think or want, but what they have reason to want. However, there are two important points, mentioned by Scanlon (ibid., p. 341), which I completely accept:

1. What people have reason to want is not independent from the condition in which they live, including facts about what most people around them want, believe and accept.

2. It is not permissible to intervene, against their wishes, in the name of their interests. Indeed, "One of the things people have reason to want is to be able to control their lives in certain ways, what people actually want makes a difference to how they may be treated . . . What people have reason to want determines how and when what they actually want makes a moral difference" (ibid., p. 407).

Summary
In the above discussion, it was argued that normative relativism is more dubious and controversial than meta-ethical relativism, just as meta-ethical relativism was earlier shown to be more dubious and controversial than descriptive relativism. Besides difficulties in both descriptive and meta-ethical relativism, it was argued that none of them entails normative relativism. Moreover, it was argued that the supplementary argument of Wong for normative relativism suffers from some problems. It was also emphasized that there is a sharp difference between normative relativism and the Principle of Tolerance: an absolutist may support the principle of tolerance or reject the enforcement of moral norms, while a relativist may have no place for tolerance in his moral system.

Ethical absolutism and diversity of morals

Unlike relativists, absolutists usually start their moral reflections with studying the nature of moral truth by appeal to reason, intuition or common sense, and then they try to meet actual difficulties. It seems that relativists usually start by considering actual moral life and its problems, such as moral disagreements, mainly reported by anthropologists or cosmopolitans, and then they (often being preoccupied with them) try to develop a meta-ethical theory to support their observations of moral life. I now propose to examine how ethical absolutists argue for ethical absolutism and how they deal with moral diversity disagreements.

Some argue in favour of absolutism on the basis that there are objective moral values by which all people should live. It has been suggested (Harre and Krausz, 1996, p. 165) that "the most telling argument against moral relativism would be a convincing defence of moral realism". The common point to all forms of moral realism is that there are moral facts. These facts are independent of moral judgements and of what individuals or societies believe. These facts are the same for all people. Of course, there are different views among moral realists about the nature and content of moral facts.

Others might argue in favour of moral absolutism without holding that there are objective moral values, but arguing that intersubjectivity (i.e. being common to different human minds) gives certain moral values universal validity and therefore all members of all societies should live according to these universally accepted moral values.

The issue of objectivism should be discussed seriously and in the final chapter I shall argue for my own position about the subject. However, regardless of what position one may adopt my argument is a) that there is no aspect of our moral experience that absolutism falls short of explaining; b) absolutism shows better conformity to all aspects of our moral experience, including our moral common sense and our ordinary way of using factual and cognitive terms in moral language. Indeed, what makes my position absolutist is the combination of both claims, since the mere second is accepted by most relativists. Most relativists accept that generally absolutism better fits into our moral experiences. What makes relativists unhappy with absolutism is mainly the assumption that there are some aspects of our moral experience or understanding that suggest that the conformity of absolutism with common sense or our moral experience and understanding is superficial or fictitious. In the next sections, I shall show how absolutism is able to deal with moral diversity without having the undesirable implications that relativism has.

In respect to the empirical evidence that morally acceptable behaviour tends to vary both between societies and inter-temporally, I think one has to consider the following points before one can draw relativistic conclusions from that evidence:

1. Even if there were no similarities in the underlying principles of different moral systems and there were no disagreements over non-moral facts, that is, even if we suppose that the differences arise simply because people have adopted different moral standards, one cannot justifiably conclude that all alternative adopted standards or some of them must be true. As I indicated in the discussion about descriptive relativism and about the second argument for meta-ethical relativism, one cannot argue from what is believed to be morally right for what should be believed to be so.

2. There are important moral similarities across cultures. There are at least some moral principles or standards that seem to be universally acceptable. Examination of what *seems* to be a dramatic difference

between cultures shows that cultures do not differ as much as it appears. For example, all rational human beings agree that it is wrong to torture people for fun. Even if we find in some part of the world a person who seems to torture for fun, we never doubt about the rightness of our judgement. What rather we might do is to seek to find what is wrong with the person who enjoys torture. We would ask, "Isn't that person irrational? Isn't that person morally deficient?"; or is there any one who could deny that equals should be treated equally or that the unnecessary destruction of value is wrong?

In fact, some general moral standards have been empirically observed to apply across many societies, such as rules against murder and rules for taking care of children and educating the young. Some anthropologists and philosophers have introduced lists of such common rules. Spiro, an outstanding anthropologist, says:

> In short, [my field studies] convinced me that many motivational dispositions are culturally invariant [and] many cognitive orientations [are so] as well. These invariant dispositions and orientations stem... from panhuman biological and cultural constants, and they comprise that universal human nature, which, together with received anthropological opinion, I had formerly rejected as yet another ethnocentric bias (Spiro, 1978, pp. 349 and 350, cited in Geertz, 1989, p. 24).

As a philosopher, Pojman introduces a list of common principles that includes prohibitions against torture for fun, killing innocent people, causing unnecessary pain or suffering, cheating or stealing, and principles that enjoin keeping one's promise, honouring one's contracts, doing justice (treating equals equally and unequals unequally), telling the truth, obeying just laws, reciprocating (showing gratitude for services rendered) and helping other people, at least when the cost to oneself is minimal.[1]

Besides the empirical data about the existence of similar general moral standards and principles, there is a rational ground to argue for the existence of such similarities. We should not think that these similarities are arbitrary. All the above-mentioned norms help people to achieve social cohesion and integration and to have peaceful and happy lives. Those norms improve social interactions and solve or at

---

1. See Pojman, 1998, pp. 47 and 48.

least decrease conflicts. Is it not the case that all human societies have felt that they have been in need of morality as a set of guidelines to help them in achieving these goals? In this way, I agree with Pojman that those common principles are examples of core morality. Core moral rules are like vitamins necessary for us, but different people may come to have them in different forms and combinations. Each of us needs certain quantities of vitamins, but in prescribing the necessary sorts of vitamins we do not need to describe recipes or specific foods or place settings.

Indeed, some moral requirements are so important that no society could survive, at least in anything like its present situation, without them. Hence, I also agree with James Rachels that the following core values are common to all societies, and are in fact necessary for any society to exist: a) we should care for children, b) we should tell the truth and c) we should not murder.[1]

How could a group survive without valuing its young? All cultural groups must be protective of their infants. Human infants cannot survive without help and care. A group's continued existence shows that this group must have cared for its young. Similarly, if a society does not place value on telling the truth it would have found no way to communicate, and complex societies could not exist without regular communication. However, complex societies do exist, so there *must* be a presumption of truthfulness. Likewise, a society could not exist without prohibiting murder. The general theoretical point is that *there are some universal moral rules for all societies; otherwise no society could survive.*

Of course, there may be differences in what each society regards as legitimate exceptions to those rules or as conditions for their fulfilment, but this disagreement has to be considered against a background of agreement on the larger issues, against a background of common outlines. The general agreed-upon principles, indeed, outline all moral systems to a considerable extent. (As I shall explain later, many of the differences arise from the ways in which different systems settle moral conflicts.) Thus, I disagree with people such as Michael Walzer in his *Interpretation and Social Criticism* (1987), who think that these common principles or values tend to be trivial or extremely general and that once they take concrete forms in different societies, they vary significantly.

---

1.   See Rachels, 1993, pp. 25 and 26.

3. The existence of moral differences and disagreements is compatible with the existence of general moral principles. There is no reason to think that, if there is a fact, all people must be aware of it or agree about it. For many centuries, people did not know that the earth is round. The history of science is full of the cases in which people either totally ignored some facts or at least disagreed about them. Of course, the success of modern science in producing a remarkable degree of convergence of belief about the basic structure of the physical world has encouraged some people to overemphasize the difference between science and morality and hold scepticism about the objectivity of moral judgements. The difference between science and morality does not change the fact that the existence of disagreements on any subject does not disprove its objectivity.

Indeed, it may be argued that the existence of moral conflicts and controversies (inside a person or inside the society) supports moral objectivism. A somewhat similar point is mentioned by Bernard Williams, who claims that if there is one thing that affirms moral objectivity it is the experience of moral conflict. He says, "That there is nothing that one decently, honourably or adequately *can* do seems a kind of truth as firmly independent of the will and inclination as anything in morality."[1]

In general, we should notice that both opponents and proponents of relativism recognize what I call "application variation" (sometimes called "application relativism"), the endeavour to apply moral rules where there is a conflict between rules or where a rule can be applied in different ways. (Application variation is acceptable even to *moral monists*.)[2] Two cultures or individuals may hold the same underlying principle but apply it differently owing to different metaphysical beliefs

---

1. Bernard Williams, "Conflicts of Values", *Moral Luck* (Cambridge: Cambridge University Press, 1981), p. 75, cited in Steven Lukes, 1991, p. 4. The reader should note that I have extended Williams's argument to moral controversies inside societies. I am not sure whether he himself had this in his mind, but I think that there is a good reason for such extension. The reason is that different parties in social debates on moral issues such as abortion usually respond to different values, which are as such accepted by all. What makes them disagree is the means they suggest solving *the conflict of values*.

2. The idea that diversity exists only at the surface and that at some deeper level there is only one set of moral standards, which is binding on all human beings and also capable of discovery through rational means, is sometimes called "moral monism" or "moral singularism". See Bimal K. Matilal, 1989, p. 339.

or different situations. For example, the ancient Callatians ate their deceased parents and considered the practice of burying as disrespectful, whereas contemporary society has the opposite attitudes about the care of dead relatives; but both practices exemplify the principle of respect for the dead. Another example is that some nations show their respect by covering the feet and uncovering the head, whereas others do the opposite. Again the principle of respect is shared.

It is noteworthy that an absolutist does not need to explain why individuals or cultures fail to have an adequate set of moral principles in order to be able to defend what the absolutist himself or herself thinks to be the adequate set of moral principles. However, as I shall try to explain below, there are various causes of failure to discover the adequate set of moral principles and therefore to have different moral views. According to non-relativism, cultures or forms of life can fail to exemplify an adequate moral unity in at least one of the following ways.

a. Some people are insufficiently intelligent or too lazy to put moral principles or values in a hierarchy, and therefore they may not know or recognize what to do when the principles or values conflict. Although moral reasoning is possible for all human beings, it gets complicated when it goes into great detail. This is one of the main reasons why people have different moral systems and this is why almost all human beings experience situations in which they feel that they are in need of moral advice or consultation. In any case, as Socrates pointed out, we have reason to listen only to the wise among us (*Crito*, 44cd).

b. Principles and rules can be applied in different ways according to the varying conditions that obtain across times or societies. For example, if the number of women in one society is much greater than the number of men, it would not be surprising if polygamy were acceptable there, while in another society, where the number of women is equal to men, monogamy might be required. Differences in the type of marriage may reflect the difference in the proportion of women to men. There may be no difference in basic moral ideals of marriage.

Lukes (1991, p. 13) refers to non-relativists who appeal to Hume's thought that "mankind is much the same in all times and places", and interpret differences of belief and practice as best explained by differences in the circumstances human beings face.[1] (Of course, Lukes himself is not pleased with the above idea and thinks that there is a deep problem in interpreting the moral thought and action of others.)

c. Many differences are the result of different applications of common values or principles in different contexts of beliefs, such as those about human nature, about the "natural" differences between the sexes or different groups or races and about the relation of human beings to the natural world and to the supernatural. Many moral beliefs presuppose certain religious beliefs and metaphysical views about the world and about human beings. For example, it would be no surprise to us to learn that those who ate the bodies of their dead parents during the time of Darius viewed it as a way of preserving their spiritual substance. Another example concerns members of an African tribe who throw their deformed children into the river, because they believe that such infants *belong* to the hippopotamus, the god of the river. We can see that a principle of respect for property underlies this practice, but a false belief in the god of the river and its possession of deformed infants has caused that strange practice. Even today the debate on the rightness or wrongness of abortion is, at least partly, due to different non-moral beliefs about the status of the foetus; what really is in dispute is whether a foetus is a person or not, rather than whether it is right to kill a person.[2]

Yet another interesting example concerns different beliefs about eating cows. If we see a group of people who are poor and may face a shortage of food, yet refuse to eat or even touch cows, we should not conclude that their values are completely different from ours. Couldn't the reason for this apparent difference be the fact that they believe in a kind of reincarnation? They may believe that after death souls of men reside in bodies of cows. To repeat Rachels's words, "The disagreement is not in our values: that we should not eat Grandma. We simply disagree about whether the cow *is* (or could be) Grandma" (Rachels, 1993, p. 23).

---

1. See Lukes, 1991, "Making Sense of Moral Conflict", p. 13. Quotation from Hume is taken by Lukes from David Hume, *Essays Moral and Political*, ii. 68.

2. For examples like these, see Rachels, 1993; Wong, 1996; Pojman, 1990, pp. 22 and 25, and Pojman 1998, p. 45.

d. Sometimes people are under considerable stress, so it becomes too burdensome to live by moral principles. Those who fail to observe moral rules may try to find some excuses and justify their moral shortcomings by saying that it was not clear what they had to do or that there were different views and so forth. Gradually they themselves may come to think that they are not really required to observe one single morality and they may develop different feelings about morals. Furthermore, the subject matter of ethics is such that people have intense practical interest in it, and surely this interest engenders passions that may obscure their moral judgements.[1]

e. Combination of the previous.

4. There are some intolerable implications of denying universally valid moral standards and rules. Of course, undesirable implications of ethical relativism may get weakened or lessened when more refined versions of ethical relativism are developed. For example, if a relativist supports only meta-ethical relativism and not normative relativism, or if he admits that morality is subject to rational constraints, there will be fewer problems. I hope now to explain some undesirable implications of ethical relativism. The first four apply to both meta-ethical relativism and normative relativism. The fifth applies only to normative relativism, since some moral relativists may allow for judging others' standards on the basis of one's own ethical system.

a. *Uselessness of consulting the standards of others*: If moral relativism were true, then we could decide whether actions are right or wrong just by consulting the standards of our society. However, few people think that their society has perfect moral standards.

b. *Implausibility of trying for moral reform*: If moral relativism is true, then there is no justification for moral reform and moral reformers are wrong, since they go against established standards. For example, those who struggled in the eighteenth century to abolish slavery were wrong, since they opposed slavery when slavery was popular; or it was wrong to oppose *suttee*, the burning of widows with their dead husbands, in India when it was popular. Accordingly, now it

---

1. For a similar point, see Nagel, 1986, pp. 185–8.

would not be morally wrong to campaign against slavery and *suttee*, since they are now illegal. But isn't this too late for reform?

If ethical relativism were true the only way to make sense of reform would be to suppose a society that is not living up to its own ideals. The reformer's task would be restricted to fulfilling social standards, and not to challenging the ideals themselves.

c. *Meaninglessness of the concepts of moral progress and ideal morality*: Usually, we think that at least some changes in our society have been for the better. For example, slavery is abolished. Regarding improvement in women's rights, Rachels says:

> Throughout most of Western history the place of women in society was very narrowly circumscribed. They could not own property; they could not vote or hold political office; with a few exceptions, they were not permitted to have paying jobs; and generally they were under the almost absolute control of their husbands. Recently most of this has changed, and most people think of it as progress. (Rachels, 1993, p. 22).

Moral progress makes sense only if we suppose that there are independent standards against which we can judge our actions and values. This is an idea that is unacceptable to both meta-ethical and normative relativists. According to most relativists, morality is based completely upon the actual adherence of people, so any actual morality is as true or justified as every other. To suppose that there is an ideal morality, which means by definition that it is the best morality, is not possible for relativists. Indeed, to them an actual morality must be even truer or more justified than ideal morality, since the ideal morality is not adhered to by any culture.

d. *Uselessness of moral criticism*: If custom or convention is to determine what is fine and just (and not just to influence what people think is fine and ugly, just and unjust) there will be no place to criticize them. If relativism were true, people could make internal criticisms, in the light of their own standards or conventions, but the standards and conventions themselves would not be subject to criticism. However, we know that one real aspect of our moral life is that we criticize customs and conventions and they sometimes change under the pressure of moral criticism. We also criticize the moral standards of individuals. We cannot stop criticizing mass murderers merely because they act according to their own moral values. If this were the case, every person could justifiably do whatever he desired, provided that his morality were culturally accepted or that he were able to make laws or establish a group of people who accepted his values consistently. This was the philosophy of Hitler. When some of his generals asked him about morality, he responded that if they were victorious history would say that the Nazis were right.

e. *Lack of moral conviction leading to nihilism*: Relativism is usually associated with a lack of moral conviction and a tendency towards nihilism. To be fair, this is partly due to the fact that relativism is sometimes identified with its most extreme forms, which hold that everything is permitted. But there is also the fact that moral confidence and commitment depend on viewing one's morality as the only true or the most justified one.

Wong (1996, p. 449, and 1998, p. 541) responds that one may adopt a relativist view and still continue to prize one's moral standards simply because they are as good as any other and because they help to constitute a way of life that is one's own. He believes that taking one's morality to be the only true or most justified morality would not guarantee a commitment to act. What commitment to one's morality requires is to be happy with what that morality means to oneself; one needs to know that one's morality can secure one's desires and aspirations. This is what makes morality so important for us in allowing us to avoid nihilism. Wong maintains that our belief that our morality is the only true or most justified morality does not create this kind of importance, nor is it a necessary condition for this kind of importance, because it makes no difference to us that other reasonable persons would accept or recognize something else to be true or most justified.

I think it may well be argued that other people are not required to accept our moral values, but we ourselves have to believe that ours are the best to be committed to, and we must be spiritually powerful enough to act according to them. In very hard and difficult situations, in which the cost of being moral may be one's life or most precious belongings, the thought that others, equally justifiably, enjoy easier moral systems will be discouraging and weakening.

Another point on which I disagree with Wong is his belief that, although those who have certitude may find it easier to make sacrifices required by morality, moral certitude has its own problems, e.g. it has contributed to the endless cruelty that human beings have inflicted upon each other.[1]

I can agree that sometimes, but not always, absolutists have had disrespect for others' moralities. I can also agree that ethical relativism may give us the insight that many of the practices that seem natural to us are no more than cultural products and that ethical relativism may help us to be tolerant and open-minded. However, as I argued in the discussion about normative relativism, I believe that disrespect and arrogance are not necessary implications of absolutism. What some or even all absolutists do is not necessarily an implication of absolutism. Practically and even in theory, an absolutist may support the value of tolerance or the principle of non-interference. On the other hand, it is worth pointing out that many, perhaps all, great improvements and reforms in the history of human beings were achieved only after people became certain that there was no other worthwhile choice before them. It would be a very unusual reformer or politician or cleric who admitted that most of the matters on which he or she held a reformist or political or religious conviction could be seen in a different, but equally valid way.

It is also worth mentioning that tolerance or indifference towards others' actions and moral codes is not a necessary application of relativism. There may be relativists who do not believe in normative relativism and have no value of tolerance in their moral system. Even people like Wong, who believe in normative relativism in one way or another – independently or jointly with contractual liberalism – admit that there are cases in which they feel justified to interfere in others' affairs.[2]

    f. *Failure to evaluate the moral standards of others*: According to ethical

---

1. See Wong, 1998, p. 541.

2. See my discussion about normative relativism.

relativism, particularly normative relativism, each society's moral standards could not be judged right or wrong by others. Therefore Nazi aggression was not immoral because any moral justification used by the Nazis could be validated against their own moral principles, which in themselves would be perfectly valid. Normative relativism prevents us from saying practices of a society that waged war on its neighbours for the purpose of taking slaves was wrong. Likewise, we should not condemn Aztec rituals that involved a form of human sacrifice to the sun god, in which as many as 20,000 people a year "were marched up temple stairs, killed, then had their bodies tossed into large piles".[1] We should not say that some customs of other societies are morally inferior to our own. We would be stopped from criticising practices of other societies. The failure to condemn such practices does not seem reasonable. Slavery seems wrong *wherever* it occurs. We feel justified in condemning the slave-holding or racist practices of other cultures.

Let us finish this part with the inspiring final paragraph of *Varieties of Relativism*:

> Different aspects of the world are available to different kinds of creatures, insofar as their sensory systems differ, and to different groups of human beings insofar as they are differently placed and differently equipped. In this sense knowledge of the world tends to the relative. But all such aspects are aspects of one and the same world, and in that sense knowledge of the world tends to the absolute. (Harre and Krausz, 1996, p. 224).

Summary
In this chapter, I first discussed different types of ethical relativism: the descriptive, the meta-ethical and the normative. My purpose was to distinguish between different relativist claims and evaluate correspondingly arguments developed by relativists.

The conclusion of the first part was that, as far as I know, no sufficient reason for any type of ethical relativism is given:

---

1.   To find more about the Aztecs see *Encarta 98 Desk Encyclopedia* and *Britannica 1997*. The example is taken from *Internet Encyclopaedia of Philosophy*, 1996. The quotation is taken from Fieser, 1996.

1. Descriptive relativism in its strongest form suffers from lack of evidence. It is, in fact, practically impossible to investigate the truth of such a claim inductively. Moreover, descriptive relativism in its strongest form is in conflict with the fact that many moral principles and values have been shown to be common to the majority of people and in some cases among all reasonable human beings and typical civilized societies. Descriptive relativism in its moderate form is more tenable, but it still suffers from the fact that many examples mentioned by relativists are either irrelevant to morality or do not show fundamental differences. In any case, I argued that descriptive relativism in both strong and moderate versions can do no harm to objectivists, because their belief in a single true or most justified morality does not require any level of agreement, just as physical facts may be both true and disputed.

2. In respect to meta-ethical relativism, I studied eleven arguments, or more precisely, eleven grounds for relativist positions, along with the standard objections and my own objections and comments on each case. When appropriate, I referred the reader to further discussions in the present work or elsewhere. In general, I argued that none of the above arguments for meta-ethical relativism works. However, the importance of two recent theories of ethical relativism, those of Harman and of Wong, warrants separate discussion, to which we shall come later. We shall see whether the modifications or supplementation made by Harman and Wong enable their theories to meet challenges or not.

3. In my discussion about normative relativism, I argued that it is more dubious than meta-ethical relativism, just as meta-ethical relativism was earlier shown to be more dubious than descriptive relativism. I mentioned that arguments for normative relativism are premised on at least one of descriptive relativism or meta-ethical relativism. Then I argued that none of them entails normative relativism. Moreover, I argued that the supplementary argument, which is developed by Wong, faces some difficulties. I also emphasized the difference between normative relativism and the principle of tolerance.

In the second part of this chapter, Ethical Absolutism and Diversity of Morals, I presented a short but comprehensive account of absolutists' policy in dealing with the issue of ethical relativism. The main result was to show that a non-relativist account of morality is capable of explaining our moral experiences, including moral diversity and disagreements, without having undesirable implications of ethical relativism.

CHAPTER FOUR

Gilbert Harman and Ethical Relativism

Introduction

One of the most widely discussed recent theories of moral relativism is that of Gilbert Harman. Harman has published several works on morality, especially moral relativism, including: *The Nature of Morality* (Oxford: Oxford University Press, 1977); "Moral Relativism Defended", *Philosophical Review,* 84 (1975), pp. 3–22; "What Is Moral Relativism?", in A. I. Goldman and J. Kim, eds, *Values and Morals* (Dordrecht and Boston: D. Reidel, 1978); G. Harman and J. Thomson, *Moral Relativism and Moral Objectivity* (Oxford: Blackwell, 1996); "Précis of Moral Relativism and Moral Objectivity – Précis of Part One" and "Responses to Critics", *Philosophy and Phenomenological Research*, Vol. LVIII, No. 1, March 1998.[1]

There are several studies of Harman's theory of moral relativism.[2] Unlike

---

1. He has published many other works on moral relativism, such as: "Moral Relativism" in *The Encyclopaedia of Philosophy: Supplement*, edited by D. M. Borchert (New York: Macmillan, 1996), pp. 383–4; "Moral Diversity as an Argument for Moral Relativism" in *Perspectives on Moral Relativism*, edited by Douglas Odegard and Carole Stewart (Milliken, Ontario: Agathon, 1991), pp. 13–31; "Relativism", *The London Correspondent*, March 4, 1990, p. 22; "Is There a Single True Morality?" in *Morality, Reason and Truth*, edited by David Copp and David Zimmerman (Totowa, New Jersey: Rowan and Littlefield, 1985), pp. 27–48 (reprinted in Michael Krausz, ed., *Relativism: Interpretation and Confrontation* (Notre Dame, Indiana: University of Notre Dame Press, 1989), pp. 363–87; "Metaphysical Realism and Moral Relativism: Reflections on Hilary Putnam's Reason, Truth, and History", *Journal of Philosophy* 79, 1982, pp. 568–75 [reprinted in Paul Horwich, ed., *Theories of Truth*, The International Research Library of Philosophy (Aldershot, Hampshire, England: Dartmouth, 1994), pp. 421–8]; "Moral Relativism as a Foundation for Natural Rights", *Journal of Libertarian Studies* 4, 1980, pp. 367–71.

2. For example: Robert M. Stewart and Lynn L. Thomas, "Recent Work on Ethical

(continued...)

most previous studies, this study includes Harman's recent works: *Moral Relativism and Moral Objectivity*, "Précis of Moral Relativism and Moral Objectivity – Précis of Part One" and "Reply to Critics". This study also considers the recent literature on Harman's relativism.

As I mentioned earlier in the discussion about meta-ethical relativism, Gilbert Harman and David Wong have tried to reconstruct ethical relativism. They both believe that standard versions of ethical relativism do not work. Therefore, they have developed subtle or moderate forms of relativism to meet standard objections on relativism. Their relativism strictly dismisses the idea that in morality anything goes. They both believe that morality is subject to some rational constraints; there are good and bad arguments for the moral positions that people take. They both are also cognitivists, since they accept that moral claims have truth values. I shall explain how Harman has restricted his relativism to *moral judgements* in contrast to *evaluative judgements*. I shall also explain how Wong has gone further and accepted most of the claims made by objectivists. Naturally he also is not a fully-fledged relativist.

In my account of Harman's theory of ethical relativism, I shall try to make it clear how it avoids some of the previously mentioned objections and yet remains subject to some of them. Indeed, it seems that there are some problems that no relativist account of morality can avoid, such as some of the undesirable implications mentioned in the last chapter. In this chapter I wish also to introduce and discuss some new aspects in Harman's theory. Harman has adopted different order or sequences of subjects in his works on ethical relativism. In my discussion, I shall follow mostly the sequence of his last co-written book, *Moral Relativism and Moral Objectivity*, which presumably presents his final preferences in this regard.

In the next chapter, I shall try first to explain the main features of Wong's theory of ethical relativism and then indicate their similarities and differences, along with their advantages and disadvantages.

(...continued)

Relativism", *American Philosophical Quarterly*, Vol. 28, No. 2, April 1991; Robert. L. Arrington, *Rationality, Realism, and Relativism* (New York: Cornell University Press, 1989); Steven Darwall, "Harman and Moral Relativism", *The Personalist*, Vol. 58, 1977, pp. 199–207; Louis P. Pojman, "Gilbert Harman's Internalist Moral Relativism", *The Modern Schoolman*, Vol. 68, Nov. 1990, pp. 19–39. There is a symposium on Harman and Thomson's *Moral Relativism and Moral Objectivity* in *Philosophy and Phenomenological Research*, Vol. LVIII, No. 1, March 1998.

Moral relativism, moral absolutism and moral nihilism

Harman studies moral relativism in contrast to moral absolutism, which holds that there is a single true morality. Of course, presumably thanks to his internalist approach, Harman takes moral absolutism to be a view about the moral reasons that people have for their actions. He says, "I will understand a belief about absolute values to be a belief that there are things that everyone has a reason to hope or wish for. To say that there is a moral law that 'applies to everyone' is, I hereby stipulate, to say that everyone has sufficient reasons to follow that law" (Harman, 1989, p. 370).

Moral relativism is also different from moral nihilism. According to both, there is no single true morality, but moral nihilism "takes this to be a reason to reject morality altogether including any sort of relative morality" (Harman, 1996, p. 5). The most moderate form of nihilism asserts that there are moral facts, but that there is no way to know them.[1] On the other hand, we normally assume that moral responsibility depends on knowledge. This can explain why we consider animals not to be subject to morality. The striking conclusion would be that no one could ever do anything morally wrong. Therefore, nihilism completely undermines morality.[2] Moral relativism rather asserts that "morality should not be abandoned" and "relative moral judgements can continue to play a serious role in moral thinking" (ibid., p. 6).

Moral relativism as a logical thesis

Harman tries to present moral relativism as a logical thesis. In *The Nature of Morality*, he mentions that he is not denying (nor he is asserting) that some moralities are "objectively" better than others or that there are objective standards for moral assessment. He also writes, "My moral relativism is a soberly logical thesis – a thesis about logical form, if you like. Just as the judgement that something is large makes sense only in relation to one or another comparison class, so too, I will argue, the judgement that it is wrong

---

1. Harman also discusses nihilism in the second chapter of *The Nature of Morality*. Referring to part of the literature on moral nihilism, Harman mentions Fyodor Dostoevsky, who examines the implications of moral nihilism in his novels, *Crime and Punishment* and *The Brothers Karamazov*, and Friedrich Nietzsche, who argues in *Twilight of the Idols* that there are no moral facts and that morality as it has existed until now must be rejected.

2. For a discussion about this problem and moral knowledge in general, see *The Nature of Morality*, Chapter Six.

of someone to do something makes sense only in relation to an agreement or understanding" (Harman, 1975, p. 3). For example, Harman formulates relative "ought" judgements as a logical thesis as follows: "Ought (A, D, C, M) means roughly that for the agent A with the motivating attitude M under condition C, D is the course of action which is supported by the best reason".

Presumably, Harman does not mean that his relativism is a logical thesis only in the sense that it can be presented in a logical form, because this does not guarantee any soundness in his theory. Therefore, Harman seems to believe that his theory is based on a logical fact. Now let us see what that logical fact might be. If by his comparison of moral wrongness with largeness he wants to suggest that wrongness is a correlative concept and therefore *logically* it has to be relative, I have to say that there is a big difference between correlative concepts such as large and small and concepts such as right and wrong. Correlative concepts to be conceived need to be considered with each other as a pair, such as large and small, up and down, and parent and child. You cannot conceive the concept of "large" without also conceiving the concept of "small". Consequently you cannot apply the concept of "large" to something without any comparison. But "right" and "wrong" are completely different. You may define "right" without any reference to "wrong". A moral relativist can claim "right" and "wrong" to be relational at most, but not correlative such as large and small.

Therefore, we should look for another way in which Harman's relativism could be considered as a logical thesis. An alternative account is suggested by Pojman (1990, p. 20). Speaking about internalism as the second aspect of Harman's relativism – contractualism being the first – Pojman says that for Harman internalism is a logical thesis about the form of a moral judgement. Harman claims that moral judgements have two logical properties, or, as I will suggest later, two implications: they imply that the agent has a good reason to act in a certain way, and that the speaker approves that reason and presumes that the hearer or the subject of the judgement does so as well. Thus, Harman claims that it is *logically* inappropriate to say, "Hitler should not have acted in the way that he acted", since he did not share our moral principles.

Again the problem arises that there is no clear *logical* implication between the moral judgement and these two properties. What a moral judgement really implies is that there must be in reality a good reason to act in a certain way, but whether it has to be *actually* realized and approved by the hearer or the subject of the argument seems to be logically unnecessary. It seems to me that in *Moral Relativism and Moral Objectivity* (1996) Harman tries to solve the problem by some "terminological proposals". He tries to relate judgements about a person's reason to judgements about what is reasonable for that person. Harman suggests that someone has *sufficient reason* to do something if and only if it would be reasonable for him to do so. However, it is possible that one has sufficient reasons for doing one of two or more options, such as eating this apple or that apple from a tray of apples. Therefore, the agent has compelling reasons to do something if and only if, all things considered, it would be reasonable for him to do so and it would not be reasonable for him not to do so. Harman adds:

> So, to say that there are compelling reasons for S to D is to say there are considerations the awareness of which would provide S with compelling reasons to D.
> ... if S does not D, S is aware of all relevant considerations, and S is not in any way unreasonable, then it is not the case that there are compelling reasons for S to D (Harman, 1996, p. 46).

Referring to those who do not observe rules against killing and stealing, or politicians whose only interest is power or simple egoists who are interested only in themselves, Harman claims that these people lack the motivation to observe basic moral requirements. Their problem is not that they suffer moral ignorance or failure to reason correctly or weakness of will. Harman's conclusion is:

> Considerations of [the above] cases suggest that what moral requirements a person has compelling reason to follow will depend on that person's principles and values ... If people have different enough starting positions with respect to their desires, goals, intentions, and values, then they will be subject to different practical reasons even given the facts as they really are (Harman, 1986).
> ... According to moral relativism, whether someone is reasonable or unreasonable in this sense is a relative matter, depending on the values in question (Harman, 1996, pp. 47 and 48).

In this way, to see whether someone is reasonable or not we have to consider the person's values themselves. Some other aspects of Harman's internalism will be examined in future. However, I think that this discussion has shown that there is no point in introducing Harman's theory as a logical thesis.

Moral relativism as similar to physical relativism

In *Moral Relativism and Moral Objectivity*, Harman tries to compare moral relativism to Einstein's Theory of Relativity, according to which an object can have different masses in relation to different spatio-temporal frameworks and there is no privileged spatio-temporal framework that determines its real mass.[1] Harman argues for a similar idea in morality. Moral right and wrong are always relative to a certain moral framework and no moral framework is objectively privileged as the one true morality. Speaking recently about the main features of his account of relativism, Harman says, "The relativity of moral right and wrong to a moral framework is comparable to the relativity of notion and mass to a spatio-temporal framework and the relativity of legal rights and duties to a legal system" (Harman, 1998a, p. 161).

Indeed, this idea of the similarity between ethical relativism and physical relativity was suggested earlier. For example, Charles L. Stevenson in his *Facts and Values* (1967, pp. 72 and 73) picks up the topic of motion to illustrate the concept of relativism. He starts with a simple case in which people may make different statements about the speed of a single object, owing to different frames of reference. He then says, "although the relativity of motion leads to a sophisticated theory, it begins with the simple point that I have made, that 'is moving' is a relative term" (ibid., p. 73).

Prior to that, Richard B. Brandt in his *Ethical Theory: The Problems of Normative and Critical Ethics* (1959) pointed out the similarity between Protagoras' relativism and the special theory of relativity in physics. He added:

> All the careful observations in *one* frame will give the *same* result; and in this sense there is a "right" answer for this frame. But different frames will have different "right" answers, and there is in principle no way of showing that one of these is the "really right" answer. (Reprinted in *Readings in Ethical Theory*, edited by Wilfrid Sellars and John Hospers (New York: Appleton-Century-Crofts, 1952, 2nd edition, 1970), p. 335.)[2]

---

1. Instead of the term "relativity", Harman uses the term "relativism" here.
2. Probably some traces of Harman's idea of Quasi Absolutism, discussed later, can be traced back to Brandt, when he wrote, "However, certain quantities (like the spatio-temporal distance between two events) are absolutes, in the sense that careful measurements will give one right answer for everybody" (ibid.).

Brandt himself admitted the dissimilarity between one type of ethical relativism, that is the methodological or sceptical relativism, and relativism in physics. To him the difference is that in relativity physics, there are methods to come to *correct* judgements for each frame of reference, while according to methodological relativism in ethics there is no *method* to find out truth.[1]

In any case, I think that there is a great difference between disagreements concerning motion and morals. Two persons within two different spatio-temporal frameworks may make different judgements as to whether a third person is moving or not. When they interpret their judgements as being relative to their own frameworks they conclude that they have not really disagreed. It is not the case with some moral disagreements. Suppose A believes that there is a substantial duty to help others and B believes there is none. Again, suppose that this disagreement is because of their fundamentally different principles rather than different assessments of the "facts of the case". (Harman himself believes in the possibility of such disagreements and even considers that they favour moral relativism since moral relativism is able to explain the persistence of fundamental ethical disagreements.) Now, if A and B note their differing moral frameworks they do not conclude that they have not really disagreed.

Darwall thinks that the dissimilarity between motion and morals derives from the fact that we *occupy* different spatio-temporal co-ordinates, while we *accept* different moral co-ordinates. He adds:

A does not simply believe that not helping those in need is wrong in relation to his values, principles, and norms. Rather, he *accepts* those values and norms and, in doing so, thinks that going counter to them is wrong, *period*. And contrariwise for B. Hence the remaining disagreement (Darwall, 1998, p. 186).

As I have explained in the discussion about the concept of relative truth, we take our views to be true in reality regardless of their mental context, partly constructed by our moral frameworks. For example, in ordinary perceptual cases, by saying that this rose is red I mean that the real rose outside my mind is red, not the rose in my mind: that is, the rose is red, period, not relatively red. However, my only means to make such a judgement is the mental notion of rose. Therefore, even if I say that this rose, which I conceived through my perceptual image, is red it does not change the

---

1.　See Brandt, 1970, p. 338. For Brandt's definition of methodological and non-methodological relativism, refer to the first chapter of the present work.

reality of the subject of the judgement. Of course, I can make "the mental rose" itself a subject for some other types of judgements. In respect to morality too, I can make judgements and express them relationally or non-relationally. I can say, "cheating is wrong, period", "cheating in my mind is wrong" or "cheating is wrong in relation to my moral system", but in all cases I may believe that the reality is the same. Cheating is really wrong, as my moral system is really right; otherwise, I could have no confidence in my moral life. Therefore, if A holds that cheating is wrong and B holds that cheating is not wrong they may quite well disagree with each other – even if they have different moral standards. The reason is that A and B take their moral outlooks just like a mirror, through which they look at the external world, and not like some objects for looking at.

Harman's response to Darwall's criticism is simply this: "But not everyone reacts to such a situation by saying that something is wrong, period. Many people (perhaps a majority of Princeton undergraduates, for example) have a more relativistic reaction. On the other hand in Galileo's day, many people had the absolutist reaction with respect to motion!" (Harman, 1998a, p. 210).

I think the emphasis on the fact that many people have a relativistic reaction or that non-relativists sometimes have made mistakes cannot settle the debate in favour of ethical relativism. Some people may ignore the non-relevance of certain facts in their judgements, e.g. someone may think that when I say to my children that cheating is wrong, some factors such as myself, the listeners, the date and the place are also relevant. However, a careful investigation may show, for example, that although *I* have made the judgement, the wrongness of cheating does not depend on me, otherwise there would be no point in advising others, including my children, not to cheat. On the other hand, it is quite possible that we sometimes ignore some relevant factors. Socrates' dialogues are good examples for showing how people may think at the beginning that their judgements are not conditional or restricted and then after a process of mutual enquiry come to recognize some hidden conditions or factors. Indeed, one of the important causes of moral disagreements is the very failure to identify correctly all relevant factors.

The debate between relativism and non-relativism cannot be settled through voting or through counting the mistakes of certain relativists or non-relativists. The debate can be settled only by defining the nature and foundations of morality, considering these two views themselves and their logical implications and analysing the reality of human moral experiences and moral language.

Although statistics cannot settle this debate, the reality of public opinion about relativism is not what seems to be accepted by "perhaps a majority of

Princeton undergraduates". I personally have had another experience. In ethics tutorials with two groups of first year undergraduates of the University of Manchester in 1997, I introduced different schools of moral philosophy, including relativism, utilitarianism and so forth, and then we went through some exemplary cases to find out what would be the judgement according to each school. After the students became familiar with each school, I asked them to express their view on what they thought to be the most appropriate approach to ethics. The majority was against relativism, although they appreciated moral tolerance and they were not yet aware of my own view.[1]

In any case, it seems to me that Harman sometimes, perhaps unintentionally, uses the acceptability and plausibility of Einstein's Theory of Relativity to supplement his arguments. For example, he asserts that belief in moral relativism does not require a speaker's recognition of the fact that he is making a judgement in relation to a certain set of moral co-ordinates. Then the only argument that Harman presents is that Einstein's Theory of Relativity also does not require people's recognition of the relevance of their judgements to a particular spatio-temporal framework. The problem is that there is a difference between these two types of judgements; how can one make a moral judgement without understanding one's moral framework? It is possible that one does not know what is going on in the external world, but one cannot ignore the conditions of one's own internal judgement. Another example comes below in a discussion about the second case in which Harman admits the existence of universal moral truths.

It must be noted that Harman's relativism is not simply a claim that moral judgements are made relative to a moral framework. There are several theories interwoven in his version of moral relativism, such as internalism and conventionalism. I shall now move on to explain different features and constituents of his theory of ethical relativism, e.g. what Harman means by a "moral framework" and the extent and constraints of his relativism. Then I shall try to analyse and evaluate his arguments and supportive theories, such

---

1. To be able to define whether a certain individual believes in relativism we have first to make sure that he or she has proper understanding of ethical theories and their implications. For example, Pojman (1998, p. 39) says that the polls that he took in his Ethics and Introduction to Philosophy Courses showed a 2:1 ratio in favour of ethical relativism over moral absolutism. However, we should know that Pojman means by moral absolutism the extremist view that moral principles are exceptionless and cannot be overridden. He adds that less than 5 per cent recognized a third position between two polar opposites. He also mentions that many of those who said they were relativists contended in the same polls that abortion is always wrong except to save the mother's life and that suicide is never morally permissible.

as the argument from diversity, moral conventionalism and social custom theory. We take as our starting point Harman's plans in his different works, especially in *Moral Relativism and Moral Objectivity* (1996).

Features of Harman's theory of ethical relativism

In brief, Harman's policy in Chapter One of *Moral Relativism and Moral Objectivity* is to argue that every moral judgement is relative to a moral framework and then that there is no single true framework. Harman holds that there are many different moral frameworks and none of them is more correct than others.[1]

Harman's preferred formulation of ethical relativism is as follows. For the purpose of assigning truth-conditions a judgement of the form *"it would be morally wrong of P to D"* has to be understood as elliptical for a judgement of the form *"in relation to moral framework M it would be morally wrong of P to D"*.[2]

Moral frameworks

Harman means by "moral framework" or a "moral system of co-ordinates" a set of values, standards or principles. Harman suggests that a moral framework can be understood on the model of the laws of one state, where the laws together with the "facts of the case" determine whether something is legal or not.[3]

The moral framework is determined by actual values, standards and principles that one accepts, but it cannot be identified with them. Harman thinks that it is this distinction that makes it possible to conceive of people making mistakes about moral issues in relation to their moral frameworks. Harman says that there is no common answer among relativists as to how

---

1. For example, see Harman, 1996, p. 5. See also Harman, 1998a, p. 161, and 1998b, p. 208. For a recent criticism of both his claims, i.e. that every moral judgement is relative to a moral framework and that there is no single true framework, see "Moral Relativism and Quasi-Absolutism" by Sarah Stroud, 1998, p. 189. One main objection is, "If moral frameworks could themselves be true or false, correct or incorrect, then particular moral claims *would* be susceptible of a form of truth or falsity which is not purely relative." (ibid.).

2. See Harman, 1996, p. 39.

3. For example, see Harman, 1996, pp. 13 and 17, 1998a, p. 163, and Darwall, "Expressivist Relativism", p.185.

one's actual values determine the relevant moral framework.

Harman believes that moral right and wrong are relative to one or other moral framework. As I mentioned above, he believes that there may be various different moral frameworks, none of which is objectively more correct than the others. To assess a moral judgement for truth, we first translate it into a moral framework. This moral framework frequently will be our own moral framework, but it could also be the moral framework of the maker of the judgement or of the audience of the judgement or of the person who is the object of the judgement.

Harman believes that any moral framework has to be consistent.[1] Therefore, inconsistent moral frameworks are not acceptable. He also admits that some moral claims might be true in relation to all moral frameworks, just like the physical claim that nothing moves faster than light which is true in relation to all spatio-temporal frameworks. Naturally, every moral claim that is not compatible with these universal claims is wrong in relation to all moral frameworks, but he believes that no substantive central core of morality is universally recognized. Harman says:

> Can a moral relativist agree with Stroud that a judgment whose truth value is the same in all moral frameworks has that truth value absolutely and not merely in relation to one or another such framework? Maybe, although that is in some ways like agreeing that "The universe is at least as large as" is true absolutely because true in relation to everything (Harman, 1998b, p. 209).

But I think that there is a great difference here between two types of cases. In the case of Harman's example ("The universe is at least as large as"), there is an inherently relational sense that makes the meaning of the phrase incomplete unless the omitted part is mentioned, but in the case of relative moral values (such as "For me, cheating is wrong"), there is a complete sentence, but the truth (and not the meaning) of that sentence depends on some fundamental and underlying facts.

When there is a moral judgement whose truth is the same in all moral frameworks or in relation to all moral frameworks, this requires that there is a common underlying fact, on which its truth depends. Therefore, both the underlying fact and the derivative judgement are absolute, just like universal claims in physics. When we see that the physical claim that nothing moves faster than light is true in all spatio-temporal frameworks, we realize that there

---

1. See Harman, 1998b, p. 208.

is one truth and that what makes it true must be something general, which is common to all the frameworks. We do not suppose that there are infinite truths brought about by infinite frameworks, each separately; or when we see that there are people in a desert who are near death from starvation and then we see that they are saved by drinking some milk or apple juice or other drink, we come to the conclusion that there is something in common between milk, apple juice and the like, which the people needed and the provision of which saved them, namely water. It would be superficial to say that in relation to one case milk was the saviour and in relation to another case apple juice was the saviour and so forth. In general, my argument is that when *a single* fact is true in relation to several cases it is, indeed, true in relation to something shared by all those cases. Even if one is not satisfied with my argument one has to admit that the principle of *simplicity* requires us to think so, unless we have compelling reason to think otherwise.

In respect to the above formulation of ethical relativism by Harman, Thomson (1996, pp. 188–96) objects that the two italicized sentences, "*it would be morally wrong of P to D*" and "*in relation to moral framework M it would be morally wrong of P to D*", are not equivalent. Thomson shows that a moral framework naturally should be construed as a set of moral commitments that either includes or implies that it is wrong of P to D, in which case the second italicized sentence is logically true, or does not include or imply this, in which case the second italicized sentence is logically false. Thus, the second italicized sentence is not equivalent with the first, since as Blackburn (1998, p. 197) puts it, "the second will typically be a truth or falsity of logic, while the first is not." In other words, one can hold many truths of the second type without holding any of the first. There may be many moral frameworks, in relation to which "it may be wrong to skip church", but one might still hold that it is permissible all the same.

Appreciating Thomson's "devastating objection", Blackburn adds that Harman's mistake surely is to displace the subject's moral framework from other presuppositions. He says, "when I judge any proposition to be true, I will be presupposing or using a tacit set of epistemological principles but it does not follow, and it is not typically true, that the truth-conditions of my judgement contain reference to those principles" (Blackburn, 1998, pp. 197 and 198).[1]

1.　See also my comment on the similarity between relativity of motions and relativity of morals above.

Evaluative relativity: "good for"

The question here is what kind of relativity has to be assumed in moral relativism. Harman compares the relativity of morals with the possibility that something may be good for one person and bad for another, that is, with the idea of *evaluative relativity*. Consider two people who have bet on a horse race. Tom has bet on a horse that can run well in the rain and Sue has bet on a horse that cannot run well in the rain. Surely the rain is good for Tom and bad for Sue. More precisely, the rain is good in relation to Tom's goals and bad in relation to Sue's goals.

Now, consider the example of abortion. Abortion may be moral in relation to moral co-ordinates determined by Tom's values and immoral in relation to moral co-ordinates determined by Sue's values. Harman believes that it can be so even if they do not recognize it, just like the previous case in which the rain could be bad for Sue even if she did not know that her horse could not run well in the rain. Harman insists that he does not identify what is right in relation to a given moral framework with whatever is taken to be right by those who accept that framework. I will speak more about this matter in the next section.

Relativism and moral language

Harman suggests that the speaker is not always required to mention all details of his judgement. For example, if the speaker and the hearer both share a system of values or moral co-ordinates that forbids abortion, the speaker can just say, "Abortion is morally wrong". Harman appears in this way to want to explain why, in most cases when speaking about morality or moral judgements, people do not refer to any particular moral framework nor do they mention that the truth of their judgements is *relative* to one set of moral co-ordinates.

However, one problem remains, which is, why in many cases, when the speaker does not share the same moral framework with the hearer or at least has doubt about this matter, he still does not make the judgement relational. This shows that the speaker himself does not take his judgement to be relative to a certain framework. Perhaps this is why Harman insists in several places that in his view moral relativism does not make any claim about the meaning or the intention of the speaker. Just as Einstein's Theory of Relativity does not involve a claim about meaning or about what people intend to be claiming when they make judgements about an object's mass,[1] neither is Harman's moral relativism a claim about "what people *mean* by their moral judgements" (Harman, 1996, p. 5). In this way Harman suggests that judgements made without recognition of the idea of relativism in physics or morality can be true if and only if they match with the relevant framework. He says:

> Similarly, we moral relativists need not adopt an error theory about the judgements of those whose moral judgements presuppose moral absolutism. Instead of counting all such judgements false, we can evaluate them as we would evaluate the corresponding relativistic judgements in relation to moral frameworks conspicuous to the people making those judgements (Harman, 1998a, p. 162).

Harman also insists that he does not identify what is right in relation to a given moral framework with whatever is actually taken to be right by those who accept that framework. Thus, Harman tries to make his theory capable of accounting for the way in which people may make mistakes. For if rightness just requires conformity to one's framework then there is the difficulty that, apart from deliberate wrongdoers, people usually think that what they are doing or saying is in harmony with their moral system, so they cannot be taken to be wrong.

I think that Harman's account here has some advantages. For example, he admits that many actual moral judgements may be falsified, owing to their incompatibility with the relevant moral frameworks. He also admits that people usually do not make moral judgements in a relational form and even they may have intended them to be absolute. However, it seems to me that there are still problems with this account of moral judgement. First, the speaker in one way or another needs to have in mind in advance a clear idea of what he or she wants to say, and, even more precisely, what he or she wants to judge. So if Harman's theory is true one must make one's judgement, at least in one's mind and intention, relative to one's moral framework. Second, his account is not compatible with our moral experience. Indeed, Harman's account does not explain the conventional usage of moral utterances; rather it tries to decide what they have to mean. Perhaps Darwall also refers to this point when he says, "Harman is careful to stress that this is not an account of what people mean by their moral judgements. Rather, it is

---

1. For example, Harman says: "Einstein's theory does not make a claim about speakers' intentions. It does not claim that speakers intend to be making relational judgements when they speak of mass or simultaneity" (Harman, 1996, p. 18).

an interpretation of what their moral judgements would have to mean if they are to be *objectively true*" (Darwall, 1998, p. 184) Unfortunately, Harman's response to Darwall does not seem to be sufficient, since he just says:

> If I may quibble about this, my suggested account of truth conditions is meant to apply to ordinary moral judgements whether or not they are intended as relative judgements, even if they are meant to be absolute judgements (Harman, 1998b, pp. 207 and 208).

The extent of ethical relativism; moral ought versus evaluative ought

Harman's relativism is a restricted one. He is not a relativist about all types of ethical claims. Harman distinguishes *moral judgements,* in which one makes a moral demand, from *evaluative judgements,* which describe what would be better for a society, or people or the world in general. It is only with respect to moral judgements that Harman is a relativist. For Harman, moral judgements are relative to the moral framework shared by the person formulating the judgement and the person who is the subject of the judgement; moral truth and falsity are relative to a shared set of values. Harman calls judgements that pertain to the relationship between an agent and his act "inner judgements".[1] He tells us (1977, p. 59) that these judgements involve *a moral ought.* There are also evaluative judgements about good and evil or about what would make the world a better or worse place. These judgements involve *an evaluative ought.*

Harman believes that inner judgements have two implications: they imply that the agent has a good reason to act as required, and that the speaker approves that reason and presumes that the hearer does likewise. Other judgements do not imply that the agent has such a reason to do what the speaker approves of. Giving an example of evaluative judgements, Harman (ibid., p. 87) says that one can consistently say that it ought to be the case that Rockefeller give his money to the poor and that the world would be a better place if he did, even though Rockefeller has no reason to give his money to the poor. In what I think to be one of his most direct statements, Harman writes:

---

1. On "inner judgements", see, for example, "Moral Relativism Defended", reprinted in *Relativism: Cognitive and Moral,* edited by M. Krausz and J. W. Meiland, especially pp. 190–5. Pojman says that for Harman "moral judgements are 'inner judgements' in the sense that their assertion supposes adherence to a moral frame of reference shared by the agent, the speaker, and the audience" (Pojman, 1990, p. 20).

As a moral relativist, in judging other people, should you judge them in the light of your own values or in the light of their values? It depends on what you say about them. If you are simply evaluating them, your own values are relevant. If you imply something about their objective moral reasons, then their values may be relevant too (Harman, 1998a, p. 167).

Thus, it becomes clear that Harman's theory is an internalist one, since it holds that moral judgements do not apply to agents unless they have motivating reasons to act in the prescribed way. However, his internalism is a limited one, since he believes that one can evaluate the acts of others, regardless of the values or motivations that they have.

Constraints of ethical relativism: intuitive or rational?

Harman thinks that a moral theory should be as consistent as possible with our common intuitions about morality. Therefore, Harman's relativism allows for intuitional or rational constraints upon morality. Any irrational conventional or socially approved set of rules or moral code must be rejected.

Harman believes that one of our strongest intuitions is that matters of right or wrong are not up to the *individual*. This can be considered as his admittance of a minimum degree of objectivity. (I will talk about this later on as *the externality requirement*.) Even with respect to moral claims, about which Harman is a relativist, he is not a subjectivist. He does not believe that moral principles describe attitudes and feelings. A subjectivist theory, for Harman, is not consistent with our ordinary moral discourse. Harman argues that we are ordinarily inclined to suppose that a person's intentions, goals, plans and projects are different from morality. We ordinarily suppose that a particular individual's decisions and principles do not determine right and wrong. "We are inclined to think that morality has an external source, not an internal one"(Harman, 1977, p. 92). We have no reluctance to speak of moral truth, knowledge and facts. These linguistic practices count against the theory of emotivism.

Argument for moral relativism

Now let us consider Harman's plan for proving moral relativism or disproving moral absolutism. Describing his plan in his last co-authored book,

Harman (1996, p. 6) asserts that in the second and third sections of the first chapter he mainly argues against moral absolutism and in favour of moral relativism.[1] Naturally, the reader expects Harman to present some reasons against moral absolutism, but Harman's argument there consists simply of presenting moral relativism as the most reasonable and plausible account of contemporary moral experience. Of course, Harman sometimes just argues that moral relativism is *a* plausible theory, and not the *only* plausible one. For example, at the beginning of the second section, Harman says, "In this and the following section I argue that the following claim is a reasonable inference from the most plausible explanation of moral diversity" (ibid., p. 8). Elsewhere he says, "Moral relativism is a plausible inference from the most plausible account of existing moral diversity" (ibid., p. 63).

Argument from diversity

Does the argument from diversity disprove moral absolutism? It may be thought that Harman has invoked moral diversity in an attempt to disprove moral absolutism. For example, on his strategy in *Moral Relativism and Moral Objectivity,* Harman says, "I argue that existing moral diversity between societies and within contemporary American society is strong evidence against moral absolutism" (1998b, p. 207). It has to be noted that Harman himself indicates that the mere fact of "moral diversity is not a disproof of moral absolutism," because differences in customs are often results of the differences in circumstances.[2] Even disagreements in the same circumstances do not lead necessarily to relativism, any more than in natural sciences. It can be just a matter of failing or not failing to grasp independent or external facts.

What Harman does say is that there is much diversity and disagreement in morality and a reasonable inference from this would be in favour of ethical relativism and, by implication, against ethical absolutism. Thus, a) he has no direct argument to disprove ethical absolutism, and b) he has no argument for ethical relativism other than saying that moral diversity and disagreements can better be explained by ethical relativism. (He sometimes says that it is hard to find another account and sometimes he says that he has no other alternative in mind.) Harman says:

---

1. See Harman, 1996, p. 6.

2. It seems that Harman here does not distinguish morality from customs. We will discuss the difference between morals and customs in the final chapter.

Really, it might be better for me to say that I put this forward as a hypothesis, since I cannot pretend to be able to prove that it is true. I will argue, however, that this hypothesis accounts for an otherwise puzzling aspect of our moral views that, as far as I know, there is no other way to account for (Harman, "Moral Relativism Defended", reprinted in Pojman, 1998, p. 56).

It is hard to see how to account for all such moral disagreements in terms of differences in situation or beliefs about non-moral facts. Many of these disagreements seem to rest instead on basic differences in moral outlook (Harman, 1998a, p. 162).

In any case, Harman begins his argument by mentioning the nature and extent of moral diversity. "Members of different cultures often have very different beliefs about right and wrong and often act quite differently on their beliefs" (1996, p. 8). He mentions examples such as rules of politeness and etiquette (like burping after eating) and, less trivially, cannibalism, slavery (or a caste system) and polygamy, or more generally the moral status of women. "It is unlikely that any nontrivial moral principles are universally accepted in all societies." (ibid.) He says that even in a single society, such as the United States, there are serious disagreements on moral issues such as eating meat or abortion (See Harman, 1998a, p.162).

According to Harman, there are various sets of moral co-ordinates or moral outlooks with different standards of right and wrong. He mentions as an example the difference among people on the extent of moral community to be protected by moral rules: family and friends, a certain race or caste or country, all human beings, human beings and animals and, finally, all living beings. People also disagree, for example, on the importance of liberty versus equality and general welfare versus the development of art and science.

In general, Harman seems to deny universal moral truths except in two cases:

First, when universal moral truths are well defined. Of course, he believes that this makes them trivial in the sense of being tautologous, e.g. "One must not kill or harm members of a certain group, namely the group of people one must not kill or harm!" Harman disagrees with the idea of Judith Thomson that there are certain principles whose negations could not be accommodated in any moral code. She means principles such as: other things being equal, one ought to do what one promised, one ought not act rudely, one ought not cause others pain or one ought not torture babies to death for fun. Harman thinks that these principles without phrases such as "other things being equal" are not universal, since many moral codes have denied them by limiting them to insiders. And if we add "other things being equal" those principles become trivial.

In my view, the phrase: "other things being equal" is equal to "considered in itself". For example, "other things being equal, one ought to do what one promised," means that keeping the promise as such or in itself is morally necessary. This by no means leads to triviality. It just means that there is a relation between keeping the promise and its moral value. Rightness or obligation is deserved by this act, but it is not fixed and it may be overriden by an additional factor. In fact, these common-sense principles that serve as the grounds for morality seem to be acceptable to all rational agents. Disagreements usually appear when a conflict happens between these principles.

Secondly, when (in my words) universal moral truths are *about* moral frameworks and not *within* moral frameworks. They are then just like universal truths about spatio-temporal frameworks in Einstein's Theory of Relativity, e.g. "all spatio-temporal frameworks must admit of motion and rest." Harman says, "perhaps all moralities have some rules against killing, harm, and deception" (Harman, 1996, p. 9).

It is unclear how Harman can consider these moral rules, which perhaps exist in all moralities as governing moral frameworks, and not be governed by them. It seems once again that comparing ethical relativism to Einstein's Theory of Relativity cannot solve the problem.

Moral conventionalism

To support his theory of moral relativism, Harman develops his theory about the nature of morality, i.e. moral conventionalism. Presumably Harman in this way tries to suggest that the main reason beyond diversity in moral views is that morality lacks objective grounds;[1] hence, there will be no single true

---

1. Harman thinks that conventional theory is in agreement with the Kantian theory in that moral principles have objectivity and interpersonal character. Morality is essentially social (See Harman, 1977, p. 112). However, he means by objectivity just intersubjectivity and not necessarily having any reality independent from the
(continued...)

morality and there will be no point in trying to terminate moral disputes by finding some objective resolutions.

Harman's approach to this point in his last co-authored book (1996) is noteworthy. He first starts with the refutation of moral nihilism and then concludes with moral conventionalism. Morality is as useful and as seriously needed as law. For Harman law lacks any objective ground. He does not believe in natural law. There is no predecided content for law. It is only after bargaining between people or groups in each society that law becomes defined. For Harman, morality also is the result of a kind of bargaining. Of course, there are some differences between law and morality. For example, unlike morality, law requires a relatively formal system that is recognized by a determinate group of people.[1]

In an informative and clear statement on moral conventionalism, Harman says:

> Before any conventions were established, there would be no such thing as right and wrong; it would not make sense to judge what people morally ought not to do. But once a group of people developed conventional patterns of action in order to avoid conflicts with each other, their actions could be judged with reference to those conventions. People who remained outside the relevant group and still in a state of nature, could, however, not be so judged (Harman, 1977, p. 110).

Bargaining: Harman believes it "is likely that most people's values reflect conventions that are maintained by continual tacit bargaining and adjustment" (Harman, 1996, p. 22; without "likely", 1998a, p. 164). Referring to an example from Hume (1739) about two people rowing a boat, Harman (1996) suggests that conventions develop from scratch in the same way that people might arrive at a rate of rowing from scratch. There are different examples of conventions among people, such as those that give rise to the institutions of money, language, property, explicit contracts and promises.

In fact, Harman is inspired by the Humean idea of "convention" in

---

(...continued)
  people. I will speak more about this later when discussing the *externality requirement*.

1.   See Harman, 1996, pp. 6 and 7.

morality, though there are some differences between his account and Hume's.[1] Hume says that some, but not all, aspects of morality rest on "convention"[2] Hume does not think that everything about morality is conventional. Hume believes that sympathy can lead us to approve or disapprove of something regardless of prior conventions. For example, we would approve of kindness to others even in a state of nature. Essentially for Hume, justice requires a convention, but benevolence does not.

Being happy with social contract theories of morality, Harman maintains that the whole of morality and politics arises from conventions adopted for self-interested reasons.[3] Indeed, Harman takes morality to be a form of politics in that it originates in a bargaining situation; different parties decide what are their common basic wants. "A custom of truth-telling arises because it is useful to be able to get information from others and others will tell truth to you only if you make a practice of telling the truth to you [presumably, them]" (Harman, 1996, p. 23). He also gives the examples of keeping promises and the institution of property. As David Gauthier said, we need to "bargain our way into morality". The way of doing so is to establish sufficient sanctions to ensure that, if we respect other people's interests, they must respect ours as well.

Argument for moral conventionalism

Harman argues for moral conventionalism by showing "how taking morality to have a source in actual bargains, reached among actual people who have different powers and resources, might explain aspects of the contemporary moral view" (Harman, 1996, p. 63). In this way, Harman seems to have preserved his argument in *The Nature of Morality* that one reason for moral conventionalism is to consider some "element in our actual moral views that seem to reflect what would be the result of implicit bargaining and mutual adjustments between people of different powers and resources" (Harman, 1977, p. 110).

He suggests (1977, p. 123) one additional support for the social convention

---

1. Hume speaks of this idea in *Enquiry Concerning the Principles of Morals* and *Treatise on Human Nature*, Book 3, Part II, Section II. For an exhaustive discussion, see David Lewis, *Convention* (Cambridge, Mass: Harvard University Press, 1969).

2. See Harman, 1977, p. 103.

3. Two good sources on social contract theories are D. Gauthier, *Morals by Agreement* (Oxford: Oxford University Press, 1986), and R. Hardin, *Morality within the Limits of the Reason* (Chicago: University of Chicago Press, 1988).

theory of morality, namely, the fact that "ought" has the same sense in respect to rules of law, clubs, etiquette, games and so forth. Accordingly, we can say that people accept moral conventions exactly in the same way that they accept those rules. In those contexts rules are certainly conventional, so moral rules also must be conventional.

Harman (ibid., p. 132) also holds that there is empirical evidence for moral conventionalism. We know that Harman denies absolute facts of right and wrong. Instead, he believes that there are facts relative to one set of conventions or another. The empirical evidence for the existence of such facts is that we often must appeal to these facts to explain why people do what they do or believe what they believe. For example, as he proceeds to show, we appeal to relative facts to explain the relative strength of harming versus not helping and to explain why animals are treated and ranked lower than people.

Harming versus not helping: For Harman, one aspect of the contemporary moral view that reflects the role of implicit bargaining and mutual adjustment is the relative strength of the duty not to harm others compared with the duty to help others. He argues (ibid., p. 111) that if our moral principles were not the outcome of bargaining and adjustment, it would be hard to see why there is this moral difference between harming and not helping. Thus, this is evidence in favour of the tacit convention theory.

The reason for such a suggestion is that according to moral conventionalism, "morality represents a compromise between people of different powers and resources" (Harman, 1996, p.24). Everyone is prepared to agree on the prohibition of harming others, because all can benefit from that. However, the same is not true of helping others, because only the needy and the poor will benefit from that. Comparing Hume's actual convention theory with hypothetical agreement theories, Harman (1977, pp. 111 and 112) maintains that the moral difference we recognize between harming and not helping can be explained on the assumption that our morality depends on an *actual* convention among people of different powers and resources. If we were supposed to bargain in a position of equality, we would not come to agree on our present moral principles.

Treatment of animals: In most contemporary moral views animals are ranked lower than people. Most people believe that there are fewer moral limits to action with animals than with human beings. Animals can be "kept as pets, raised as food, hunted for sport and used for medical experiments" (Harman,

1996, p. 25). Harman argues that it is not possible to give a utilitarian account of this difference. For animals are also sentient beings just like human beings, so they should count the same in the utilitarian calculus. Again Harman believes that it is moral conventionalism that can explain this difference. Morality is a set of human conventions and animals have no role in the process of bargaining and convention making; hence, it is quite simple and natural that our moral conventions favour us.

On the other hand, it is not clear why, if Harman is right, there should be any such thing as our concern for animals at all. Harman responds that at first our concerns are restricted to a narrowly defined group of people, i.e. those who have participated in our conventions. Then there will be a tendency to generalize that limited concern and extend it to outsiders and after that to animals. Let us consider exactly Harman's words:

> Given a disposition to feel concern and respect for certain people, there will be a tendency for the disposition to apply to similar cases, so one may find oneself with concern and respect for outsiders, too. One might even come through stimulus generalization to be disposed to feel a certain concern for animals (Harman, 1996, p.27).

Given that the only factors bearing on morality according to Harman are conventions adopted for *self-interested reasons,* I can find no reason for such a generalisation compatible with moral conventionalism or social contract theories. Harman himself seems not entirely happy with the above idea. Perhaps this is why he says, "This is highly speculative, of course – just a possibility" (ibid.).

Implicit and actual agreement

One of the important aspects of Harman's ethical relativism is his emphasis on *implicit* agreements or conventions that the members of a group develop as their morality. These agreements give rise to "inner judgements" that constitute agents' applications of the morality. Harman believes that there is no need to have explicit agreement among the members of the society or among people who participate in bargaining. There need be only tacit agreement. They agree (in intention, not in any ritualistic way) to follow the rules because in this way they can benefit from, and not be harmed by, one another's actions. Harman tries to make clear that his theory requires an agreement only in intention and is not in need of supposing some specific and ritualistic act of agreement. It is enough that the members of a group show through their behaviour that they are willing to obey moral rules, provided that others do so as well.[1]

Harman maintains that in implicit agreements "there is no given moment at which one agrees, since one continues to agree in this sense as long as one continues to have the relevant intentions" (Harman, "Moral Relativism Defended", reprinted in Pojman, 1998, p. 60). Therefore, Harman does not believe that it is necessary to give an exact date and characterization of the event of making an agreement, and his view cannot be rejected simply on the basis that we do not remember that we have ever agreed with someone on what our moral rules should be. I agree with Harman that agreements are not always required to be explicit or ritualistic. But I think that every implicit agreement or knowledge or judgement has to be recognizable and even explicable when one starts to reflect on them and consider them consciously. Otherwise there will remain no difference between truth and illusion.

Harman (1977, pp. 111 and 112) also believes that agreements have to be actual. Each member must have *actually* agreed to follow the rules on the condition that others do so as well. No *hypothetical* agreement is at work here. Harman distinguishes between Hume's theory and hypothetical agreement theories. Hume believed that duties and obligations are derived from *actual*, not hypothetical conventions. We know that actually in all societies people have different conditions of life. For example, some people are very rich and powerful, while others are needy, poor and weak. Hypothetical agreement theories hold that "The correct moral rules are those that *people would* agree to under certain conditions of equality". Harman believes that there is no point in assuming that people in unequal conditions have to make conventions for equal conditions. Why does a rich man, who is not in need of help and whose interest goes no further than bargaining about not harming each other, have to suppose that he is equal to a poor man? Therefore, Harman rejects hypothetical agreement theories.

The social custom theory

According to Harman, subject to rational constraints, morality derives from social customs and rules that are socially enforced and transmitted to the

---

1. See, for example, Harman, 1977, pp. 196, 201 and 202, Arrington, 1989, p. 211, and Robert M. Stewart and Lynn L. Thomas, p. 91.

members of the group. By his loose definition (1977, p. 93), social custom holds that morality derives from the rules or customs that society enforces in a certain way. These rules and customs are external to the individual: hence, they have a degree of objectivity that the individual's personal goals and feelings lack. Since the members of the society internalize these rules, they provide motivation for moral behaviour. A member of society who has internalized the society's moral code is thereby provided with reasons for acting in certain ways.

Harman warns us that we must not oversimplify the social custom theory. The theory does not mean that whatever is customary is right. Slavery may be customary in one society and still be wrong. Based on basic socially enforced facts and certain factual beliefs, members of the society enforce the derivative principles. Members of the society may make mistakes in discovering factual assumptions. They may not recognize the conflict that can arise between basic and derivative principles "because of ignorance of fact, stupidity, and self-deception" (Harman, 1977, p. 94).

Harman's theory develops out of two very strong intuitions. One is that morality, as we discussed above, has to have some external source; otherwise we should be forced to defend a counterintuitive form of subjectivism. Arrington calls this the *externality requirement.* Harman argues that "we do not ordinarily suppose that right and wrong are determined by a particular individual's decisions and principles. We are inclined to think that morality has an external source, not an internal one" (Harman, 1977, p. 92). He also says, "If externalism is dead, everything is permitted" (ibid., p. 93). Harman tries to satisfy the first requirement by locating the source of morality in social conventions, those of a group transcending the individual. Morality is based on socially enforced rules and customs.

The second intuition is that the proper usage of moral language implies that when we say a person ought to do something he has reasons for doing so, reasons deriving from the principles he himself accepts. Arrington calls this the *motivation requirement.* Harman satisfies the second requirement through his idea of inner judgement, which restricts the scope of moral judgement about agents to those agents who at least tacitly accept the speaker's conventions.

Harman thinks that there are two advantages in social custom theory. First, it is compatible with our intuitive feeling that morality has external sanctions. Second, it can explain "why morality has the particular content we normally suppose it has" (Harman, 1977, p. 94). For example, since society has interests in being honest or helpful to others or respectful of others' property, there are social pressures to act accordingly. If our society had enforced different rules, what is right and what is wrong would have changed.

The externality requirement

To get from the externality requirement to the social custom theory, Harman tries to show that alternative ways do not work. In *The Nature of Morality* (1977), he asserts that there could be only two external sources for morality: a divine source and human sources. He immediately dismisses the first possibility to argue for the latter. "If these [sanctions] are not divine, they must be human; that is, they must be social. Morality must then depend essentially on some social law enforced by custom and social pressure" (Harman, 1977, p. 93).

In *Moral Relativism and Moral Objectivity* (1996, Chapters 2 and 6), Harman studies and criticizes ethical naturalism and rationalism as alternatives to his theory. He argues against reductive forms of naturalism, because he holds that the same natural features and facts can be found in different societies with different moralities. Furthermore, naturalists frequently ignore, or fail to explain, the important role of principles in the moral life. Therefore, naturalism fails in its attempt to equate moral facts with a specific set of natural facts.

Rationalism does stress moral principles, and a rationalist such as Kant thinks that the moral life consists of following principles derived from reason itself, principles that are binding on all rational agents, but Harman argues against the universal features of Kant's ethics. According to Kant, if you are to act morally, your basic principle or maxim must be universalizable. This means that what you accept as a principle or maxim you have to accept as a maxim for all rational beings. Kant claims that one must always act in conformity with a maxim that one would accept for all human beings, but Harman counters that while we must act according to maxims that would be rational for all others to act upon, we need not think that it would be irrational for others to reject them. According to Harman, there are a number of mutually exclusive sets of maxims, any of which it would be rational for all human beings to follow. In short, Harman rejects a number of arguments that there are universally applicable objective moral reasons. Instead, he suggests (1996, p. 63) adopting a quasi-absolutist way of talking about moral reasons.

Quasi-absolutism: Harman tries to develop an idea about the meaning and the use of the terms that can be both acceptable and helpful for moral relativists. He calls this idea "quasi-absolutism". It is also sometimes called "projectivism". Harman says:

> In perhaps the simplest form of quasi-absolutism, a moral relativist projects his or her moral framework onto the world and then uses moral terminology as if the projected morality were the single true morality, while at the same time admitting that this way of talking is only "as if" (Harman, 1996, p. 34).

Thus, a moral relativist, instead of saying, "This is wrong in relation to my moral co-ordinates", says only, "This is wrong". For example, if Tom considers raising animals for food to be wrong in relation to his moral standards he can say, "Raising animals for food is wrong in relation to my moral co-ordinates", but, instead, he may just say, "Raising animals for food is wrong". If so, what Tom has done is to suppose reality to be in conformity with his moral outlook. In other words, he has projected his belief on to the external world.

In using the expression "quasi-absolutism" and perhaps introducing the idea beyond that expression, Harman was inspired by Blackburn's expression of "quasi-realism" in *Essays in Quasi-Realism* (1993).[1] Harman says:

> The central assumption behind such quasi-absolutism (as I will call it, echoing Blackburn's "quasi-realism") is that words can be given meaning by being given a use. I do not know whether this assumption is correct but will suppose that it is for the sake of argument (Harman, 1998a, p. 165).

It is noteworthy that Blackburn criticizes Harman for speaking of quasi-absolutism as a re-bandaged quasi-realism and considering the quasi-absolutist as a moral relativist who adopts a way of talking "as if" there were moral absolutes. Blackburn, the person who introduced the idea of quasi-realism and whom Harman considers a quasi-absolutist, says:

> I am sorry to say that I do not accept this way of putting it. Insofar as the term makes sense to me, I am not a moral relativist (I don't accept Harman's relational account of the truth-conditions of moral

---

1.   As I mentioned earlier, some traces of this idea may be traced back to Brandt.

judgments, and in fact doubt whether any relativistic construction is coherent) and I am a moral absolutist (I hold, for example, that it is wrong to kick dogs for fun whether you want to or not, and that it would have been wrong whatever anyone had thought about it.) I do *not* recognize my position as one of talking "as if" there were values, rights and duties, when "really" there are none (see, for example, my *Essay in Quasi-Realism*, pp. 55–8). I hold there are values, rights, and duties. And I am pleased to have this opportunity to express such healthy attitudes, which I hope you share. (Blackburn, 1998, p. 198).

For Harman, one advantage of the quasi-absolutist way of speaking and presenting ideas is to give a chance for moral relativists to disagree with each other. In the above example, if Tom and Sue mention the details of their moral judgements there will be no disagreement. If Tom asserts that raising animals for food is wrong in respect to his moral standards Sue also will agree that raising animals for food is wrong in respect to Tom's moral standards, and vice versa, but if Tom omits the relational part of the judgement and just says that raising animals for food is wrong, Sue may disagree with him. Harman says:

Self-conscious moral relativists might adopt a special quasi-absolutist terminology in order to express their disagreements with each other, and judgements made using that terminology can be counted true or false, even if not objectively true or false (Harman, 1996, p. 63).

or, more clearly:

Then the first point of usage is that Veronica and Archie are to be able to express their disagreement in affective attitude using the QA terminology (Harman, 1998a, p. 165).

Therefore, Harman believes that as long as a moral relativist, who uses quasi-absolutist terminology, accepts X is WRONG (absolutely wrong) if and only if X is wrong in relation to the relevant moral framework, he can use quasi-absolutist terminology to express moral disagreements, while purely relativist semantics cannot allow people with different moral frameworks to express moral disagreements.[1] Stroud believes that Harman introduced quasi-absolutism in Chapter three of *Moral Relativism and Moral Objectivity* "in order to repair a defect he sees with his original formulation of moral relativism" (Stroud, 1998, p. 192). That defect is the difficulty of expressing basic moral disagreements.

I agree with Stroud (ibid., pp. 192–4) that if Harman's moral relativism is not a claim about meaning, as Harman himself asserts, then his moral relativism would seem to pose no threat to univocality of moral terms, since both parties intend to speak in an absolute manner. Therefore, if A says, "Raising animals for food is wrong", and B says, "Raising animals for food is not wrong", A and B are really disagreeing with each other, or more precisely, they are expressing their disagreements. If someone on behalf of Harman says that disagreements *in affective attitudes* cannot be expressed without appeal to quasi-absolutism, the answer would be that it is quite possible to express even disagreements in attitudes through relativistic usage of language. For example, Joe can sincerely say, "I am against (standards that permit) raising animals for food", and Jane can sincerely reply, "I am not". If so, then we can say that they have expressed their clashing attitudes.[2] Of course, the relativist view about moral language allows people only to pretend to express moral disagreements, since if both parties and the hearer reflect a little they will realize that they are not talking about one object in relation to the same framework; they are talking about what is right for each, regardless of the others. However, the situation for quasi-absolutism is not better, because quasi-absolutism is no more than a mask (see Comment 8 at the end of this chapter).

The motivation requirement

Harman believes that it does not make any sense (and is logically improper) to make a moral appeal to a person who does not have common fundamental moral principles with oneself. For example, in one society human sacrifice may be practised regularly. In that society, the sacrifice is seen as necessary in order to maintain the cosmic order or to please the gods. When an outsider comes and claims that it is wrong to go forward with another planned sacrifice

---

1. See Harman, 1996, p. 33, and Darwall, 1998, p. 186.
2. The final judgement of Stroud on Harman's relativism is obtainable from the following passage: "I note in closing that I have not commented at all on Harman's arguments for moral relativism; I have merely attempted to bring out some difficulties which attend even the *formulation* of such a view" (Stroud, 1998, p. 194).

there is no reason for them to accept this, since they do not share that moral vision. Those who object to the sacrifice can offer no morally relevant reason for refraining from their practice. However, Harman grants that one could attempt to dissuade those who sacrifice by making an evaluative claim to the effect that the world would be a better place in which to live if human sacrifice were not practised.

In *Moral Relativism and Moral Objectivity,* Harman relies considerably on examples: the example of a group of cannibals and the example of Hitler in contrast to Stalin. Hitler did not have a reason not to do what he did, so he is evil rather than wrong. On the other hand, although Stalin was a mass murderer, it is possible, Harman believes, that he was trying to do the right thing. He knew that it was bad to kill masses, but he found it the lesser of two evils. Not ordering the purges could lead to the collapse of the revolution. Of course, Harman does not pardon Stalin's actions.[1]

He believes that in such cases we refuse to judge them to be morally wrong in their actions simply because they do not share our moral principles. If we said that they were morally wrong it would imply that they had good reasons for not doing those acts. Of course, we can say that the world would be a better place if there were no cannibalism or the deeds of a Hitler. We might even use the evaluative "ought" and say there ought to be no such practices in the world.

This is one of the crucial and, at the same time, most controversial aspects of Harman's theory. There has been great resistance to Harman's motivation requirement. For example, it has been suggested that our refusal to pass judgements on others' actions is simply because of our acknowledged inability to convince them.[2] In response, Arrington says, "Harman can reply that if we cannot convince them that what they have done was wrong it means that they could not understand that what they have done was wrong. Then it follows that they did not have reasons for not acting in that way and finally it is logically improper to say that they were wrong" (Arrington, 1989, p. 208). I

---

1. See Harman, 1977, pp. 97–8 and 105–9, and "Moral Relativism Defended", reprinted in M. Krausz and J. W. Meiland, eds, *Relativism: Cognitive and Moral* (1982, pp. 192 and 193). For example, Harman says, "Hitler is beyond the pale in a way that Stalin was not. Hitler was not just immoral, he was amoral, he was evil. Stalin was terrible and also, perhaps, evil; but he was not wholly beyond the reaches of morality or at least that part of morality that we invoke in judging him to be an evil man" (Harman, 1977, p. 108).

2. See, for example, the editors' introduction to "Moral Relativism Defended", reprinted in M. Krausz and J. W. Meiland (1982, pp. 186–8).

think our inability to convince people such as Hitler is not because they cannot understand since they are mad or foolish. It is rather due to their bias, their insistence on their own views and their refusal to pay attention to what is said to them; indeed, they do not want to understand.

One fundamental problem that Harman himself realizes is that the motivation requirement is in conflict with one aspect of our moral view. As Kant observed, we can make moral judgements about anyone, regardless of his moral principles, but if we accept the motivation requirement and take for granted that people do not have the same moral principles, it appears that "something is wrong with our ordinary view that we can make moral 'ought' judgements about anyone, no matter what their principles" (Harman, 1977, p. 90). Arrington tries to reply on behalf of Harman and says, "Another possibility, not considered by Harman, is that the *ought*-judgements we make about anyone, no matter what their principles, are really evaluative *ought*-judgements rather than moral ones" (Arrington, 1989, p.208).

Showing his sympathy with Judith Thomson's (1996) criticism of Harman's internalism, Blackburn says, "I have always been puzzled why anyone should hold that moral judgement is inapplicable to anyone who is bad enough. Hitler's character was certainly one to cause comment, so why not moral comment?" (Blackburn, 1998, p. 198). Blackburn thinks that perhaps Harman is overly influenced by Wong's idea, that "one should not interfere with the ends of others unless one can justify the interference to be acceptable to them were they fully rational and informed of all the relevant circumstances".[1] Blackburn thinks that Wong's idea is not applicable to this case, because "a fully rational and informed Hitler who is nevertheless brimful of bad desires can surely be *stopped,* even if according to Harman he cannot be judged" (ibid.).

General comments

1. In his last book, Harman supports moral relativism with moral conventionalism, and not with a social custom theory. He says that in each society people through bargaining agree on some moral rules or (you can say) on some conventional values. Since there is no objective way to prefer one society's rules to another there can be no single true

---

1. See my discussion earlier about Wong's idea in the section on Normative Relativism.

morality. It seems to me that there is a noticeable change in Harman's whole theory of moral relativism.[1] In *Moral Relativism and Moral*

---

1. The change in Harman's ideas is noticed in a recent work by Wong in 1998. Wong (1998, p. 542) introduces *Moral Relativism and Moral Objectivity* by G. Harman and J. Thomson (1996) as the "most comprehensive statement of Harman's relativism. Modifies some earlier position taken." However, he does not mention anything about the characteristics of the modified positions.

    There is also a controversy between Nicholas Sturgeon (1998) on the one hand and Harman (1998b) and Railton (1998) on the other about changes in Harman's view in *Moral Relativism and Moral Objectivity*.

    Sturgeon says, "Harman is well known for having argued that supposed moral facts never seem relevant to the explanation of nonmoral facts. [Gilbert Harman, *The Nature of Morality* (New York: Oxford University Press, 1977), Ch.1] He does not repeat that argument, however; when he mentions moral explanations, he concedes that many appear perfectly reasonable, insisting only they are of little help in settling deep moral disagreements [Harman, 1998a, pp. 168–70]." (Nicholas L. Sturgeon, "Thomson Against Moral Explanations", *Philosophy and Phenomenological Research*, Vol. LVIII, March 1998, p.199).

    On the contrary, Railton says, "Now since his earlier book, *The Nature of Morality*, Harman has been widely perceived as rejecting any sort of 'moral explanation.' But in his contribution to *Moral Relativism and Moral Objectivity* he reaffirms earlier claims that the issue for him is not whether there are any moral explanations, but whether these explanations could provide the sort of evidence we'd need to adjudicate epistemically between rival moral theories or frameworks [Harman, 1998, p. 171]" (Railton, Peter, "Moral Explanation and Moral Objectivity", 1998a, p. 177).

    In the footnote, Railton says about Harman, "As he previously [in 'Moral Explanations of Natural Facts – Can Moral Claims Be Tested Against Moral Reality?', *The Southern Journal of Philosophy 14*, Suppl. (1986): 57–68, p. 60] wrote: . . . the question is not just whether there are 'moral explanations.' It is rather whether there is the sort of moral explanations that would make moral claims empirically testable in the way that scientific claims are empirically testable . . . Thomson identifies the Thesis of Moral Objectivity as 'It is possible to find out about some moral sentences that they are true' (p. 68). To put the thesis in Harmanian terms, 'It is possible to find out about some nonrelativistic moral proposition that it is (objectively) true' (compare 174). Harman believes that even the most plausible moral explanations would not support such a finding."

    Harman replies to Sturgeon. "In fact, my interest in moral explanations has always [in the footnote, Harman refers to the first chapter of *The Nature of Morality*] been an interest in the extent to which uncontroversial data might be better explained by one rather than another competing moral framework, so that the data could provide evidential support for the one framework over the other. (Railton cites a 1986 paper in which I tried to make this clear.) I agree with Sturgeon that there are many interesting issues about moral explanations over and above the one just mentioned" (Harman, "Responses to Critics", 1998, pp. 207 and

(continued...)

Objectivity Harman gives an account of the process of the establishment of moral rules that is noticeably more individualistic. For example, individuals are said to think about their benefits in respect to animals and then to make a convention in this regard, and people negotiate with each other on social ties and through bargaining decide to be faithful to their promises, to tell the truth and so on.

Thus, there can be morality without any need to assume that morality is derived from social customs and rules, as social custom theory holds. Harman admits that there can be a moral system for one person only. He says: "There is even a limiting case (in morality, not in law) where a person sets standards for him or herself – a one-person group" (Harman, 1996, p. 7). According to this account, the role of society comes only after the establishment of individual-made conventions. Harman maintains that when a set of moral conventions or conventional morals gets established it becomes difficult to modify it. There will be social pressure to follow them and penalties for offenders as well. People who feel unhappy "may try to renegotiate a more favorable outcome" (ibid., p. 24).

However, it seems that in his previous works Harman had developed another account about the origin of morality and its source of power. Harman's theory there is not simply a claim that moral judgements are made relative to conventional rules, but rather, his moral conventionalism is a form of social custom theory.[1] According to social custom theory, morality is derived from social customs and rules enforced by the society and internalized by the members of the society. There is a role for a new generation of any society in producing

---

(...continued)
   208).

1.   Having studied crucial cases such as cannibalism in which our intuitions are unclear and conflicting, Harman asserts that it is hard to decide whether a social custom theory agrees or conflicts with our intuitions. On the one hand, we feel that we cannot blame members of those societies who have the custom of cannibalism, since they do not know it as wrong. On the other hand, we believe that their practice is objectionable and therefore it is not definitely the case that if we visit their society it will still be right for us to say "when in Rome, do as the Romans do". Harman feels that the problem is partly due to the vagueness of social custom theories and tries to solve the problems by "a more precise theory that supposes that morality rests on tacit convention among the members of society" (Harman, 1977, p. 99).
      Therefore, Harman seems to believe that his idea of conventionalism is a version of social custom theory, which is free from the vagueness of the ordinary version.

contemporary conventional morals. From the beginning, they have faced a well-established moral system and at most they could open negotiations about it.

Actually it helps Harman's argument to maintain that moral systems and moral rules are external to people and that society provides sanctions for violating them; hence, they can enjoy some degree of objectivity. Since these rules are internalized in the members and, therefore, the members accept them, they have the motivation to conform to them. Therefore, in Harman's old account the role of bargaining comes after the establishment of a moral system, but in his new account a moral system can be made through bargaining only.

In my view the only solution for this inconsistency is to suppose that Harman still believes in a social custom theory but for some reason, probably such as shortage of space in the co-authored volume of *Moral Relativism and Moral Objectivity* and/or to prevent criticisms made by others of his social custom theory, he did not present a comprehensive account of his multi-aspect theory of moral relativism. The full account will be as follows. There is an obvious diversity in moral values. Most of contemporary moral debates are not terminable, since there is no objectively privileged moral system. Our ancestors adopted a set of conventional moral standards or rules and we inherited a well-established moral system. This moral system enforces its standards and values upon us and since we have internalized these standards and values we have the motivation to follow them. However, we do not have to follow them without considering our own interests. Some people might violate the rules and some might ask for renegotiations to reach a new agreement through bargaining.[1]

However, it is not clear why Harman should not have referred to this overall account, if this is what Harman really wants to develop in *Moral Relativism and Moral Objectivity*. What is suspicious is that Harman speaks of moral conventions and bargaining as if it is completely up to us to make decisions and there are no social pressures now interfering in our decisions. I strongly feel that the atmosphere as well as the reasoning in this book is quite different from the previous works, even though it can be made consistent with them.

---

1. Harman clearly says that according to moral conventionalism the principles that apply to you are not simply what "the surrounding group" conventionally accepted. It is up to you to accept the conventions.

2. Arrington believes that the "implicit bargaining" aspect of Harman's overall theory is not an essential part of his relativism, and that it sits uncomfortably with his relativism. Belief in the social custom theory requires no specific theory about the origin of these rules. All that the social custom theory needs is that the rules be seen as binding because they are enforced by society. If relativism requires diversity of rules, this diversity could easily be explained in terms of rules having different ecclesiastical, political or biological origins. There is no need to adopt the implicit bargaining theory.

The other problem is that the implicit bargaining theory is even incompatible with Harman's ethical relativism, since it leads to the expectation that all societies that are similar in the distribution of wealth and power will reach the same outcome in their bargaining and especially they will reach the same balance struck between the harm and help principles (I say "especially", because in this case it would be enough that there are the rich and the poor or the powerful and the weak) and that the moral rules prohibiting lying, murder and other forms of harm will be universal. Arrington says:

> Thus the implicit bargaining theory would predict that principles proscribing lying and murder would be common – that is, that there would be widespread agreement on basic moral matters. Relativism, on the other hand, seems to be based on the conviction that there is widespread moral disagreement. At a minimum, it is committed to the likelihood that different social groups subscribe to different basic moral principles. Hence relativism and the implicit bargaining theory go in opposite directions (Arrington, 1989, p. 212).

Unlike Arrington, I think Harman's theory is in need of implicit bargaining theory, since he believes that there are aspects of our moral intuition that cannot be explained simply by appeal to the social custom theory. I explained in my note on the change in Harman's argument how he tried to develop a more precise version of the social custom theory in *The Nature of Morality* and why he focused only on moral conventionalism (including implicit bargaining), and not the social custom theory in *Moral Relativism and Moral Objectivism*. However, I agree that Harman's adoption of implicit bargaining theory weakens his theory of the relativity of morals and leads to absolutism, since the result of bargaining would mostly be the same in different societies, given that Harman himself admits widespread disparities of power.

3. One problem with many forms of ethical relativism, including that of Harman, arises from a failure to distinguish between morality that is relational and morality that is relative.[1] For example, Harman believes that morality is based on, or is relative to, implicit agreements, but this in itself does not grant the truth of ethical relativism, since agreements themselves can be relativist or universal in character, depending on whether they are binding on all rational human beings or only on a special group. Therefore, to suppose that morality is relational to, say, agreements does not necessarily mean that morality is relative and not absolute.

4. Social custom theory assumes that if there is no society and people live quite separately there will be no right or wrong. Harman himself also insists that morality is a social phenomenon. However, he suggests that there may be some cases in which the relevant "group" is constituted by one person only. This is a limiting case of morality. Harman asserts, "If there were only individual moralities, only sets of personal principles and no group conventions, morality as we normally think of it would not yet exist." That one person cannot judge others according to his principles, and we usually take morality as capable of giving guidelines for judging more than one person. Moreover, there remains no room for externality.

Unlike Harman, I think it is quite possible to conceive of situations in which there is only one person engaged and morality, as we usually take it, has something to say to direct his actions. He would have sufficient grounds to treat something as right or wrong, at least in respect of his personal affairs. Human values or virtues do not always have a social feature.

Another point is that Harman himself admits that many people think that, even in a state of nature, murder is wrong and justice is good. However, Harman tries to defend the social custom theory by saying, first, that it is too difficult to understand what a state of nature

---

1. Indeed, Bunting believes that Harman's theory is a classic example of this confusion. See Bunting, pp. 84 and 85.

would be like to be able to judge about moral rules there and, secondly, "it is not *clearly* essential to our conception of morality that moral constraints should apply in a state of nature". (Harman, 1977, p. 96). My argument in the whole of this work, especially in the final chapter on the foundations of morality, is that moral standards are independent of our choice or bargaining; there is a real relationship between the act itself and its moral status. Even if there were no other people to negotiate or bargain with in order to come to an agreement, I would still believe that torturing for fun is against our goodness, interest or perfection, and is wrong.

5. It seems strange that moral relativism is claimed to be rooted in moral disagreements, but relativists such as Harman face serious problems in explaining how a real disagreement is possible. The reason is that ethical relativism proposes a structure in which moral claims can conflict only apparently; in reality, conflicting claims refer to different relative facts and everything may be acceptable in its place. The relativist faces the puzzle of explaining why they first appeared to conflict. Also, as Lukes suggested, the other difficulty with ethical relativism is that it is not clear how it can explain conflicts *within* cultural boundaries.[1] Here, relativists have no way other than appeal to what absolutists say in explaining moral disagreements and diversity. In the discussion about absolutism and diversity of morals, I tried to investigate all possible ways for such explanation.

6. As I explained above, Harman's ethical relativism is an internalist theory, since it denies that moral judgements apply to agents who do not have reasons to follow them. Unless one has a reason (a motive) to perform a moral duty, it is incoherent to say one has a duty, but externalist theories hold that an act can be judged on the basis of objective standards, regardless of whether or not the agent had motives at the moment of action to follow those standards.

One main problem with Harman's internalism is that he does not give a rationale for his claim that the applicability of moral judgements requires that the agent have a good reason for acting in a certain way – in a sense of "reason", which depends on the intentions, desires, aims

---

1.   See Steven Lukes, 1991, p. 4.

or motivations of agents.[1] As I said earlier (in the discussion about moral relativism as a logical thesis), in the more reasonable account of what Harman means by a logical thesis, he gives us merely some "terminological proposals".[2] His proposals are based on the assumption that "ought implies can", so if the person has currently no motivation to do A he could have no moral obligation to do A. Harman does not give us any reason why we cannot suppose that the necessary condition for moral responsibility is the possibility of having reason or motivation to do a certain act and not the actuality of that.

A more plausible alternative can be understood by considering that we usually regard a person who has acted so immorally that he has lost his motivation to observe moral rules to be still morally responsible. More generally, one may say that one condition for moral responsibility is free will. To exercise free will, one needs to have knowledge, motivation and power. However, if one has deliberately in one way or another through one's previous free decisions left no room to exercise one's free will, yet one will still be morally responsible for one's actions. Think of a person who has attempted suicide and is going to die in a few seconds. This person now has no power to keep himself alive and will certainly die, but we do not hesitate to consider him responsible for what he did, since he deliberately did something in the past that led to his current situation, in which he has no room to exercise his free will. Therefore, I think that the Aristotelian thesis about moral responsibility, that "ought implies could have", is more plausible than Harman's account.[3]

Internalism tries to show why we should be moral and therefore says that being moral depends on having a good reason, i.e. a motive, for being so, but there are two problems here. One problem is that there is no sufficient reason put forward for believing in internalism. The other problem is to explain, "How can one be immoral?" It is undeniable that part of human moral experience is deliberate wrongdoing and intentionally immoral advice.

Unlike what internalists might have thought, I will argue in the final chapter that we can be committed to objectivism or externalism and still be able to give a clear answer to the question, " Why should we be

---

1. See, for example, Stewart and Thomas, 1991, pp. 91 and 92.
2. See also Harman, 1996, p. 46.
3. See Shomali, 1996, and Pojman, 1990.

moral?". To answer this question we must not neglect another important aspect of our moral experience, i.e. the possibility of being immoral.

As I mentioned earlier, Harman takes morality as a form of politics, since it originates from implicit bargaining of different parties. Now the question that arises here is why, in the case of law, obligations do not depend on having a reason to do so, in the sense mentioned above; why "moral demands have to be acceptable to those to whom they apply in the way that legal demands do not."[1] I see no reason to prevent us from saying that one has a moral duty not to torture for fun when one has no reason not to do so and at the same time allow us to say one has a legal duty not to do so.

The only answer that occurs to me is that Harman may claim that in the case of law there is a well-established set of norms, so what we can do is to bargain on legal systems in toto. We are obliged to obey that legal system that we have a good reason to choose. Therefore, it is not necessary to have a good reason for any single legal demand. However, in the case of morality there is no such strong and established set of norms and we need a good reason for any single moral demand.

7. It is striking that, according to Harman, evaluative judgements, which are made with reference to the principles or standards of the speaker, are not restricted in any way with respect to their scope. We can evaluate the acts of any person even if he does not share our moral principles and say that he ought not have acted as he did, if we mean by this that *evaluatively* the world would have been a better place had he not so acted. In such cases, we evaluate the act and we do not pass judgement on the moral relationship between the act and the agent. Harman has had this opinion at least since he wrote *The Nature of Morality*, where he expressly says that his relativism is only about what he calls "inner judgements" and that his relativism is not meant to apply, for example, to the judgement that someone is evil or that a given institution is unjust.[2]

Harman's distinction between evaluative judgements and moral judgements is not sound. Indeed, all evaluative judgements are made with reference to the principles or standards of the speaker and are

1. Harman, 1978, p. 152.
2. See Harman, 1977, p. 4.

reducible to moral judgements. How can one coherently say that "Hitler's aggression was wrong, but it was not wrong of him to aggress"? I cannot agree with Harman that a member of Murder, Inc. can *only* be called *evil* in our vocabulary and cannot be *judged* to be a wrongdoer.

Moreover, Harman's distinction between *evil* and *wrong* is not sound. To suppose that Hitler was evil but not morally wrong leads to the absence of any moral significance in the notion of evil. This is contrary to what we usually mean by using the term "evil". It has been suggested (Pojman, 1990, p. 29) that this distinction between "evil" and "wrong" leads one to suppose that "evil" is equal to non-cognitive expressions, such as "boo" or "I don't like that", and this in turn makes Harman's view liable to standard objections to non-cognitivism.

Harman may argue that psychologically speaking it is more convenient for us to call Hitler evil than simply say that what he was doing was wrong, but there is no compelling reason to suppose that psychological convenience is a good reason for a correct doctrine. Neither is there any reason to think that Harman's idea is backed up by a correct linguistic intuition. Matilal says:

> It does not seem too odd to say in English that Hitler, being a rational human being, turned into a madman and committed most serious crimes against humanity, while it could be counter-intuitive to say that he reached an inner "moral" judgement following his *own* set of "moral" principles (Matilal, 1989, pp. 344 and 345).

8. Harman seems to speak of quasi-absolutism as if he has really discovered some hidden reality and tries to solve many problems with that. For example, he refers to Wong's idea about the morality of non-interference with the practices of others as an implication of both meta-ethical relativism and a liberal-contractualist morality in the West. Wong believes that this implies that one should not interfere in others' practices unless one could justify this to them, were they fully rational and informed. Harman replies that if what is required is *justification* in terms of quasi-absolutism, there will be no need for tolerance, but if we mean objective justification, tolerance is required.

It seems that quasi-absolutism does not solve such problems and it is likely to be simply a linguistic point. What liberal-contractualist morality requires is a real justification that convinces the other side, not just presenting or projecting one's views or reasons as if they are the absolute ones. It is rather a deception. In his final work, Harman himself says, "Although I am not sure the terminology really makes sense, I describe what I take to be the best possible way I know of to introduce such a terminology" (1998b, p. 210).

9. One objection to Harman's theory of bargaining is that defining moral standards, values and duties through bargaining among participants with various social positions and different amounts of power and wealth leads to unjust outcomes in relation to the poor and to animals, who did not take part in the bargaining.

In *Moral Relativism and Moral Objectivity*, Harman himself mentions this objection and replies that there is no acceptable way other than moral conventionalism to explain those two aspects of today's moral experiences. Therefore, we have three alternatives:

a. To consider the relevant agreements null and void. This implies that there is no reason to refrain from harming other people. This is not acceptable.
b. To see nothing unjust and unfair in those agreements.
c. To consider unjust agreements as not completely null and void, at least when they are basic moral disagreements. We can at most only negotiate about them.

Harman mentions that people with a superior power of bargaining tend to accept the second possibility and people with an inferior position tend to accept the third position. The dispute can be solved "when some new, consistent consensus is reached". However, Harman thinks the problem is not very serious. He says:

> In fact, most people do not seem to think that vast differences in power by themselves make an agreement invalid. For example, it is widely thought that contracts made by individuals with large banks and other corporations are often legally and morally binding, despite extreme differences in bargaining power of those involved. So it is possible that there is no real problem here (1996, p. 29).

I think that there is a big gap between Harman's examples and morality. Unlike legal contracts, all moral contracts, and especially the basic ones, which are to serve as foundations of morality, as moral conventionalism suggests, have to be free from any element of injustice and bias. Morality in any form and of any kind has to serve human ideals and one of the most crucial and important ideals of all human beings is justice.

Of course, there may happen some cases in which one morally has to be committed to some unjust or unfair contracts, but it does not contradict the above-mentioned point. For example, a mother may be in urgent need of money to afford a very expensive operation to save the life of her child who will otherwise die. The cost of the operation is defined by the authorities and is excessive. She has no way to change their decision, at least in the short term, and there is no other option for her. So she agrees to pay the due amount. This agreement is legally valid from both sides, but morally the mother is definitely right to agree to pay the proposed amount, whereas the authorities of the hospital are not right. However, both sides of the agreement morally and legally have to fulfil the requirements of the agreement as far as they can.

Now, suppose that the situation becomes more complicated. The mother has to sell her house to collect the money. Since she is in a rush she has to sell it at half price. A potential purchaser comes and without any bargaining or pressure accepts the price and agrees to pay the *price* (half of the real price). Again this agreement is legally valid and both sides have to observe it. What about the moral point of view? The poor mother is definitely right, but the second person may be considered morally condemned. Although the purchaser is helping in some way and has not exercised any force or pressure on her and has not used any deception, he has misused this opportunity and has observed only his own immediate interests. Morally he is required to propose voluntarily some reasonable and fair price. How far morality is from bargaining!

10. In *Moral Relativism and Moral Objectivity*, Harman himself mentions the following criticisms as well, and then tries to answer them.

   a. Failure to resolve moral disputes objectively. Responding to the objection that moral conventionalism deprives us of objective solutions to moral disputes, Harman asserts that even if we accept the existence of objective solutions we cannot accept that there are no other rational solutions for moral disputes. Bargaining counts as a rational solution. In politics and ethics, disputes often involve bargaining. We argue with each other, not only by showing facts but also by giving practical reasons to modify moral understandings. For example, we say, "If you don't do this we won't do that." "Disadvantaged groups can threaten to withhold full participation in a moral framework unless their disadvantage is lessened or removed" (1996, p. 22).

b. Lack of normative force. It may be objected that morality, when based on bargaining, contracts and conventions, loses its force. Morality is thus based on morally irrelevant considerations. Harman replies that morality does not lose objective absolute normative force, simply because it never had that. "Morality has and will continue to have its relative force" (ibid., p. 28).

Evaluation of Harman's responses to these two objections needs an independent discussion about the objectivity of morality. Some aspects of the subject will be discussed in the final chapter.

Summary

For an overall study of Harman's ethical relativism my discussions in this chapter should be taken together with my examination of the arguments for meta-ethical relativism and absolutist accounts of diversity of morals in the third chapter and of the foundations of morality in the final chapter. In short, Harman's theory of relativism has some advantages and at the same time suffers from some problems.

Here, I should like to mention what I consider the advantages of Harman's theory.

1. Harman's theory takes the problem of relativity of morals seriously, in the sense that it admits that it cannot be settled by collecting some anthropological data about the diversity of morals and neglecting the philosophical nature of the discussion. Harman admits that the mere existence of diversity cannot be an argument for ethical relativism.

2. Harman is very well aware that the debate over ethical relativism is

interwoven with the debate about the foundations or origins of morality. Hence, he develops his theory of moral conventionalism (and the social custom theory).

3. Harman also tries to be faithful to our moral experiences, including those aspects that suggest objectivity of morals. We saw that he is a cognitivist and believes in the truth value of moral judgements. We also saw how he puts emphasis on the externality requirement and rejects the idea that right and wrong are determined by a particular individual's decisions and principles. "If externalism is dead everything is permitted" (Harman, 1977, p.93).

4. Harman acknowledges that most people do not intend their judgements to be relational and this is why he says that his theory is not about the meaning of moral statements.

5. Harman admits that one problem with relativist accounts of morality is that they cannot explain how people can disagree with each other, and this is why he develops quasi-absolutism.

6. Harman accepts that people do not hesitate to pass judgements beyond cultural boundaries and this is why he distinguishes between the evaluative ought, which describes what would be better for a society or people or the world in general, and moral judgements, in which one makes a moral appeal. Harman clearly says that his relativism is a restricted one; his relativism is about moral ought or inner judgements only.

On the other hand, there are some disadvantages in Harman's theory, as it also suffers from some problems of ethical relativism in general. There is no need to repeat my criticisms and comments on Harman's theory. However, I should like to indicate that the advantages of Harman's theory are mostly in recognizing symptoms, but his treatments of them are not acceptable. In particular, my main objections concern his internalism, his moral conventionalism, the distinction between evaluative ought and moral ought, the notion of quasi-absolutism and the ambiguity of his argument in some of his works (see general comment no. 1).

I also disagree with Harman about explaining moral disagreements and aspects of our moral experience, which Harman takes to serve as evidence for his theory of moral conventionalism, such as the relative strength of the duty not to harm others compared with the duty to help and the fact that in most moral views animals get ranked lower than people. In the second part of the third chapter, Moral Absolutism and Diversity of Morals, I showed how an absolutist account of morality can explain all types of disagreements. I also believe that the reason for the difference between harming and helping originates from our conception of individual rights and mutual responsibilities. Although helping others is good, we cannot make it obligatory, since it is not appropriate to compel someone to help others solve their problems by inflicting troublesome demands on him. Moreover, morality sometimes loses its point, i.e. the promotion of our human compassion and benevolence, when it is compelled or enforced.

Hence, I believe that *except in vital norms and the least expectations* (in the sense that all ordinary and average human beings can be expected to carry out)*, without which social order gets disturbed and without which one loses one's chance to exercise even voluntary aspects of morality, no moral value must be enforced or compelled.* I think this account can also explain one of the differences between morality and law. Law, indeed, makes formal arrangements to make sure that all members of the society observe and carry out those vital and minimum norms and expectations. Thus, you may not expect all people to trouble themselves to help others, but you strongly expect and even require them not to harm others.

I also disagree with Harman in respect of his explanation of the fact that in most moral views animals get ranked lower than people. Unlike Harman, I think the reason lies in the fact that in any moral system there has to be a hierarchy of values, which prescribes what to do when prioritization is needed. For example, an adequate moral system has to tell us what to do when there is a conflict between two moral duties, e.g. the duty to fight against invading enemies and the duty to take care of one's old mother, as Sartre suggested. Indeed, what distinguishes a moral system from a set of separate moral rules is the existence of such ranking. Of course, this ranking is not arbitrary; ranking of the duties has to be made in accordance with their relationship to ideal/s of a given moral system. Those duties that unveil or embody values that are closer to the ideal/s are prior to those that are farther away. Thus, duty to respect one's mother can be considered more important than or prior to the duty to respect one's friend, because our moral system takes reciprocating (showing gratitude for services rendered) to be more important than helping, or because our moral system considers the merits and virtues of the recipient in its judgement concerning the amount of respect that the recipient deserves.

Now, with respect to our treatment of people and animals, I think the reason for the difference lies in the priority that most moral systems give to protection of human beings compared with protection of animals or plants, for example, because human beings for their dignity and merits deserve more attention, or because human beings can be more useful to society or because every human being is indeed related to a group of people, such as relatives and friends and his or her suffering causes suffering of all those people, which is presumably not the case with animals or plants. I think this account can better explain the difference than Harman's claim that animals are ranked lower because they cannot participate in our moral bargaining. Harman's account must also explain why animals have any position in our morality at all, granted that they have not participated in the bargaining at all.

Therefore, Harman's theory of relativism suffers because of the weakness of his grounds (I have discussed internalism and moral conventionalism), the weakness of his arguments (I have discussed his argument that ethical relativism is the best explanation of our moral experiences, such as moral disagreements, the relative strength of the duty not to harm others compared with the duty to help and the lower rank of animals in our moral views compared with people), inconsistency (I have discussed his distinction between "moral ought" and "evaluative ought"), ambiguity (in his method of argumentation and his premises as they appear in different works) and the practical uselessness of some of his suggestions (such as his idea of quasi-absolutism). Among these problems, the most important to me is that his grounds are not sound; indeed, every type of ethical relativism has to be classified according to its grounds and the extent of relativism that they imply.

In the next chapter, I shall discuss Wong's theory of relativism, which has gone further in accepting more aspects of moral objectivity and has embodied a more modified version of ethical relativism.

CHAPTER FIVE

David Wong and Ethical Relativism

Introduction

One of the most widely discussed recent theories of ethical relativism is that of David Wong. Wong's works on ethical relativism include: *Moral Relativity* (Berkeley: University of California Press, 1984), "Three Kinds of Incommensurability" in *Relativism: Interpretation and Confrontation*, ed. Michael Krausz (Notre Dame: University of Notre Dame Press, 1989), "Relativism" in *A Companion to Ethics*, ed. Peter Singer (Oxford and Cambridge: Blackwell Publishers Ltd, 1991, second edition 1996), "Moral Relativism" in *Encyclopedia of Ethics*, ed. Lawrence C. Becker (New York and London: Garland Publishing, Inc., 1992); and "Moral Relativism" in *Routledge Encyclopedia of Philosophy*, ed. Edward Craig (London and New York: Routledge, 1998).[1] I shall try in this chapter to give a clear and critical account of his theory, some aspects of which have already been discussed in the first three chapters.

Wong believes that there are weaknesses in some of the standard arguments for ethical relativism, such as the argument from diversity and the

---

1. He has published many other works on moral relativism, such as: "A Relativist Alternative to Anti-Realism" (abstract of commentary on Stephen Schiffer's "Meaning and Value", given at the 1990 Eastern Division Meeting of the American Philosophical Association), *Journal of Philosophy 87* (1990), pp. 617-8; "Pluralistic Relativism", *Midwest Studies in Philosophy*, Vol. 20, *Moral Concepts* (1996), University of Notre Dame Press, pp. 378-400; "Response to Kupperman's Review of Moral Relativity", invited response to Joel Kupperman's "Wong's Relativism and Comparative Philosophy", *Philosophy East & West 36* (1986), pp. 275-82; Review of *Integrity and Moral Relativism* by Samuel Fleischacker, *Ethics 104* (1994), pp. 882-3; "The author responds: Wong to Fuller", invited response to Steven Fuller's "Towards Objectivism and Relativism", *Social Epistemology 1* (1987), pp. 365-72; "Commentary on Sayre-McCord's 'Being a Realist about Relativism'", *Philosophical Studies 61* (1991), pp. 177-86.

functionalist argument.[1] However, he believes that despite the weaknesses of these arguments, moral relativism has always been rooted in the impressiveness of the variation in ethical belief across human history and culture. Therefore, he says, "moral relativists must chart some other more complicated path from the existence of diversity to the conclusion that there is no single true morality" (Wong, 1996, p. 445). He follows the same path.

Wong's theory of ethical relativism is premised on the claim that there is no single true morality and that morality is a social creation designed to resolve internal and interpersonal conflicts. He thinks that the main difficulty in explaining moral experience is the reconciliation of features of our moral experience that suggest the objectivity of morality with other features that suggest the subjectivity of morality. Wong argues that his theory can give us the best explanation of all features of moral experience. He believes that his theory of relativism allows individuals and societies to make mistakes in their moral judgements. He thinks that his theory can explain other cognitive aspects of our moral language. At the same time, it allows and explains the obvious fact that people frequently disagree on moral subjects. His theory accommodates the concept of "truth", but makes it relative. There is no objective, independent foundation for morality. According to this theory, morality is based on human interests and desires.

Now, let me try to explain the above points in detail. I shall also refer to the difficulties of his theory, and compare his view with that of Harman.

Three kinds of incommensurability

Wong believes that there are three kinds or versions of incommensurability theory. One version is that there is incommensurability with respect to translation. It holds that there are terms in at least some other languages that cannot be translated into any terms in our own language. The second version is that there is incommensurability with respect to justification. It holds that there are at least some other justifiable theories that have different fundamental premises about the nature of the world or fundamental forms of reasoning. The third version is what can be called "evaluative incommensurability". It holds that we cannot say that our own theory is better than all other theories. There are at least some other theories about which we have to be silent.

---

1. For my discussion about these arguments, see Chapter Two, the second and fifth arguments for meta-ethical relativism.

A popular way of arguing for evaluative incommensurability is to start with either the first or the second type of incommensurability. For example, it may be argued that there are languages that are radically untranslatable, and therefore we cannot compare our ideas with the ideas expressed in those languages as we have no proper understanding of both sides and are unable to make a judgement of superiority.

Donald Davidson has refuted this kind of argument.[1] In principle, it makes no sense, he argues, to recognize something both as a *language* and as untranslatable. It is actually striking and odd that some advocates of the untranslatability of other languages argue for their claim by lengthy explanations of those ideas or theories expressed in other languages to make us think that they are so odd, alien and strange that we should not have any *temptation* to understand them.[2]

Wong argues that it is our ability to understand other people's beliefs and ideas that make "the most interesting and substantial" cases for evaluative incommensurability. When we understand how their beliefs are tied to a life that such people would like to have, we realize what they have gained from that sort of life and what we may have lost.

With respect to the argument from the second type of incommensurability for the third, the popular and usual way is to argue that we have no justification for our own most basic premises and forms of reasoning, so there is no way to show that others' views are inferior to ours.

Wong in several places insists that evaluative incommensurability does not require a sceptical view about the existence of an independent and neutral standard for judgement between theories. Indeed, it arises from "a solid sense of what is satisfying in alternative forms of life" (Wong, 1989, p. 156). Wong writes:

> I want to stress the fact that I am not making the argument for incommensurability from a skeptical position. I am assuming that we know our own "style" of reasoning is more reliable. But I am also assuming that our knowledge and experience of other cultures and of the diversity of our own cultural roots has had a broadening effect on our notion of what a good human life is. We may reject the notion that all forms of life are equally good and accept the notion that there is

---

1. See "On the Very Idea of Conceptual Scheme," in *Proceedings and Addresses of the APA* 47 (1974).

2. See discussions about the problem of translation in the present work, Chapter Three, Descriptive Relativism, and the fifth argument for meta-ethical relativism.

more than one form of life that is best. We need not be skeptical about the objectivity of value judgments to introduce a reasonable amount of pluralism into those judgments (ibid., pp. 154 and 155).

Now, we know that Wong is not against the objectivity of moral judgements. Neither is he sceptical about the possibility of understanding our culture or other cultures. I shall now try to elaborate on his general argument for ethical relativism.

Objectivity or subjectivity?

Wong believes that in morality, the terms "objective" and "subjective" connote a family of characteristics that are frequently found together in descriptions of the nature of morality, but are not necessarily related. Characteristics of objectivity are "several and perhaps all of the following claims:

1. Moral statements have truth values.

2. There are good and bad arguments for the moral positions people take.

3. Non-moral facts (states of affairs that obtain in the world and that can be described without use of moral terms such as "ought", "good" and "right") are relevant to the assessment of the truth value of moral statements.

4. There are moral facts (which may or may not be claimed to be reducible in some way to non-moral facts).

5. When two moral statements conflict as recommendations to action, only one statement can be true.

6. There is a single true morality" (Wong, 1984, p. 1).

By contrast, moral subjectivism denies several and sometimes all of these claims. Wong argues that one feature of our moral experience that suggests moral objectivity is that we commonly call moral beliefs true or false (claim 1). The other feature is that we argue for or against these beliefs, while we maintain that our arguments may be good or bad (claim 2). Then he mentions an example from Iris Murdoch to show that people *mature in making moral judgements*. The example is of a mother who has hostility towards her daughter-in-law, judging her to have a childish and crude character. The mother, however, reflects on her own attitude and concludes that she has been narrow-minded and certainly jealous. Then she looks again at her daughter-in-law and finds her to be refreshingly simple and candid. The mother now has a moral reason to treat her daughter-in-law differently. People can reflect on their moral attitudes and find reasons to change their attitudes. Therefore, there must be some facts that are relevant to our moral assessment, whether we are aware of them or not. Thus, Wong brings some evidence for claim 3 and denies the strict separation between matters of natural fact and value by contending that states of affairs that can be described without the use of specifically moral language are relevant to the assessment of the truth value of moral statements.

Wong also accepts claim 4, but he denies claims 5 and 6.[1] On claim 4, Wong maintains that, although there is no strict entailment, claims 1 to 3 are often taken as evidence for 4. He thinks that claim 4 provides a plausible explanation of the truth of 1 to 3. I think his view is or can be based on a recent account of the connection between evidence and explanation. Let us first consider an example. When Smith has a bullet in his head, and Jones is standing over Smith's body with a smoking gun, there is no strict entailment that Jones has killed Smith. However, the first two facts can be considered as evidence for the claim that Jones has killed Smith.

The question here is how the truth of those facts counts as evidence for this claim. What kind of relationship is there between two sides that makes one of them act as evidence for the other? Thomson says: "An attractive recent account of the connection is this: the truth of SS is evidence for S just in case the truth of S would *explain* the truth of SS" (Thomson, 1996). She then refers to Harman's "Inference to the Best Explanation" (1965) in *Philosophical Review* (No. 74).

It seems to me that what Thomson suggests about the relation between the evidence and what is explained does not always hold true. There are some cases in which something can be evidence for another, but the other does not explain the former. For example, if there are two exclusive and co-existent symptoms for a disease, each can be evidence for the other (as well as the disease) but they cannot explain each other. It is only the disease that can explain both of them. In general, I would say that two effects of the same

---

1.   Wong believes that there are moral facts that are reducible to non-moral facts.

cause can act as evidence for each other, but they cannot explain each other. Of course, each effect can lead us towards the cause that certainly can explain the other effect and in this way serve in the process of explanation.[1]

In any case, Wong's theory of relativism accommodates claims 1 to 4, but does not agree with claims 5 and 6. However, Wong tries to give an account of how some people come to believe 5, that is, that when two moral statements conflict as recommendations to action, only one statement can be true, and 6, that is, that there is a single true morality. According to what Wong has mentioned previously, we can infer that for him a plausible theory has to explain all features of people's moral experiences, even why and how they make mistakes. Wong argues that we normally take admitting the truth of a moral statement to be a reason to act in accordance with that statement when it has implications for how to act. Again in Murdoch's example, if the mother admits she truly ought not to act coldly towards her daughter in-law, she is normally taken as admitting a reason to act otherwise. Thus, when two moral statements conflict with each other they are indeed directing the agent towards two opposite directions, which is not acceptable. Therefore, only one of them can be true (claim 5).

Absolutists who hold claims 1 to 6 may argue that claims 1 to 5 lead to claim 6, because if there cannot be two conflicting true moral statements for the same reason there cannot be two sets of such statements or, in other words, there can be only one true morality. The other way to come to 6, Wong suggests, is to adopt a correspondence theory about moral truth or falsity. For there can be only one true morality that can accurately picture and correspond to moral facts.

Relativists deny 6 and usually 5 (and quite often 4 and sometimes all the claims). Of course, Wong believes that the best strategy is to consider the denial or acceptance of 6 as a criterion for classifying theories as relativist or absolutist and then to make finer discriminations within each category according to the denial or acceptance of the other claims (1 to 5).

In respect to those aspects of today's moral experience that suggest

---

1. Thomson herself also has a modification of the above thesis on the relation between evidence and explanation. Thomson (1998) describes her positions in Harman and Thomson (1996) in short by saying that it is not necessary to suppose that a is evidence for b if and only if b explains a. It is quite possible that a is both evidence for and explanation of b. For example, "Alfred is gorging on hamburgers" is evidence for "Alfred will soon feel ill" and at the same time explains it. She also gives non-causal examples, such as the fact that a painting has such and such features, which explain its being an impressionist painting (Thomson, 1998, pp. 171 and 172).

subjectivism, Wong asks his readers to note deep disagreements on issues such as abortion, and also to note that comparative ethics, sociology and anthropology indicate significant diversity in moral belief, across societies and within many of them. Wong claims that none of these fundamentally different types is closer to the moral truth. He thinks those who assume that only one of these types can be true and others are adopted through mistakes face a difficulty in explaining *how* members of those societies made such mistakes. Of course, I personally believe that non-relativists can explain sources of disagreements and diversity without facing any problem. Earlier in this work (Chapter Three, Absolutism and Diversity of Morals), I showed how absolutists can explain diversity of morals. Moreover, I believe that even relativists have to appeal to those explanations, at least some of them, to be able to explain disagreements among members of a single homogeneous society.

Inference from the best explanation

Wong takes his relativist theory to provide the maximal reconciliation of the features of our moral experience suggesting objectivity with the features suggesting subjectivity. This maximal reconciliation is made possible by replacing the philosophy of language presupposed by previous theories with a more satisfactory one. Contemporary theories of the nature of morality have focused on moral language in order to reconcile the opposing features of moral experience. Because of their failure many philosophers no longer appeal to the analysis of moral language. Wong is optimistic and thinks that a much more successful analysis can be given. He tries to use the last achievements of the philosophy of language and particularly truth-conditional semantics, causal theory of reference and translation theory.

Let me list some changes that have happened in the philosophy of language that are important to Wong. A kind of verificationism that underlies emotivist theories such as Stevenson's "has lost all credibility". The analytic-synthetic distinction that underlies Moore's open-question argument against naturalism in favour of the existence of a non-natural property of goodness and Hare's argument against naturalism in favour of the existence of an "evaluative" element of moral meaning are forcefully attacked by Quine.[1] Another change

---

1. Moore's open question is, "Is pleasure really good after all?" He means that because this question is worth asking, good cannot be identified with pleasure. It is the case

(continued...)

is that there have been new ways of approaching the study of meaning. Among different developments in this field, Wong refers to theories developed by Quine and others on the way of translating the languages of alien cultures. Wong tries to apply theories of translation to the debate between moral absolutism and relativism to determine whether people of different societies and groups within a single society are talking about the same things when they use moral terms.

Fundamentally different moralities

Wong believes that the relativist argument is best conducted by pointing to fundamental differences in moral beliefs, and then by claiming that they are best explained under a relativist theory that denies a single true morality. Wong believes that *actually* there are fundamentally different moralities. As I discussed earlier, all those who hold to descriptive ethical relativism believe that there are fundamental differences concerning all or some moral values. Fundamental differences are those differences that are not results of different applications of common values or principles.[1]

For Wong, the best example of fundamental differences between moral outlooks is the difference between virtue-centred and rights-centred moralities. This example is so crucial for him that he puts great emphasis on it in all his works on moral relativism. In *Moral Relativity*, he says, "I will focus on differences between virtue-centered and rights-centered moralities, and differences between interpretations of each type of morality" (Wong, 1984, p. 3). He makes it clear (1992) that virtue-centred moralities emphasize the ideal of a certain sort of community life in which the individual is conceived and may flourish, while rights-centred moralities emphasize individual rights to liberty or to other goods, which are necessary to secure one's well-being. As we saw earlier, elsewhere he says:

> One apparent and striking ethical difference that would be a good candidate for this sort of argument concerns the emphasis on individual rights that is embodied in the ethical culture of the modern West and

---

(...continued)

> with other natural properties. Hare argues that since we can use "good" to commend pleasurable things, "pleasure is good" is not an analytic proposition, and "good" must have an element of meaning that allows the use of commendation.

1. For a detailed absolutist account of all types of differences and diversities, see my discussion about absolutism and diversity of morals.

that seems absent in traditional cultures found in Africa, China, Japan and India. The content of duties in such traditional cultures instead seems organized around the central value of a common good that consists in a certain sort of ideal community life, a network of relationships, partially defined by social roles, again, ideal, but imperfectly embodied in ongoing existing practice. The ideal for members is composed of various virtues that enable them, given their place in the network of relationships, to promote and sustain the common good. (Wong, 1996, p. 445).

In short, we can say that a virtue-centred morality operates with the concept of a good common to a community of persons. It defines as virtuous those kinds of character and action that are necessary to achieve a common good. An important part of such morality is the notion of social function and roles. On the contrary, a rights-centred morality operates with some conceptions of personal interests prior to or independent of the participation in a community. Such morality attributes some rights or entitlements to individuals to protect their interests. As Arrington (1989) puts it, these rights allow individuals to pursue their private interests with maximum freedom, balanced only by a consideration of the freedom of others and (at times) considerations of equality. These two moralities are irreducible to each other. What they mean by an adequate moral system is quite different.

Wong also believes that even within each type of these two moralities there are various extensions. For example, Rawls and Nozick both believe in a right-centred ethics. However Rawls's ideals are freedom and a fair method for the distribution of goods, but Nozick's ideal makes an absolute of the right of a person to his property entitlement.

Wong believes that previous relativist analyses such as those of Hare and Stevenson failed in explaining features of our moral experience that suggest objectivity. They failed to explain why people use a highly cognitive vocabulary to express their moral attitudes and why they assume their own attitudes to be well-argued and true and their alternatives to be false. Recent theories like that of Harman show better understanding of those features, but they still need improvement. Using those findings of recent philosophy of language, Wong tries to develop a relativist theory that is more faithful to those objective features and at the same time accommodates subjective features as well.

I personally think that Wong's theory and its assessment are not much based on those linguistic points. In his recent articles on moral relativism one hardly finds any references to those points. Therefore, I appreciate Arrington's statement that "Wong's analysis can be presented and understood without the trappings of these semantic theories, and I shall attempt to expound his views without appealing to them" (Arrington, 1989, p. 221). It is noteworthy that recently Wong himself in the bibliography of "Moral Relativism" (1998), introduces his *Moral Relativity* in this way, "A defence of moderate relativism based on a naturalistic approach. Some chapters presuppose contemporary philosophy of language that some may regard as technical" (1998, p. 542).

Wong believes that absolutist theories fail to explain features of our moral experience suggesting subjectivism, i.e. the existence of apparently irresolvable moral disagreements and apparent diversity of belief. Moral statements, Wong believes, have to be interpreted in a way that they can be said to correspond or not correspond to some facts and therefore be liable to truth or falsity. At the same time, Wong believes that those facts are produced in each society separately, so they may vary from one society to another. What are those facts? Wong believes that those facts are "relationships among acts, persons and rules". The truth or falsity of moral judgements depends on whether or not these judgements accurately describe this relationship.

Unlike Harman, Wong does not believe that moral rules are the results of implicit agreements. Moral rules are not to be necessarily agreed on through a process of bargaining by the members of a society. According to Wong, "there are certain aspects of moral experience suggesting that morality possesses an objectivity independent of any implicit agreements made within groups" (Wong, 1984, p. 24).

Overall he has four arguments against Harman. First, many of us recognize some basic moral duties when there are no implicit agreements. "Suppose that in the next Great Depression, the fabric of society unravels into a Hobbesian war of all against all. Many of us think we would still have the elementary duty not to kill each other for amusement, even if we know that others had no intention of reciprocating" (ibid.). Harman may simply deny this duty, but anyway he has to explain how so many of us came to be so mistaken. Otherwise, we had better look for another conception of morality.

Secondly, we find it quite acceptable and usual that a speaker applies his moral rules to people from other groups or societies, which have no implicit agreement with the speaker's group. "Members can judge the moralities of other groups by application of their own adequate moral system" (Wong, 1984, p. 63).

Thirdly, another aspect of moral experience is that sometimes we can and do criticize people of other societies for their unfair agreements. For example, if they agree on rules working to the extreme disadvantage of a majority of the population because a powerful elite was able to impose that agreement on them, we can say that the elite ought not to have taken advantage of the weaker position of others.[1]

Fourthly, there are alternative ways to explain the oddity of saying, for example, that "Hitler morally ought not to have behaved in that way". For instance, we can say that Hitler was so beyond the reach of moral motivation that there is no point in saying such a thing, or we can say that the sentence is odd because it does not show the enormity of Hitler's crimes.[2]

For Wong morality contains any rules to which members of the society are committed for resolving internal or interpersonal conflicts, whatever the origin of this commitment. Now, let us look at his views on moral rules and their formulation.

The formulation of rules

Wong considers rules as "the first means by which people began to formulate and to recommend to each other actions or policies of action" (Wong, 1984, p. 37). The simplest form of a rule is "A is to do X". Later people noted conditions for rules, so they used rules of the form "If C, A is to do X". "C" is a place holder for a sentence type used to identify conditions under which A is to do X. Then they developed general rules of the form "If C, everyone is to do X", from which more specific rules about particular agents could be derived.

Wong recognizes three types of rules: the set of rules indicating necessary

---

1. Wong says, "Harman can reply that an agreement is subject to criticism on the grounds of coherence, a requirement that includes the avoidance of arbitrary distinctions. Perhaps the elite have rules of fair dealing among themselves, and it is possible to criticize as arbitrary the limited application of these rules. There is no guarantee, however, that we will always find rules of fair dealing, even among an elite, and it isn't necessary for the intelligibility or correctness of our criticism of an agreement that we find within it such rules. It is enough that no such rules are applied to dealings between the elite and the others" (Wong, 1984, p. 25). Later Harman (1996) himself has actually tried to respond to this argument. For an account of Harman's response and my criticism, refer to Chapter Three, general comments, no. 9.

2. For an account of Harman's argument and its criticism refer to Chapter Three, motivation requirement, and also general comments, no. 6.

or efficient means of achieving a given end, the set of rules defining social manners or etiquette, and the set for resolving internal and interpersonal conflicts. For the first two, Wong gives these examples: "when someone says, 'One ought always to thank the host before leaving a party', the point is to instruct the audience in etiquette; or the speaker's purpose may be to identify an action that is necessary and/or sufficient for an end, as in, 'If you want to start the car, you ought to put it in gear'" (Wong, 1984, p. 67). Internal conflicts of requirements stem from an individual's different needs, desires and goals, and interpersonal conflicts stem from people's different interests. The third type originates morality. Thus, a moral ought, which might be expressed in the form "A ought to do X" means that under certain conditions, A would be breaking a rule belonging to a set of rules for resolving internal and inter-personal conflicts, if he does not perform X. (There will be soon a discussion about the analysis of the moral "A ought to do X".)

Wong distinguishes morality from law by saying that law exists only to resolve interpersonal conflicts. He also distinguishes morality from psychotherapy by saying that psychotherapy is only to resolve internal conflicts. Morality has both functions. Of course, there have to be other differences between morality and law or between morality and psychotherapy, otherwise morality would be a combination of law and psychotherapy.

Certainly there has to be a set of rules indicating appropriate behaviour or treatment in different cases. However, Wong believes that it is more informative to talk of a "system" of rules than a set, because there have to be some priorities or orderings among rules. For example, saving lives is prior to promise-keeping and truth-telling. Wong also mentions Rawls's theory of justice as another example. According to this theory, maximizing equal liberty is more important than the just distribution of other primary social goods, such as income and wealth.

Criteria for an adequate moral system

There are many possible systems of rules. Some moral systems are *adequate* with respect to some ideal of morality. Wong says, "True moral 'A ought to do X' statements are founded on moral systems that are adequate with respect to some ideal of morality (that includes an ideal of moral change). The simplest way to do this is to analyse such statements as referring to an 'adequate' moral system" (Wong, 1984, p. 39). He also says: "'Adequate moral system' is not used frequently in ordinary moral discourse. The term is a modest idealization in the sense that I have chosen it as a more explicit rendering of what people have in mind when they use terms such as 'the right moral rules'" (ibid., p. 40).

Indeed, the distinctive aspect of Wong's relativist analysis is the notion of an "adequate moral system". With this notion, Wong makes clear that when people speak of moral duties they do not simply report what is required by social rules, because they may consider these as arising from superstition or prejudice or errors and therefore reject them. In our moral judgements, Wong believes that we consider ideal rules or adequate rules rather than prevailing moral rules or actual rules.[1]

The validity of an adequate moral system comes from moral standards. Standards specify ideals to be fulfilled. In other words, an adequate moral system meets the standards for moral systems. A complete list of such standards specifies the ideal of morality. For example, the ideals of harmonizing the maximal self-fulfilment of all agents or treating humanity as an end in itself could be spelled out in terms of some standards.

Wong speaks of different kinds of processes through which a group may settle on the standards for adequate moral systems. Those standards may be settled because members of the group have implicitly agreed on them, because some members of the society have presented them as sanctioned by a powerful and wise deity, or because one powerful and influential segment of the group has favoured them. It is also probable that a combination of such factors bears on a group's selection of standards.[2]

One advantage of Wong's theory of ethical relativism is that it allows for false beliefs about the nature of adequate moral systems. There can be false beliefs, through simple misinformation about relevant facts, self-deception, and false beliefs about the consequences of actions or failures to act. There can also be false beliefs arising from the fact that the set of adequate moral systems may contain more than one member for a group of speakers, so different members of the set may be applicable to different groups and societies, depending on variable conditions such as the availability of human and

---

1. I have a reservation here, that if this is the case relativists cannot take actual disagreements to imply that there are genuine disagreements among members of a society or different societies on moral ideals. Accordingly, they cannot argue from actual moral disagreements for descriptive relativism. The only option for them is to show that regardless of agreements and disagreements people really have different moral ideals.

2. See Wong, 1984, pp. 53 and 54.

material resources. Therefore, it could very well be a complex matter to determine which system is applicable to a given group or society. Much knowledge of human psychology, political science, sociology and economics is required. "The possibility for error is endless. False doctrines about human nature, about the way economic systems work, and so on, could all result in false beliefs about which adequate moral systems apply, given the conditions of a group or society" (Wong, 1984, p. 62).

The other advantage of Wong's theory is that it holds that there are universal constraints on what an adequate morality must be like. These universal constraints may be the results of certain determinate features of human nature along with similarities in the circumstances and requirements of social co-operation. For example, a common feature of adequate moralities might be the specification of duties to care for (because of the prolonged dependency of human children) and educate the young (because they must become able to play their roles in society). Likewise, another common feature of adequate moralities might be the specifications of duties of the young to respect those who bring them up in order to ensure that the latter are adequately motivated. They cannot bring children up properly unless they have sufficient motivation (and the children's obedience).[1]

An analysis of the moral "A ought to do X"

Wong interprets "A ought to do X" statements in this way: "By not doing X under actual conditions C, A will be breaking a rule of an adequate moral system applying to him or her". Of course, we have to remember that end of every moral ought is to resolve internal conflicts between requirements and interpersonal conflicts of interest. An "A ought to do X" statement is always implicitly or explicitly relative to conditions in which we have to act.

Wong thinks that it is desirable to allow for a kind of variation in moral systems that results in systematic and widespread differences in moral rules. Wong uses two examples provided by Castaneda and Rawls. Castaneda believes that monogamy is morally right in a community in which there are almost equal numbers of men and women, but in a community in which women form just, say, ten per cent of the population the polyandric family is right. Rawls believes that the liberty of individuals may be restricted only for the sake of obtaining a better balance within the total system of liberties, not for the sake of achieving a more just distribution of other primary social

---

1. See Wong, 1998, p. 541.

goods, such as income and wealth. It may be reasonable to sacrifice certain political liberties and rights, if and only if it leads to greater and fuller long-run liberties.[1]

The kinds of conditions to which Castaneda and Rawls refer concern the human and material resources available to whole groups and societies. Conditions also include what we have done or been in the past (such as having made a promise or assumed an office with responsibilities) and what others have done that affect the society or environment. For example, a group that is constantly attacked by enemies may tolerate aggression and violence in its members, since these qualities are needed in its defence.

This implies that a number of moral systems may be equally adequate from the standpoint of an ideal of morality. Wong calls the set of systems that satisfy the sentential function "Y is an adequate moral system" the "extension" of the term "adequate moral system". The extension may contain a number of moral systems that conflict with each other with regard to the content of rules or to priority orderings among the same rules. Conditions determined by the human and material resources available to whole groups and societies and by the effects of other groups and societies on the environment may define which moral system applies to a given group or society.

However, the possibility remains that more than one system may meet what is required by those conditions, because Wong believes that, although human nature and natural resources restrict ways of preventing internal and interpersonal conflicts, human nature is so plastic and flexible that it allows different solutions. In this case, the relevant system would be determined by the "subscriptions" of the members of the group or society. Wong uses the term "subscription" to refer "to desires to act in accordance with a system of rules" (Wong, 1984, p. 44).

The other source of relativity in what one morally ought to do is variation in the ideal of morality. Wong believes that adequate moral systems may vary in this way to a large extent. For example, some moralities could place the most emphasis on community-centred values of a common life, some other moralities on individual rights, and "still others could emphasize the promotion of utility" (Wong, 1998, p. 541).

---

1. I think it is clear that there might be conditions in which people are starving and their suffering may be such that the need for, say, bread seems to be prior to the need for liberty.

An analysis of "X is a good Y" statement

Unlike Harman, Wong extends his relativistic analysis to judgements of the form "X is a good Y" (moral goodness) as well as the judgements of the form "A ought to do X" (moral obligation). Wong believes that it is possible to present a relativist analysis of moral "X is a good Y" statements based on the same ideas that underlie the moral "ought". Using the same concepts of standards and adequate moral systems, Wong analyses "X is a good Y" in this way: "Under actual conditions C, X satisfies those standards for Ys contained in adequate moral systems applying to X" (Wong, 1984, p. 69). This analysis is relativistic because it allows for different extensions of "adequate moral system", with different standards.

As there are different types of "ought", there are different types of "good" as well. Wong refers to a list of familiar uses of "good" provided by G. H. Von Wright.[1] This list includes:

- Instrumental good. This kind of goodness relates to tools, instruments or activities involving them, such as "a good knife", "a good house" and "a good way of doing something, such as unlocking the door".

- Technical good. This relates to people who are good *at* some activity and who require special training to be good at it, such as "a good scientist or physician".

- Utilitarian good. This is what serves some end or purpose, deliberately or accidentally, such as "good plan", "good luck" or "good advice".

Von Wright admits that there are more categories and that some kinds of "good" might fall between these categories. Wong believes that there is no need, and that it is in fact unwise, to define each kind of "good" separately. There are no systems of standards especially devoted to each type. Every kind of goodness is relative to a multiplicity of ends, purposes and interests. Therefore, the general truth condition analysis of "X is a good Y" can be: "Under actual conditions C, X satisfies the appropriate standards for Ys". Wong believes that evaluative comparison is a derivative of this formulation. "X is a better Y than Z" means that under conditions C, X satisfies to a greater degree the appropriate standards that apply to X and Y.

1.　See Wong, 1984, p. 70.

Moral truth

One more advantage of Wong's theory of ethical relativism is that it is a cognitivist theory: he believes that moral statements have truth values. The foundation of his analysis is a correspondence theory of the truth, because he thinks that moral statements refer to rules and standards that are distinct from those statements. Of course, these rules and standards are not independent from human will and invention. They are developed by people to resolve internal and interpersonal conflicts. Wong believes that despite these points that might suggest a coherence theory of truth, his analysis meets the requirements of a correspondence theory and accordingly has the advantages of such theories. This analysis can explain why we may falsify the morality of another group of language users, even if it is a coherent system of moral beliefs very different from ours.

This analysis allows for different sets of adequate moral systems corresponding to different ideals. Aren't ideals of morality also subject to rational criticism? Wong mentions some aspects in which moral ideals are liable to rational criticism, but he insists that there are some restrictions to these criticisms. Moral ideals might be based on some factual errors concerning, for example, human nature or religion. These factual errors can be criticized, so the room for human choice in the adoption of a moral system becomes limited. As we mentioned earlier, there are also constraints imposed by human and material resources or effects of other groups and societies on the environment. Since morality is a social creation designed to solve internal and interpersonal conflicts, we can also criticize an ideal if it does not promote the function of morality.

Therefore, Wong is not happy with those conceptions of moral relativism that suppose that everything is permitted once relativism is admitted. He says:

> This is to arbitrarily associate with relativism the ludicrous view that a group could choose a morality as one chooses what to have for breakfast, with as much neglect of the past history of the group and of its present conditions, such as the availability of its human and material resources and the balance of power among its classes (Wong, 1984, p. 75).

Wong believes that actually relatively few people choose their morality for themselves. In most cases people simply come to adopt a moral system when they learn the moral language. Those few people who choose for themselves have to face the constraints mentioned above for groups and other constraints arising from individual psychology. Any morality requires a set of desires and intentions that may be very difficult to acquire. Sometimes one needs to change one's habits and qualities. "He could *try* to accept this morality; he could *choose to try* to change himself, but it would be silly to say he could simply choose to change himself" (Wong, 1984, p. 76).

Thus, one positive point about Wong's relativism is that it does not allow that all moral systems are true. A problem may arise here that relativism is contrary to common sense. In response, Wong denies that this is the common belief. Wong thinks that absolutists can claim only that many intelligent and informed people have the belief that there is a single true morality. Wong tries to explain why these people have such a false belief.

Wong agrees with Mackie that there are two reasons why many people believe there is a single true morality. First, there is a tendency among human beings to project their moral views onto the world. Second, morality is a social creation designed to regulate interpersonal relations, so it has some externality to the individual.[1] However, he disagrees with Mackie on some major points.

Unlike Mackie, Wong believes that it is not necessary to suppose that all moral statements have to be either false or without truth value. Wong believes that moral statements have truth value and at the same time they can be true. He points out that there can be genuine truth conditions concerning the rules and standards of adequate moral systems. (We have referred earlier in this chapter to Wong's view on the general truth condition.)

Wong adds that a serious challenge for relativism and a common path to absolutism is the Aristotelian approach. According to this approach, morality is for the fulfilment of human nature and only one morality serves the greatest fulfilment. Wong believes that his relativist analysis is compatible with this and all other paths to a belief in absolutism. Wong accepts that morality is for the fulfilment of human nature, but he believes that what constitutes human fulfilment is not fixed and the same for all groups and societies. Wong says:

> . . . such variation results in different extensions for "adequate moral system" as the term is used among different groups and societies. If this kind of variation exists, it is not difficult to explain why absolutists should fail to recognize it. Our conceptions of what constitutes human fulfilment are to a large extent shaped by our personal experience,

---

1. For Harman's similar view, see Chapter Three, externality requirement.

observations of those around us, and what we are taught on the subject. Relatively few of us have been in the position of being pressed to confront an alien conception of human fulfilment and to understand it. Even fewer of us will be pressed to justify our judgments of alien conceptions as misguided or perverse (Wong, 1984, p. 79).

It is possible that in the above passage Wong somehow is referring to his own experience as a first-generation Chinese American. Elsewhere, he explains how he faced a kind of conflict between inherited values and the values of the adopted country. As a child he had to struggle with the differences between what was expected of him as a good Chinese son and what was expected by his non-Chinese friends. Compared with his non-Chinese friends, he had to fulfil expectations in the matter of honouring parents and upholding the family name duties, which were much more rigorous, but at the same time he was supposed to feel superior to them because of that. He says, "It added to my confusion that I sometimes felt envy at their freedom"(Wong, 1996, p. 442).

General comments

In different parts of this work, I have referred to Harman's and Wong's ideas about different subjects relevant to ethical relativism. For example, in respect to Wong, I have studied his ideas about definition and divisions of ethical relativism, history of ethical relativism, descriptive relativism and existence of fundamental differences, argument for meta-ethical relativism as inference to best explanation of moral fundamental differences, normative relativism and lack of moral conviction as an undesirable implication of ethical relativism in the first three chapters of this work. Here, at the end of this chapter on Wong's theory of ethical relativism, I should like to undertake an overall assessment of his theory by focusing on what I think to be the most important aspects of Wong's theory of ethical relativism.

As I mentioned earlier, Gilbert Harman and David Wong have tried to reconstruct ethical relativism. They are both aware of the problems in standard versions of ethical relativism and believe that ethical relativism has to be reformulated to be able to work. Therefore, they have developed subtle or moderate forms of relativism to meet standard objections on relativism. There are some common advantages in their way of treating the issue of ethical relativism. In the following pages, I shall mention some of these advantages, along with their particular inputs to the debate.

1. They both take the problem of relativity of morals seriously. They admit that it cannot be settled by collecting some anthropological data about the diversity of morals and neglecting the philosophical nature of the discussion. Wong goes further and argues that even meta-ethical relativism in itself does not entail normative relativism.

2. They are both very well aware that the debate on ethical relativism is interwoven with the debate about foundations or origins of morality. Hence, Harman has developed his theory of moral conventionalism (and the social custom theory) and Wong has developed his theory of adequate moral system (and social creation of morality).

3. They both try to be faithful to our moral experience, including those aspects that suggest objectivity of morals. Therefore, Harman supports cognitivism and believes in the truth value of moral judgements. He also puts emphasis on externality requirement and rejects the idea that right and wrong are determined by a particular individual's decisions and principles. Wong also supports cognitivism. In respect to objectivity, Wong goes further. He believes that non-moral facts are relevant to the assessment of the truth value of moral statements and that there are moral facts.

4. They both agree that one difficulty for relativist accounts of morality is to explain how people can disagree with each other and how cross-cultural conflicts are possible. We saw earlier that Harman has developed the notion of quasi-absolutism in order to make moral disagreements and conflicts possible. Wong tries to solve the problem via the notion of adequate moral system. Referring to two different adequate moral systems, two moral judgements may equally well prescribe two different things. They are independent from each other and both can be true. Of course, the conflict is only pragmatic and not logical; two judgements recommend two different actions that cannot both be performed.

5. They both agree that part of our moral experience is that we pass judgements beyond cultural boundaries. We saw earlier that Harman

distinguishes between evaluative ought and moral ought. He believes that evaluative ought is not restricted and his relativism is about moral ought or inner judgements only. Wong believes that meta-ethical relativism itself does not prevent us from passing judgements on people from other cultures, so he does not feel any need to restrict his relativism to a special type of judgement. Therefore, his theory is more consistent. For example, we can condemn the actions of people from other cultures when they fail to adopt a proper ideal that can solve conflicts of interests or when they fail to conform to their ideals. To be able to develop a modest form of normative relativism, Wong proposes the principle of justification as an outcome of combining meta-ethical relativism with Western liberal contractualism.

6. They both strictly dismiss the idea that in morality everything goes right. They both believe that morality is subject to some rational constraints; there are good and bad arguments for the moral positions that people take. Wong accepts more constraints on morality, since he believes that ideals of morality can be shown to rest on false factual beliefs, that standards and rules can be shown to be unfeasible or out of accord with the reality of human needs, and that there are psychological constraints at the individual level on the choice of morality owing to the relatively fixed nature of most people's desires, taste and character.

7. Both theories are so different from common forms of ethical relativism that they are sometimes criticized for not being sufficiently relativist (for example, see Arrington, 1989). As Harman's moral conventionalism and particularly implicit bargaining can act as an objective criterion for recognition of a true moral system, Wong's idea that morality is for solving internal and interpersonal conflicts of interest also sets up a criterion of efficiency for distinguishing an acceptable moral system from an unacceptable one. Of course, they themselves believe that these criteria allow the existence of more than one moral system, but they cannot deny the possibility that there may be only one morality that can best fulfil the conditions.

In general, I believe that Wong's proposal has more advantages, although his proposal is thereby less relativist. The further he has stood from stereotype relativism the better results he has achieved. However, his proposal still has some problems. Here I propose to list some of the advantages of Wong's theory over that of Harman.

a. Wong's theory is more consistent, since it does not differentiate between evaluative ought and moral ought.

b. Wong's theory is not an internalist theory. His theory distinguishes between being true and providing a reason for action. Therefore, Wong's theory is not subject to difficulties that I mentioned earlier.

c. Wong does not believe in moral conventionalism and implicit bargaining. Although Wong believes that morality is a social creation, he is a realist, in the sense that he accepts the existence of specifically moral facts. For Wong, moral facts are the relation between individual, act and rule, and moral claims are true when they correspond to moral facts.

d. According to Wong's theory, morality is somehow rooted in human nature and real human needs, since he takes morality to be a response to those needs. Therefore, the only reason to allow for relativity is that human nature is plastic enough to allow alternative resolutions and, hence, alternative moral systems.

e. Although both Harman and Wong do not believe that every moral system is acceptable, Wong places more constraints on morality. Besides rational constraints, Wong believes that human nature and natural resources put some constraints on the way that internal and interpersonal conflicts can be avoided. Efficiency in solving conflicts in interests and meeting our needs is one important criterion for any acceptable morality (see comment no. 6 above).

f. Wong sees no problem in applying moral rules to people from other cultures. He broadens the scope of moral rules so that they can consistently be applied to a person outside the group. Wong gives an account of how such extension can occur.

g. Wong allows moral criticism of one's own society – to a limited extent, of course, that is, as long as accordance or conformity with ideals is concerned.

Despite these advantages, I disagree with Wong on the following issues:

I. In addition to some theoretical reservations that I have about the argument from "inference to the best explanation" itself, I do not think that it actually entails ethical relativism. I think that absolutism or objectivism can present the best explanation of our moral experience, granted that simplicity, conformity to common belief and comprehensiveness have to be considered in deciding what would be the best explanation. Absolutist or objective account is *simpler*, since it gives us the ability to explain all our experiences of the world, whether in science or in morality, in the same way. Absolutism or objectivism *better conforms to common belief* in universal and constant validity of moral values and general rules. Absolutism or objectivism is able to explain all aspects of our moral experience, but relativism faces problems in explaining all objective aspects of our moral experience, such as moral cognitive language, moral confidence, moral criticism, moral reform, moral progress, consulting the standards of others and even explaining how people could really disagree with each other or have cross-cultural conflicts.

II. I disagree with Wong about the origins of morality and, as I argued above (comment no. 7), he himself has to admit, and indeed has admitted, that morality is rooted in reality and especially in human nature.

III. I disagree with Wong about his explanation of the existence of fundamental differences between right-centred and virtue-centred moralities. There seem to be some common underlying moral principles in such cases.

IV. I disagree with him about the difference between law and morality. Although I may agree with him that law has to solve interpersonal conflicts only, psychotherapy has to solve personal conflicts and morality has to solve both internal and interpersonal conflicts, I think morality is substantially different from law; otherwise morality would be only a combination of law and psychotherapy.

V. I disagree with Wong about his principle of justification, a modest form of normative relativism, which is an outcome of combining meta-ethical relativism with Western liberal contractualism.

VI. I disagree with Wong about whether ethical relativism leads to lack of moral conviction or not.

Summary

Although I agree with Wong on many points, especially in defining symptoms and conforming better to common sense and human moral experience, there remain some aspects of his theory that I cannot accept.

Wong's theory of relativism suffers because of the weakness of some of his premises or grounds (his view about the origins of morality and about the nature of morality, as it appears in his discussion about the difference between morality and law) and the weakness of his argument (the notion of "inference to the best explanation").

There are also some problems with some aspects of his theory of relativism, such as his principle of justification as a modest form of normative relativism, his explanation of the difference between right-centred and virtue-centred moralities and his defence of ethical relativism in response to the criticism that it leads to lack of moral conviction.

Among these problems, the most crucial and fatal ones are those concerned with the grounds of his theory. As I mentioned in the case of Harman, every type of ethical relativism is recognized and classified according to its grounds and the extent of relativism that it implies.

The last point I would make in respect to Wong's theory concerns the degree of relativity involved in it. We saw that Wong believes that morality is subject to both rational constraints and constraints exerted by human nature and natural resources and has to show its efficiency in solving internal and interpersonal conflicts. I agree with Wong about all these, but it seems clear that, within such limitations, it is very unlikely that we shall have more than one moral system that has the maximum conformity to all those requirements. Therefore, it is dubious that, even granted his grounds and arguments, his theory is in a proper sense a relativist one.

My conclusion up to now has been that there are problems in all versions of ethical relativism. Modification of ethical relativism reduces these difficulties, e.g. Harman's theory was shown to have fewer problems than stereotype relativism. Wong's theory was shown to have even fewer problems, since it was more modified. Yet, it might be suggested that refutation of available versions of ethical relativism does not disprove it. It is still possible to have a perfect version in future. Therefore, as I argued earlier, the ultimate solution for the debate is to settle first the issue of the foundations of morality. For example, if the foundations of morality are proven to be real and not dependent on subjective factors, there will be no way to argue for meta-ethical relativism. On the other hand, if morality is proven to be founded on individual tastes or decisions or social acceptance, there will be sufficient grounds to argue for ethical relativism.

In the next chapter, we shall discuss the foundations of morality. The first step will be to try to discover the nature of morality.

CHAPTER SIX

Foundations of Morality

Morals and customs

Introduction

Any judgement on the foundations of morality requires a clear understanding of the nature of morality: what does it mean to be "moral"? To answer this question we have to set up some criteria to distinguish morals from customs, though both serve to regulate our behaviour or ways of life. This problem gains more importance in the present study of ethical relativism, because many cases of differences between cultures that are mentioned by relativists are indeed related to customs, rather than morals.

Robert Cavalier makes a good distinction between customs and morals, or in his words between mores and morals. He says, "There is a distinction between 'morals' and 'mores' – the latter can be defined as 'harmless customs' (e.g. 'tea at 4'); the former as 'treatment of others' (e.g. 'the practice of Apartheid')."[1] Then he adds that in the discussion about ethical relativism we need to be aware of confusing "harmless conventions" with "harmful practices." In discussing relativism, we are concerned only with "moral practices". I shall try in this section to develop my theory about the nature of morality via distinguishing between the functions of customs and morals.

An analysis of customs

Customs and morals require us to act in certain ways. In other words, they direct our voluntary actions. Failure to do so usually causes blame, just as conformity to them brings about praise. I think pure customs – and I mean

---

1. Robert Cavalier, "Section 6: Ethical Relativism", a single page on-line syllabus, Carnegie Mellon University, 1996.

by "pure customs" those customs that do not contain any moral element – are socially or culturally approved regulations for creating some harmony in a society and enabling social aspects of our actions in daily life to avoid confusion or disagreement in the society. Customs help members of each society to make their social relations harmonious, regulated and predictable. For example, the form and colour of clothes in a funeral ceremony or the rules of greeting or treating guests are defined by the society or the culture.

Harman characterizes one kind of social convention in an insightful way that can be useful for defining customs. (Of course, as we saw in the fourth chapter, Harman seems not to distinguish between morals and customs.) He maintains that social conventions of politeness, deference and etiquette are some cases concerning which we are inclined to say, "When in Rome, do as the Romans do". These conventions have a social function, which is to "help smooth relations with others, making certain activities more predictable and easier to participate in; they make it possible for one to relax in various social situations; and they reduce confusion. It does not matter very much exactly what the conventions are, as long as there are some rules. These rules are therefore very much like linguistic conventions or rules of the road" (Harman, 1977, p. 96).

In many cases uniformity and harmony are more important than the particular way of conduct decided by the society.[1] People might wear white clothes or black ones at a funeral ceremony. What is more important is that there is an established custom to harmonize them. Among Arabs and many other Middle Eastern nations it is pleasant to see that the guest has finished the food and no food remains on the table. For them it shows that the guest has enjoyed the food. By contrast, in some Far Eastern nations the host likes to see that the guest has left some of his meal in his plate since it shows that there has been food enough and more. England has had both customs. What matters is that all these cultures in one way or another have been able to establish a standard and perhaps equally good way of treatment. This example shows that there may be two contrasting ways of treatment when some of the moral aspects are identical, such as doing one's best for one's guests or being thankful to one's host.

---

1. As Scanlon (1999, p. 339) suggested, there is sometimes a need to regulate a particular kind of activity, but there are different ways of doing it to which no one could reasonably reject. He adds that what he calls the Principle of Established Practices holds that in such situations if one of these non-rejectable principles is generally accepted, then "it is wrong to violate it simply because this suits one's convenience" (ibid.).

Of course, some factual parameters, whether local or universal, may bear on the formation of customs, such as nature, the climate, the economic situation, population and religious beliefs. Rachels emphasizes the fact that there are many factors bearing on the production of customs other than the values of the society at issue. This is why mere difference in customs does not imply difference in values. He says:

> Many factors work together to produce the customs of a society. The society's values are only one of them. Other matters, such as the religious and factual beliefs held by its members and physical circumstances in which they must live, are also important. We cannot conclude, then, merely because customs differ, that there is a disagreement about values (Rachels, 1993, p. 23).

An analysis of morals

As Sidgwick (1967, p. 1) suggested, it is difficult to define the subject of ethics in a way that "can fairly claim general acceptance". He adds that the derivation of the term is to some extent misleading. Originally ethics meant what relates to character as distinct from intellect. According to this usage, which was considered as the subject of the treatise of Aristotle, ethics is more general than a study of the qualities of character, which we call virtues and vices. He writes:

> According to the Aristotelian view, which is that of Greek philosophy generally, and has been widely taken in later times, the primary subject of ethical investigation is all that is included under the notion of what is ultimately good or desirable for man; all that is reasonably chosen or sought by him, not as a means to some ulterior end, but for itself (ibid., pp. 1 and 2).

Before explaining my thoughts about the nature of morality, I should note that in this work I do not distinguish between the terms "ethical" and "moral". Of course, originally they had different meanings: "ethical" was derived from a Greek word for personal character and "moral" was derived from a Latin word for social custom.[1]

I think morals serve both to regulate our actions and to direct us towards

---

1. For more discussion about this point, see Williams, 1997, pp. 546 and 547.

some ideals. Customs do not necessarily pursue ideals. If a certain way of doing a customary act helps us in achieving our ideal/s of life, then it has a moral element in it. For example, if one way of treating the body of dead relatives shows respect to them, but other customary ways of treatment do not, then an element of morality becomes involved, unlike the case of driving on the right-hand side or the left-hand side of the road. Moreover, being committed to morality requires considerable spiritual effort and determination because it usually conflicts with one's selfishness and immediate desires, but in respect to customs there is no necessary internal conflict among personal desires. Therefore, it is much easier to observe social customs than moral rules. Furthermore, customs in general are social phenomena, so by implication they have nothing to do with one's private life considered out of social contexts, but morality involves both social and non-social aspects of life.

Morality indeed starts when one opens one's eyes to the world and finds oneself in need of defining certain relations to other beings and even to oneself, both in theory and in practice. Any response to the theoretical aspect might be considered as one's world-view or metaphysics and any set of practices proposed in response to the practical aspect constitutes one's morality. So it would not be strange to suppose that everyone is in the centre of a moral universe formed with one's relations to other relevant beings (including oneself). Of course, this does not mean that there are real separate moral worlds or that people's worlds have to be metaphysically different; it rather seems that almost all people presume that they live in one single and common world. People do not consider themselves and therefore the world around them unique. Hence, they can establish well-organized relationships with each other. Indeed, most people do not even notice that they live in such a moral universe.

Now, an important question arises: what factors can bear on defining one's relations to other beings and to oneself? This general question in turn may be divided into more particular questions, such as: what should I do in relation to my parents? What should I do in relation to my relatives? What should I do in relation to my friends? What should I do in relation to strangers? What should I do in relation to my society? What should I do in relation to the nature and the environment around me? What should I do in relation to myself – my possessions, my time, my body, my talents and so on?

Surely there are different ways of establishing these relations, and everyone somehow needs to choose among them. Every choice needs some criteria. Arbitrary or baseless choices seem impossible. It is also impossible to explain how we can prefer one of the alternatives without any kind of pre-existing preferences. For example, whether to be respectful or not to someone cannot be decided without some belief in the privilege of respect or non-respect, prior to the decision. Now let us see what candidates might be there to form our choices.

Some may say that, without considering any differences in the results or outcomes of the alternatives, we find ourselves obliged or at least recommended to respect (or not respect) a person. For example, it might be said that a person may simply *see* that one action is right or is his or her duty and, therefore, no general criteria need operate in this perception. Thus, the pre-existing preference comes out of our intuition or moral sense or conscience. It seems that this view fails to give an adequate account of the whole procedure. It might explain why we prefer one action to the other, but it does not go beyond that. It does not explain why we have perceived in a certain way, why our perceptions are not arbitrary and baseless. So we still have to seek some criteria or reasons for our choices.

Every well-grounded response to the above questions depends on two tasks: defining a relevant ideal and defining a practical way to reach that ideal. Without having an understanding of an appropriate ideal in advance, one cannot decide what to do. It is only after consideration of one's ideals that one can choose a policy of action and be able to justify it for oneself and others. Of course, it does not necessarily mean that there should be a certain interval or period between these two parts. What is important is that in a well-grounded moral policy the latter comes logically after the former. However, in practice one may come to an understanding of both at the same time, or even, in an authoritative morality, one might realize one's required actions before one's ideals.

Having defined one's ideal/s, one realizes that every possible relation that one wants to establish with other beings (or even oneself) stands in one of the three states in respect to one's ideal: harmful, neutral or useful. In other words, different ways of establishing relations may be found to be undesirable (unpleasant) or neutral or desirable (pleasant). It is noteworthy that these states in themselves cannot motivate or affect the agent. It is only after one's recognition of something as harmful, for example, that one might refrain from doing it, or after considering something as useful or pleasant that one might decide to do that. Thus, what *actually* motivates an agent is what he or she thinks to be harmful, neutral or useful, that is, what is harmful or neutral or useful *in the view of the agent*, not *in the reality*. We may drink poisonous water when we are not aware that it is poisoned, or we may cut our old friendship with a person when mistakenly we believe that he is a wrongdoer and that continuing a relationship with him therefore is harmful to our happiness. A person who knows that smoking is physically harmful to him might still smoke, if he comes to believe that after all smoking is useful or pleasant, because he gets some relief or relaxation that is greater than the harm that he receives.

However, it needs no emphasis that what really brings one nearer to one's ideal/s is the act that *really* leads one towards one's ideal/s. Therefore, despite the fact that at different times one may have different conceptions of what a proper act in a certain case is or that different observers may have different judgements about what the agent has to do to get closer to his ideal/s, the right act is only the one that *really* yields the ideal/s.

Morality and self-love

Everything that is able to motivate an agent has to have certain relations with him and has also to be reducible in one way or another to his interests; otherwise it would be irrelevant to him and he would not care about it. For example, we do not care if someone throws some bricks in a desert, but we do care if someone throws one small stone in *our* garden. Mothers, who are symbols of love for others, do not care for others' children as much as they care for *their* own children. There have always been brave and devoted soldiers or commanders who have been prepared to sacrifice all their belongings and even their lives to protect *their* people or *their* cities or *their* countries. During wars you can usually find such people on both sides. What is the reason that such people who seem to possess a quality of self-denial do not defend or try to protect the interests of the other party? Indeed, they try to destroy the interests of the other party, at least insofar as they can serve as obstacles for the interests of *their* people or *their* cities or *their* countries.

Of course, there are some people, such as physicians or lawyers or conservationists, who do not restrict their services to any particular group of people. They do their best for certain global causes, not only local or national ones, but still I think that there are three reservations here:

- There is a real doubt that these people, though trying for global causes, do not make any distinction, at least in their minds and hearts, between the difficulties and troubles of *their* own and those of others in another part of the world, though it may not necessarily be clear in their practices. If two people come before a doctor presenting a similar illness and both urgently need an operation – his only son and his enemy[1] – would he hesitate to give priority to *his* son?

- These people are usually *interested* in some special aspects of human affairs. For example, some try to stop crimes and unjust deeds against people by tyrants. They are usually indifferent to what happens to the natural environment, simply because *they* are not much *interested* in that. Similarly, there are people who are concerned only with the protection of nature and do not care for human rights.

- We might accept that there have been some benevolent people, especially among mystics, who would consider, for example, their son and their neighbour's son the same.[2] However, it is not credible to say that these people could love their neighbour's son more than their own son without the former's having any additional merit or because altruism requires more love for those who are farther removed from us. The condition "without

---

1. Assume that his enemy by no means does something harmful to others.
2. Of course, I doubt that this is a real demand of real mysticism. Actually this has been my concern for almost nine years. From the beginning of my religious studies and my acquaintance with religious mysticism, I have always been interested in understanding how real mystics devote themselves to God's service and what it costs them; how can they deny their own desires and love anything only insofar as He pleases? My conclusion, briefly, is that there are different, and at least two, levels in the mystical or spiritual journey. At a lower level it suffices that one considers His pleasure as one's highest aim. In this way one can have other aims and can love one's possessions, such as one's fame and family. The only requirement is that they should not prevent one from obedience to Him. Whenever there is an actual conflict between His pleasure and other things one has to be prepared to give priority to His pleasure. At a higher level the mystic is required to devote his love to Him. The mystic may love again the same things, such as his fame and family, but in this case all these loves derive from a unique and single love, that is, love of Him.

   Therefore, it is quite possible and reasonable that a mystic also loves, say, his father and respects his father more than his friend's father when he sees that he is in debt to his father and his father has no other to care for him. Of course, when such a mystic then finds that his friend's father is evaluatively better and is closer to God, he would then love him more than his own father. I am not here to judge these mystical beliefs. Whether these beliefs are true or not, there seems no doubt that there have been mystical experiences and sincere devotions and loyalty to this way of life. A comprehensive account of morality has to be able to explain all kinds of human moral experiences including the mystical one. I hope that the present account is able to undertake this job.

having any additional merit" is to exclude those cases in which the neighbour's son deserves more respect because of his piety and benevolent character.

Moreover, we should note that these people believe that selfishness demotes and downgrades *them* and that altruism and self-sacrifice is better for *them*. If in a complicated or imaginary case they come to the realization that to love a neighbour's son as they love their own is unnecessary and may even be harmful to their perfection they unhesitatingly cease to do so. This might be so if, for example, they think that this love might be misunderstood by others, that it would bother their own children and family or that they might lose their purity of intention and it would downgrade them.

Thus, we do not act if we believe that we will not get anything from our action. Even in non-serious acts such as playing a game, telling a joke or toying with the rings on our hands we have certain purposes, to which we are not indifferent. The purpose matters to us and we see it as useful in some way and yielding to what is precious or dear to us. To put it in a more abstract way, an act will motivate an agent if he or she has an interest in it and if it is in his or her interests of him (i.e. s/he gains benefit from it).

Thus, I think that morality is based on one's natural desire for self-improvement and one's desire to achieve one's ideal/s. This theory of morality can be called "morality of self-love". To secure one's interests perfectly one needs to satisfy all sorts of genuine desires, including benevolent desires.[1] A person who loves himself or herself also loves his/her parents, children, relatives and friends, may also love all human beings, animals and nature. Human beings do not enjoy a comfortable life when they see that others are suffering or starving. Their concern for themselves, for their happiness and perfection, requires them to be benevolent. The theory of a self-love morality thus accommodates an intrinsic and genuine desire in us all to make others happy, even if it has nothing to do with our *immediate* interests. This implies that we have a self-interest even in what has no *immediate* effect on us.

This view might also be called a "morality of self-interest". However, I hesitate to use this term because, as I explained above, for me the extent of interest is not limited to what is usually conceived of by popular egoists as

---

1. According to Harman's description of Hume's position, Hume believed that, thanks to the power of sympathy, people can sometimes have unselfish concern for others and this concern provides them "with (weak) reasons to act so as to benefit others apart from any expected gain for yourself" (Harman, 1977, p. 138).

"self-interest". (According to hedonistic egoism, happiness is defined in terms of one's own pleasure or absence of pain, which is the only thing that one intrinsically desires, like a newborn child who acts exclusively for pleasure.[1])

Thus, all voluntary actions of every agent derive from a basic desire or inclination to satisfy his or her concerns and interests.[2] The above explanation shows the essential role of self-love. As Rand said, "The achievement of his own happiness is man's highest moral purpose" (Ayn Rand, 1964, p. 27).

It has to be noted that self-love is quite different from selfishness. The difference between the selfish and the non-selfish is not the existence or non-existence of self-love. The difference concerns the way in which one considers one's interests and ends and tries to fulfil requirements of self-love. Some fail to feel the desirability of helping others, either because they have not fully grasped human nature and what is to their real benefit or because they have considered short-term interests only. This is why they prefer to have everything just for themselves. For example, if they are hungry and there is a little food they will try to appropriate that food exclusively, because they consider their hunger alone.

---

1. It has been claimed that some of the actions of adults may not be consistent with hedonistic egoism. One controversial example is that of "someone who commits suicide in order to 'get back' at others by making them feel bad" (Harman, 1977, p. 140). How can a person get pleasure (from what he has done) after his death? Some psychologists have said that such a person must be unconsciously assuming that death is not the end of life and he or she will be there to enjoy the suffering of others. That person also gets immediate pleasure by showing his or her will to others.

   I think the person can get pleasure merely by imagining what will happen to others in future, say, after his or her death. This is part of our nature. Our desire for some future act makes us take pleasure in the preparation and anticipation for it. This is why we become motivated, for example, to prepare a syllabus this year for a lecture that will not take place until next year or to reserve tickets in January for a journey that we shall make in the summer. Therefore, I think these examples do not refute hedonism.

2. Nagel (1970) believes that "we have a reason to do whatever will promote the satisfaction of any desire". In this regard, Nagel sees no difference between the satisfaction of one's own desires and that of others. It would be irrational not to help another person when you can give that help and there is no reason not to do so. In response to Aristotelian or Humean thinkers, who hold that the desires of others can bear on your action only when you have a pre-existing desire to satisfy their desires, Nagel thinks that there is no basic desire in us to satisfy their desires. This is just a reflection of the way in which practical reasoning works.

   One of the problems with Nagel's view is that he has not demonstrated why it is irrational not to care about other people (see for such argument against Nagel, Harman, 1977, p. 72).

The proper way is to consider all human desires and prefer those that are more endurable or more fundamental or more "human" (in the sense that I will explain later at the end of the discussion about motivation). If that is so, it will be better for the person to give that food to a needy person. The satisfaction and the spiritual pleasure that one gains through giving one's food is much more than one gains from eating the food oneself. Such a person acts on what *he* wants, but the object of his want is to help others. He has discovered that benevolence is improving and selfishness is degrading.[1]

Regardless of what one may come to feel in respect to benevolence and helping others, my general argument in the whole chapter is that human *genuine* desires and interests that shape morality depend on human nature, which is the same in every human being. There is a *real* relation between human nature and those desires and interests and the moral status of every action is derived from such a real relation. (See my discussion about concepts of "good" and "ought" in this chapter.) Thus, my view is completely different from Harman's internalism, which holds that moral requirements apply only to those people who are willing to adopt them.

Decision-making

Before making any decision to do something, we have to go through a complicated process that consists of different stages. Here we shall look at those stages, especially in respect to those aspects of the procedure that can explain how people may make opposing decisions.

Conception and assessment

The first step is to conceive some action, say, going to a party. It is impossible to make a decision without conceiving the subject. Then we start to think about that action and its outcomes: its benefits and/or harms. This evaluation helps us to decide whether to go to that party or not. It seems clear that unless we have already made or been given an assessment of an action, we will not decide to do it before considering its results. Later we shall throw more light

---

1. Rachels (1993, p. 67) suggests that, although almost all moral systems recommend us to behave unselfishly, it is the *object* of my want that determines whether I am selfish or not, not the mere fact that I am acting on *my* wants. If I want my own good and also want other people to be happy and I act on *that* desire, my action is not selfish.

on this point. Although people may evaluate actions differently, all people perform the action that they have, overall, evaluated positively. Even a criminal who knows that crimes are wrong commits a criminal act only when he takes that act to be good for him and actually better for him than not doing it.

There are many people who are not happy with some of their deeds or habits. They decide "never to do that again". For example, consider a drunkard who wishes not to drink any more. After a short while he gradually feels that he needs to drink, but at first he still thinks that he must not drink and so he resists. Later he feels more pressure from inside and starts to think again whether it is really or absolutely bad to drink. His affection for drink may make him think that in general or in that particular situation it is better to drink or that he has no choice other than to drink. Of course, it is quite possible that as soon as he succumbs and the pressure is removed he becomes remorseful and even wonders why he has acted so wrongly again.

It has to be noted that the evaluation is sometimes very easy, to the extent that it may be even overlooked. For example, when a person has already evaluated and performed the same action several times he may come to a decision quickly. The only thing he needs is to become certain about the required similarity of both cases, which does not necessarily take a long time. Equally, in other cases the required evaluation or assessment may take a long time, since it may not be easy for the agent to study the action, its possible consequences and the available rules. Failure to come to any conclusion leads to non-action. In other words, non-existence of a reason for action serves as *a reason* not to act, just as non-existence of a cause can be considered as *a cause* for the non-existence of its effect. For example, as the operation of a heater is the cause of the heat non-operation of the heater is rationally considered as *the cause* of non-existence of its heat. Therefore, the operation can explain the heat and non-operation can explain the relevant non-heat.

Of course, it should be noted that if we suppose that there are alternative causes for the same effect (such as sun and heater for the heat), non-existence of the effect depends on non-existence of all of the causes. Thus, non-existence of all of the causes is to be considered as a cause for non-existence of the effect. It should also be noted that sometimes we decide to act even if we have not been able to come to a decisive judgement about goodness of a given action. That is the case when acting seems to the agent more likely to produce good results. In other words, a probable or relative preference of one side leads practically to a decisive preference, given that other things are equal.

Motivation

Harman and many others distinguish between "theoretical reasoning" and "practical reasoning". The former is concerned with beliefs, whereas the latter is related to decision-making and is concerned with desire or intention. To repeat Harman's words, "to say that someone has certain reasons to do something is to say that he has practical reasoning available to him that would lead him to decide to do it" (Harman, 1977, p. 138). In my account, there is a necessary link between these two types of reasoning: theoretical reasoning and practical reasoning. I think every practical reasoning is preceded by some sort of theoretical reasoning. At first the agent finds some reason to believe that in reality a certain act is or is not conducive to his ideal/s. Then, having found some reasons to believe that one alternative is better, he will get the motivation to act accordingly. It is only after being motivated that we intend or decide or become determined to do the given action. Here and during the assessment the role of emotions and desires is very important.

In my view, there is something right with emotivism here. Emotivists have well considered the crucial role of emotions in our actions and moral judgements. They believe that to accept a moral principle is to be for or against something; and, as Harman (1997, p. 66) also suggested, that is to be motivated for bringing something about or preventing something from happening. But the problem with emotivism is that it magnifies the role of emotions to the extent that it reduces everything to emotions and thus ignores the rational aspect of the process of decision-making. Emotivism fails to explain how emotions become directed towards particular objects out of many alternatives, and why they should be.

On the other hand, rationalists are right in recognizing the role of reason in backing up our decisions.[1] The problem with some rationalists is that they have ignored the role of emotions and failed to explain how we follow our rational judgements. For example, according to Kant, reason is the only motivating source. To decide what to do you have just to ask yourself what you have reasons to do. Kant believes that basic moral principles are binding

---

1. Kant, as a typical rationalist, argues that we normally assume that there are reasons why we do what we do. This assumption is called a "practical postulate". It is not provable, but it is necessary for conceiving ourselves as agents. Harman says, "Kant does not think that you can know whether you or anyone else ever decides in this sense to act. He thinks that it is possible that your actions are always the blind result of competing desires and that you never act for one or another reason" (1977, p. 75).

on all rational beings, including angels and intelligent Martians (if they exist), since those principles can be known by all rational beings. The subtle point here is that, since any acceptance of those principles needs to be motivated, there must be a source of motivation in reason itself. To repeat Harman's words, "Kant's conclusion is that either reason alone is such a source of motivation or morality, as we ordinarily understand it, is 'a vain and chimerical notion'" (Harman, 1977, p. 67). Thomas Nagel in *The Possibility of Altruism* (1970) on a Kantian basis argues that basic desires such as hunger and thirst serve merely as some data for reason. We do simple what we have reason to do. What desires do is to give us some reasons for action.

I think Hume is right that it is dubious that reason alone can be sufficient to motivate. It seems clear that there must be a source of motivation in all rational beings, but it does not mean that the reason itself has to be such a source. Like Hume, one might hold that human beings have an innate tendency towards sympathy with others, or as I argue, one might hold that everybody is equipped with self-love. Hume maintains that it is not irrational to prefer the destruction of the world to some minor harm to yourself, like the scratching of your finger, since there is nothing in reason that compels you to care more about the world than about your finger. According to Hume, desires can be the ultimate source of motivation. Practical reasoning is brought into play just to organize already existing motivations in a chain of means-ends. The only practical irrationality is to fail to arrive at the best means for your ends. There is no irrationality in ends themselves, unless they are chosen because of false beliefs.[1] Even some philosophers who are greatly influenced by Kant do not agree with him about the power of reason, that is, that reason alone can define what sets of moral rules one should adopt. For example, Hare as a post-Kantian philosopher at one time did not think there was anything more than consistency required by rationality that can favour one set of principles over possible alternatives.[2]

Whenever we find some action good for us we become interested in doing

---

1. On Hume's idea about motivation, see Hume, 1752, Section I, and Harman, 1977, Chapters Three and Six. The other good source is Schneewind (1992, pp. 506 and 507), in which he writes, "Hume argued against rationalism by saying that reason alone cannot move us towards action, and since morality does, morality could not be rational." Benn (1998) also discusses this problem. For example, he says, "What causes more problem is the idea of objective reasons, which in some sense exist apart from desires. This is partly the familiar problem of whether we can be motivated to do something by what Hume called 'reason alone', without desire" (Benn, 1998, p. 53).

2. On Hare's different positions, see my discussion about Hare in Chapter Three.

it. There are always desires for doing whatever suits us. Usually we are not in need of any decision to create desires in ourselves, otherwise we should be in need of creating another desire for creating the first and then we should need a third desire to create the second. This leads to an endless or circular chain of desires, which is impossible and which is not what we find in ourselves when we reflect on the process of decision-making.

On the other hand, as discussed above, it is impossible to desire something in which we have no interest and out of which we think that we shall not get any pleasure or benefit. On many occasions we decide to perform some painful acts such as undergoing a surgical operation or working continuously day and night to prepare a paper for a forthcoming conference. In all such cases we are simply pleased with suffering, because we expect greater pleasures or satisfactions for which we have stronger desires. This is why those who cannot or do not appreciate those future pleasures or satisfactions tend not to undergo those pains or difficulties. For example, children resist being injected because they consider only the instant pain and fail to appreciate the importance and benefits of a healthy life, which are far greater than the pain. In such cases the best policy is usually to promise them something soon for which they have a greater desire.

Different types of desires and pleasures
When it is said that we do only those things by which we get pleasure or satisfy our desires, it does not mean that we have accepted a crude version of hedonism. There are different types of desires and, correspondingly, different types of pleasures. "Physical" or "sensual" desires are related to those things that bring about physical or sensual pleasure. Although all desires and pleasures are felt or understood by the whole "self", physical pleasures have a significant relationship with a certain part of our body, as well as a relationship with an external physical object. Indeed, physical pleasures are the outcome of a certain contact between one part of our body and a physical object, such as the pleasure that comes from having a delicious meal or smelling a rose. Of course, when a person is very preoccupied he probably gets no pleasure from smelling roses around him, although his sensory organs are working well. This fact shows that having pleasure is not identifiable with that physical contact. Indeed, pleasure is brought about only after one realizes that contact. All pleasures and pains are finally to be perceived in the same way as we perceive other facts.

There are also some more enduring pleasures that might be called "semi-abstract". The pleasure one gets from having money or high position or fame or respect is not directly caused by physical matters and therefore has nothing to do directly with any senses or parts of the body. It is true that an office worker becomes happy when he or she hears that s/he has been given a promotion or when s/he feels notes in her hands, but this pleasure has nothing to do with these physical contacts. The physical contact in these cases is just a means for understanding that what was desired is actualized; otherwise, from a sensual point of view there is no difference between hearing about his or her own promotion or someone else's promotion, or between having valid notes and invalid ones in his or her hands. However, usually people enjoy these things because in this way they can have access to what they wish. This is why one does not get any pleasure from one's money if one is not allowed to spend it, or why one does not enjoy one's fame when one is not able to introduce oneself or one's position to people around him, although that person might be the most famous writer or actor or statesman. On the other hand, one can enjoy a false claim of high position. For the pleasure is not brought about by that "semi-abstract" matter, but rather by having, say, credit to buy a good car and house or holidays, which all cause in one way or another pleasures of the first type.

There is still another type of pleasure (and accordingly another type of desire) that may be called "abstract" pleasure, such as the pleasure one gets when one has confidence or peace of mind or when one is happy with oneself or with what one has done in the past. The desire for such a pleasure is a genuine one: it is not to obtain some sensual or semi-abstract pleasure. I mean by "genuine desire" a desire that is first of all real and secondly basic or irreducible to an underlying desire. A genuine desire is a desire that we may feel directly and independently and not simply because it leads to another desire. One way of deciding whether a given desire is genuine or not is to reflect on what is desired and see whether we *really* desire it *as such* or not.[1] A

---

1. There are two alternatives. One alternative is that the reflection might show that we do not really possess any desire for it and it was just through some illusion or confusion that we came to desire it. For example, a thirsty person may desire to drink a cold drink without knowing that it is poisonous. If s/he knew that it was poisonous s/he would never have desired to drink it. The other alternative is that the reflection might show that we really desire it, but we never desire it for itself. We only desire such a thing in order to satisfy another desire. For example, a thirsty person who sees a glass of cold lemonade really desires to drink it, but this does not mean that thirsty human beings have a desire for *a cold glass of lemonade*. What they primarily desire is to have some liquid that can quench their thirst. Whether it is water or lemonade or cola makes no difference to that primary desire. (Of course,

(continued...)

pleasure that a truth-seeker gets when he discovers a new fact is not for money or job or respect. In this case, knowing more about the world and about oneself is precious.[1]

I believe that reflection on our desires and inclinations shows that *we never desire what is vicious as such*. We have no desire or inclination directed towards some vicious act or thing *in itself*. This is why a person who always observes moral principles does not necessarily feel frustrated. If there were some desires in human nature that could be satisfied only with the immoral, the result would be that all moral people would have felt unsatisfied, disappointed and frustrated. However, this seems not to be the case. I think there is no doubt that there have always been in different cultures some people who observed carefully all moral laws and at the same time they felt very happy, confident and satisfied in their life.

I believe that it is up to us to direct our desires towards the virtuous or the vicious. For example, when we are hungry we desire to have some food. This desire is usually originated by a genuine need and it is to make us aware of there being such a need to be met and to encourage us to make some efforts or undergo the required difficulties. Now the agent may decide to choose an easier way to obtain food, that is, to steal; or there is a genuine love for the opposite sex. This love or desire directs man and woman to a close relationship, through which, on the one hand, they can supplement each other and give peace and confidence to each other and, on the other hand, human reproduction can continue. A person might decide to satisfy this desire through marriage and another through adultery or a free sexual relationship. We are not now discussing which one should be blamed or praised. What is important is that there is no genuine desire that has to be satisfied with things such as stealing, adultery, oppression and the like. As I explained earlier, I mean by genuine desire some desire that is real and irreducible to another desire.

Even if we suppose that a man has a desire for a particular woman who is

---

(...continued)
   there might be a secondary desire for a special type of drink.)

1. There is a beautiful and inspiring story about Abu Reyhan Biruni (941–1021), a prominent Iranian mathematician, astronomer, historian, pharmacologist and theologian. A few minutes before his death, Al-Biruni was visited by one of his neighbours, a jurist. Biruni started to ask him something about inheritance in jurisprudence. That man was surprised and asked Biruni why he was interested to improve his knowledge when he was near to death. Biruni replied, "Which is better? To die while knowing this or to die ignorant?" Biographers say that he used to carry out research and study on all but two days in every year.

married, this does not mean that he has a genuine desire for a relationship with a *married* woman, rather it simply happens that the woman he desires is married, just as she happens to have a certain name. If we suppose further that there are some people who desire to have sex only with a married woman or with a girl without the consent of her parents, this does not imply that there must be genuine or basic desires for such experiences in this case or in countless other similar cases. What we may be seeing here is a combination of basic desires, such as desires for sex and excitement, or for sex and freedom. (I shall elaborate on this point shortly.) We may suppose that someone has a desire for food but has no money. This does not mean that he has a genuine desire for some stolen food. The desire is simply for food. If that person earns some money or is given some money he would have no reason to steal and could have his desire satisfied by the food he has bought for himself.

A potential objection to my claim may be found in the case of young Augustine, who stole some pears when he was neither hungry nor poor. He stole something of which he had "enough, and much better". Those pears were "tempting neither for colour nor taste". Augustine confesses that his joy was in "the theft and sin itself" (*The Confessions of St Augustine*, Book II, Chapter VI). Now, one may argue against my claim by saying that this example shows the possibility of acting just out of the desire for the vicious (in this case, for theft).

Another potential objection may be raised by considering the problem of *kleptomania*. Kleptomania is defined as "a persistent neurotic impulse to steal especially without economic motive" or "a recurrent compulsion to steal without regard to the value or use of the objects stolen".[1] A kleptomaniac rarely uses what he has stolen: he might hide it or give it free to other people or even secretly return it. The kleptomaniac is usually able to buy what he steals, but he obtains gratification from the theft itself.

In response, I have to say that there is a difference between acting to enjoy the theft and having *genuine* (real and irreducible desire) for the theft *as such*. St Augustine himself points out that he had no genuine desire for theft; it was his misguided desire for freedom and power that motivated him for theft. He says:

> What did I love in that theft? And wherein did I even corruptly and pervertedly imitate my Lord? Did I wish even by stealth to do contrary to Thy law, because by power I could not, so that being a prisoner, I

---

1. *Britannica*, 1997.

might mimic a maimed liberty by doing with impunity things unpermitted me, a darkened likeness of Thy Omnipotency? (ibid.).

He also adds that companionship and amusement, e.g. laughing together when deceiving others, were also influential in motivating him and enhancing his love for liberty through theft, to the extent that if he had been alone he would not have stolen those pears (ibid., Ch. IX).

With regard to kleptomania, first it should be noted that psychologists and psychotherapists consider kleptomania as a mental disorder. Indeed, the very fact that it is considered as a mental disorder to steal without regard to the value or the use of the object stolen supports my argument that we have no genuine desire for the theft as such. On the nature of this mental state, we find:

> Although widely known and sometimes used as an attempted legal defense by arrested thieves, genuine kleptomania is a fairly rare mental disorder . . .
>
> Kleptomania is classified as a disorder of impulse control, meaning that the victim is unable to overcome the urge to steal and feels an increasing tension with attempts to resist, until yielding to the impulse gives release. In some cases, the stolen objects may have a symbolic sexual or other significance for the kleptomaniac, but the sexual aspects of the disorder are not always evident.
>
> Psychotherapy can be effective in alleviating the disorder . . . (*Britannica*, 1997).

Secondly, it is not clear that even the kleptomaniac who is mentally disordered commits theft for the theft itself. It is quite possible that the object stolen has a symbolic significance for him and he feels that the object belongs to him and not to the other party or that he feels powerful or free or proud when he breaks the law and takes away possessions of other people without being noticed or stopped.

My claim – that we have no genuine desire for the vicious as such – would be refuted if we could adduce a case in which a person (presumably, a mentally healthy one) desires *primarily* something that he acknowledges to be morally wrong, such as theft. Cases in which someone desires mistakenly or unconsciously morally wrong acts, e.g. desires to give a glass of water that happens to be poisonous to a thirsty child, do not refute my claim, since such people have no real desire for such an act. Neither do cases in which someone desires deliberately morally wrong acts, but in order to satisfy some underlying desires, like the case of young Augustine who committed a theft to satisfy a combination of desires for things, which are not in themselves bad, such as freedom and amusement, and not for the theft itself.

On the combination of desires, I should like here to refer to three important non-physical desires that quite often get combined with well-known basic desires (such as the desire for food or sex). Those three are the desire for rest, the desire for freedom and the desire for excitement (or amusement). Of course, these are not the only ones, but I consider them very important, since they usually have an active and effective part to play in wrong and immoral actions. Let us first elaborate on the desire for freedom or liberty.

There seems to be no doubt that such a desire exists. Human beings want to be free to do whatever they wish. They want to be able to exercise their power or will whenever they wish and without any obstacle or barrier. It is quite clear, especially among children and young people, that sometimes the very fact of being asked not to do something motivates them to do so. There is a very famous saying in Arabic that "Man is greedy for whatsoever is prohibited". Of course, this is true only when the person himself does not have an overwhelming aversion towards "what is prohibited". For example, if you have a lazy child or student who never studies and seems to care nothing for his future or the role of education in that future, you cannot expect that prohibiting him from studying will make him study. Another example can be found in nearly all religious societies. There are many things that are forbidden in world religions, which ordinary people dislike, and prohibition does not make people like them, such as eating dirty things, drinking blood or killing one's parents or children.

I do not think that the desire for liberty drives some people to commit unlawful actions. Real liberty is the ability to do whatever a person has a *genuine* desire for. A free person is able to follow whatever is in his real interests or to his benefit, not to follow the outcome of his misguided desires or wishes. Even granted that the desire for liberty in reality may lead to immoral or illegal actions, this does not disprove my claim that *we have no genuine desire for unlawful and vicious deeds as such*. If a person steals or lies or oppresses others simply because he or she is seeking liberty, the same person with the same ambition for liberty will not desire and perform these immoral deeds if s/he happen to be obliged to do so in other circumstances. This means that s/he had no genuine or irreducible desire for those bad deeds.

There is another desire that human beings share, i.e. a desire for rest, relaxation or, one may say, ease. It could be claimed that the combination of this desire and the desire for food might result in stealing, or, similarly, that the combination of this desire and sexual desire might result in a free sexual relationship, but neither of these two desires separately or jointly directs the agent in one way or another. It is the agent himself who evaluates the different factors and finally selects one course of action. Indeed, it is part of his decision-making to invoke the desire for ease instead of, say, the desire for honesty or loyalty. It also falls to him to consider ease from various different aspects and in the short and the long term. Of course, the agent's judgement is influenced by his information and his beliefs, but having the same information and beliefs, people might still decide to behave differently.

Now, let us examine my claim that we never desire the vicious as such in relation to abstract desires. I would contend that, not only do abstract desires not direct us towards the vicious, but they even seem to carry a positive and virtuous nature. Unlike physical desires, abstract desires are exclusively human. Unlike physical desires, abstract desires do not exist merely to remind us what we need to continue living. Physical desires, which are to a great extent recognizable in all animals, encourage us to act according to our instincts in order to survive. Of course, when something is common to humans and animals it cannot have a moral implication in itself, since there is no responsibility or moral agency among animals. This point affirms what I mentioned earlier about human physical desires, that they are neutral; they are capable of being satisfied morally or immorally. Abstract desires reflect what can be considered as fully-fledged human needs. This is because the main element in the nature of every being is the part that constitutes its identity and distinguishes it from similar beings, in short, that is exclusive to it. Therefore, what is really *human* is not to be found in other animals.

Elsewhere, referring to a similar fact, however, from a different approach, I wrote:

> Most people seem to instinctively realize that every being has a different level of perfection, closely matched to that being's inherent characteristics and purpose in the scheme of things in the universe. For instance, an ordinary shade tree, which does not bear fruits, compared with an apple tree, which does the latter as well as the former, is considered of a lower status of perfection in the scheme of things. It is for this reason that an apple tree in an orchard, which grows enough leaves to provide ample shade but for some reason does not bear fruit, is most likely to be cut down and replaced with one that does. It has not lived up to its potential, its level of perfection. In other words,

although the tree remains useful in many respects, it has failed in that aspect which distinguishes it from the less perfect trees which do not bear fruits.

The same analogy works when comparing humans and animals. If a human being does not exhibit characteristics which rise above those shared with animals, i.e. eating, drinking, seeking comfort, shelter, pleasure and the continuation of the race, then that human being has not reached his or her full potential, or perfection (Shomali, 1996, pp. 14 and 15).

Of course, it does not necessarily follow that a person who does not exhibit *human* characteristics is not a human being, since it is surely the potentiality of having human characteristics that marks a human being and distinguishes him/her from other animals.

Thus, our self-love defines our ideals of life, which can be summed up as wishing to have life in the largest quantity and greatest quality. Our self-love also establishes a cluster of desires that may motivate us to perform what practical reasoning instructs us to be good means for achieving our ideals, our goals and objectives. Doing what we desire gives us a proportionate type of pleasure, though we may not have aimed at having that pleasure. For example, a mother who takes care of her child gets some pleasure, although she might not have thought about receiving pleasure at the time when she got up out of bed and went to feed her baby.

Whatever is demanded by our genuine desires (i.e. the real and irreducible desires) is of natural value for us and gives us pleasure. Physical desires and perhaps some of the semi-abstract ones (e.g. the desire to win competitions) are shared by animals and can be considered as *animative* values. Whatever is exclusively demanded by the nature of human beings is a *human* value. Achieving *human* values as such is required for *human* happiness, while achieving *animative* values plays only a secondary or preparatory role. It can be argued that it is morally good to pursue the latter values insofar as they serve the former. We feel no conflict or difference in ourselves between our moral ideals and the demands of humanity. This fact is closely related to another fact, namely, that "good" and "bad" are not conventional or contractual, but rather they really exist and they can be realized and discovered by human reason through the consideration of human nature, human talents and potentialities and their perfection.

Different factors bearing on moral judgement

My analysis of the decision-making process gives an account of the role of internal and external factors in our moral judgements. I believe that a proper understanding of these roles can settle the dispute between relativists and absolutists (or objectivists). These roles can be summarized in this way:

1. The role of beliefs, knowledge and information

One of the crucial parts of our moral judgements is the way we conceive a problem and then the way we assess the results and consequences of each side of the problem. Differences and disagreements in this realm can lead towards different judgements about the same action. Even people who share the same moral ideals or rules are not exempted from these differences and disagreements.

2. The role of desires

The desire for each alternative act is a key factor in our decision-making. Although genuine desires are the same among human beings and they lead them towards their needs for survival and happiness (or, in other words, larger quantity and greater quality of life), their interaction and application may be different. It is up to the agent to choose which desire is foremost, perhaps to lean towards one side by, say, considering different optional combinations of desires or by neglecting the weight of options on the other side. It should also be noted that one's upbringing, training and character are also very important and influential in making decisions. A person who, since childhood, has always been encouraged to be kind and benevolent to others has stronger desires to help others and to prevent their suffering, even at the cost to himself of inconvenience, time or money. Of course, there is plenty of room for the agent to make his own decision and exercise his own will.

I should emphasize again that we have no genuine desires for acting wrongly. Physical desires are from a moral point of view neutral. They can be satisfied morally or immorally. One of the important implications of this fact is that human beings never get pleasure from a wrong action *itself*, because pleasures are brought about when at least one desire is satisfied and since there is no desire for a morally wrong action *simpliciter* no pleasure is occasioned by a wrong action. When someone eats a stolen apple, he may get some pleasure, but this pleasure comes from satisfying his desire for eating delicious foods and fruits. It is not eating a stolen thing or, more precisely, the stolenness of the eaten thing that has brought the agent pleasure. The same is true of adultery. It is not the adultery that is demanded by a genuine desire. The genuine desire is for sex and the pleasure comes from the satisfaction of this desire.

In the case of the stolen apple, people may experience one of the following states:

a. Some may eat the stolen apple and get some pleasure and feel nothing wrong in it. Thus, they enjoy eating a delicious thing (not the fact that the thing is stolen) and find nothing wrong in stealing others' possessions. Of course, we are not here to explain why, but we can understand this circumstance, if we consider all the factors bearing on a moral judgement, as discussed in this chapter.

b. Some may eat the stolen apple and get some pleasure and at the same time feel guilty. There is no contradiction here. The pleasure derives from one thing and the guilt from something else. Of course, such people have not been able to practise a well-established moral system consistently.

c. Some may not eat the stolen apple, because they do not want to commit a wrong. However, they might be tempted to eat that apple, although they hate stealing or eating a stolen apple. Therefore they resist the temptation and do not eat it. The temptation and the aversion can co-exist precisely because the two feelings are attached to different aspects of the case.

d. Some may not eat the stolen apple, because they so intensely hate wrong-doing such as stealing that they will not contemplate allowing themselves the pleasure of eating a delicious apple. Such people do not face any temptations in this case.

3. The role of one's own will and decision

Although there are lots of restrictions imposed by external and internal conditions, the agent is after all free to make his decision. Without a belief in free will nothing remains as morality. The difference between different agents in exercising their free will can be seen in these parameters:

a. In adopting some ideals or values for their lives. People's ideals of life are very important in directing their actions.

b. In their readiness to acquire the necessary information and study it appropriately. Some people act quickly; others prefer to be far-sighted and cautious. Some tend to be pessimistic and others tend to consider just the positive and even to overlook unpleasant possibilities.

c. In organizing their desires and giving priority to some of them or combining some of them to outweigh another desire.

   It seems that if we allow for the fact that an agent can organize and prioritize his desires, we can believe in free will without denying the role of desires in motivating the agent. Thus I do not agree with Harman, who, like Kant and Nagel, holds that we have to consider nothing more than our desires as some data that underlie the reason. Or, to put it another way, he thinks that being faithful to free will and being rational require us to treat our desires as data and not some forces or compulsions. He admits that sometimes desires act as compulsions, but not normally.

   I think there is a middle position between the position, on the one hand, that treats desires as mere data and denies their motivational role, and, on the other hand, the position that treats desires as forces and compulsions that leave no place for free will, or reasoning. Desires motivate us towards alternative acts or an act and its negation, and it is at that point that we turn to exercise our free will or make a decision. When there is only one way in front of us we cannot speak of decision-making. Since both sides of the decision are usually desirable in one way or another, and it is up to us to tip the balance in favour of either side, as we choose, we are usually able to resist one of the sets of desires.

   Indeed, it is this view that makes free will intelligible. Two human beings in completely the same relevant conditions may decide differently. For example, one may prefer to satisfy instant desires and the other to satisfy future desires. One may prefer to satisfy the desire for comfort and relaxation, and the other the desire for acquiring knowledge. Rather it is the Kantian and Nagelian view that denies freedom. If you treat desires as mere data to be fed in along with other data and use these to fulfil logical requirements, you will come to a certain conclusion. Coming to that conclusion is not a voluntary act.

If people come to different conclusions in those same circumstances it must be only because they are mistaken or ignorant. You are not free to come to your preferred conclusion. In this case, you cannot speak of good will neither can you blame wrongdoers. They are blameworthy if and only if they failed to do their best to collect good data and develop good arguments, which in turn would suggest prior error or ignorance. The end result would be not to blame wrongdoers and criminals at all.

d. In their practice and application of their desires, such as deciding to satisfy one's desire for sex through marriage or through adultery.

4. The role of one's mental and intellectual abilities and talents
For example, analytic and critical minds may make better or quicker decisions.

5. The role of conditions
By conditions I mean characteristics or particularities that surround the case of judgement, including the agent's physical and mental condition (such as health and illness), the agent's feelings (such as happiness or sadness), the agent's capabilities, circumstances of other people who might be involved (for example, a teacher has to consider conditions of his students), time, place, laws, culture (including customs), available resources, means and aids. Any change in these conditions may require the observer and the agent to change judgements on the appropriate decision or action.

Knowing and paying attention to all the facts that, decisively or possibly, consciously or unconsciously, bear on our decision-making help us to have them in our own control. In this way, we can make a judgement that is really to our benefit.

Paul Taylor has made a very informative and insightful study about the requirements of a rational choice. I propose to give a short description of his account here. Taylor (1970, pp. 345–60) believes that a choice is rational *to the extent that* it is free, enlightened and impartial. Of course, he believes that actually no choice can ever be completely free or enlightened or impartial. He describes conditions of freedom in this way:

a. The choice is not decisively determined by unconscious motives.

b. The choice is not at all determined by internal constraint, that is, the person is not under any compulsion, such as from an irresistible impulse or an extreme desire. He is in complete control of himself.

c. The choice is not at all determined by external constraint.

d. The choice is decisively determined by the person's own preference.

Taylor describes the conditions of enlightenment in this way:

a. The nature of each way of life is fully known.

b. The probable effects of living each way of life are fully known.

c. The means necessary to bring about each way of life are fully known.

Taylor describes conditions of impartiality in this way:

a. The choice is disinterested, that is, the choice is not at all determined by bribes, by desire to protect one's privileges or one's favourite people's privileges or emotional prejudices.

b. The choice is detached or objective, that is, the choice should be made among ways of life other than that in which the person was brought up and other than that to which he is committed at the time of choice.

c. The choice is unbiased. He says, "a choice is unbiased to the extent that (i) the person's upbringing was non-authoritarian, (ii) the person's education was liberal, and (iii) the person's experience of life up to the time of choice was of considerable variety, richness and depth" (Taylor, 1970, p. 359).

Although some of the above items in Taylor's study may be controversial or impractical, bearing them in mind probably helps the agent and the observer to make better judgements and decisions.

An analysis of moral concepts

In the light of what has been argued up to now, we can start to analyse moral concepts as follows.

1. "Good" and "bad": Whatever is useful, first to protect our life and our species and secondly to make us more perfect, is good. In other words, the intrinsic goodness is "larger quantity and greater quality of life (or existence as a human being)". Whatever brings about a larger quantity of our life (such as taking care of our health) or a greater quality of our life (such as acquiring more knowledge or confidence or peace) is good. Whatever is harmful to our being and causes shorter life or lower quality of life is bad.

   When we consider some action and we find it producing something useful for our ideal we call it "good" and if we find it harmful we call it "bad". There may be some actions that are neither useful nor harmful. These actions are simply neutral, such as walking or speaking, in most cases. Here it is also possible to say that whatever is not harmful to our ideal is "good". Thus "good" extends to include neutral actions as well. It can also be said that whatever is not useful is "bad". In this case, "bad" extends to include neutral actions. I prefer the latter way of thinking, because everything that does not promote our perfection is a loss. (Consider that we have limited life, power and resources!) People are also different: some people feel guilty when they spend their time unpurposefully and others do not care. It depends on the degree they have of self-care and determination for self-improvement.

2. "Right" and "wrong": Every action that is useful, first to protect life and species and second to make us more perfect, can be called "right" as well. Every action that is harmful (to our ideals; either to the quantity or quality of life) is "wrong". Again the same can be said about neutral actions. Unlike some analyses, this analysis shows that it is not necessary to suppose "bad", "right" and "wrong" as derived from the concept of "good". Yes, it is possible that sometimes, when we have already known the goodness of some action, we take a short cut and conclude that the action when it recurs or is repeated is also right, or that its opposite is bad and wrong, instead of reconsidering the action and its relationship with the moral ideal. The reverse is also possible.

   If we use "good' in a broader sense, then it can be applied to whatever has a positive relationship with our being and nature and, therefore, is precious for us, including both non-voluntary matters such as our own existence and voluntary actions or qualities such as learning or honesty. "Right", however, seems to be exclusive to voluntary actions and qualities. The same point is true about "bad" and "wrong".

In any case, when we believe that an action is good or right we will be motivated to do it, since we have harmonious desires and motivation to do whatever is useful or pleasant for us. According to this analysis it seems pointless to seek for any additional reason. Indeed, it is impossible for our reason (intellect) alone to prove that we should be concerned with our interests and should do whatever is good for us. It is similar to another impossible task, which is to prove that we can trust reason.

3. "Ought" and "ought not": Sometimes we may have another approach to actions. We may consider the relationship between some action and our moral ideal and discover that it is necessary to perform that action in order to reach that ideal. In other words, we may find a causal relationship between our action, such as learning, and our ideal, such as perfection. It means that learning occurs in a chain of causes that lead to our perfection. Since we want to reach our ideal (i.e. perfection), it is necessary to adopt the cause (i.e. learning). We express this *necessity* in terms of "ought" and say, "We *ought* to learn". Similarly, if action *a* is preventing us from reaching our ideal, that is, its absence is necessary for us to reach our ideal, we say, "We *ought not* to do *a*."

Relativism and absolutism

We saw earlier that moral relativism generally can be defined as a view that holds that there is no single true or most justified morality. I believe that the only kind of difference in moral judgements that can be thought to support ethical relativism is the difference that comes from adopting different ideals and values. If one could support the claim that *different individuals or societies can adopt parallel ideals that are equally justified*, then one could establish meta-ethical relativism. Of course, the mere existence of different moral ideals or values does not imply that there is no single true or most justified morality, because, for instance, people may have failed to understand the true moral ideals.[1]

As I argued earlier, there is a *real* relation between *our self-love* and *genuine*

---

1. For an absolutist account of moral disagreements, see Chapter Three.

desires, our ideals and *our nature.* To be able to show that there are those parallel ideals, therefore, the relativist has to show that there are different types of human nature. People or individuals with different moral systems must be shown not to belong to a common species, to what we usually conceive of as the same human nature. One undesirable implication of this view would be that if a person or society decides to adopt a new moral position he or it has to first *change* his or its nature! Or more precisely, they cannot change their moral position, unless their nature has been already changed! I think this is something that relativists are not prepared to accept.

Human nature: The study of human nature is far greater than can be undertaken in a discussion about ethical relativism. However, I should like to give some clues for further work. It seems to me that there are good grounds for thinking that human beings have the same nature. Of course, it is clear that biologically human beings are the same. However, what I mean by human nature here is more than that. Human nature is an ontological notion that can be partly known through philosophy and partly through psychology. Historical and social manifestations of this notion can be known through sociology, history, anthropology, arts and literature. However, I think that by internal reflection everybody can understand many aspects of this notion and, to a greater extent, can grasp others' views regarding human nature.

As I have explained earlier in this chapter, there are some qualities that we share with animals and others that belong exclusively to human beings and that are the main element in constructing our identity. Another way of putting this is to say that there are some qualities without which one is no longer considered a human being and, on the other hand, there are others without which one still can be considered as a human being. For example, we can still consider as human a person who has no desire for food or sleep, but not a person who has no desire for happiness or perfection or truth or beauty. This is a truth we can find through internal reflection and, of course, philosophy and sciences, such as psychology can enrich our findings. Those qualities or characteristics that differentiate human beings from other animals can be divided into two categories: perceptions and desires. Some types of perceptions are distinctively human and this is why human beings have been able to flourish in the various fields of science and to improve their techniques. There are also some desires that are exclusive to human beings and this is why we have always pursued knowledge, perfection, benevolence and the arts.

Thus, what I mean by human nature is not just a biological identity; it is rather a more abstract identity that produces similar characteristics in all human beings. If there were no such common nature among human beings there would be no place for disciplines such as education, psychology, sociology or even economics. All these sciences presuppose that human beings are similar and behave similarly in similar conditions.

I should like to add that my notion of human nature does not involve moral commitments. As I explained earlier when analysing the concepts of "good" and "ought", all evaluative concepts are in a sense descriptive: they report the existence or non-existence of a relation between our ideals (which are in turn defined by our nature) and given states of affairs or quality. For example, when we say, "telling the truth is good" it means that there is a causal or an ontological relationship between this act and, say, our perfection; or when we say, "we ought to learn" it means that there is a causal relationship between learning and our ideal, that is to say, perfection. It means that learning occurs in a chain of causes leading to perfection. Since we want to reach our ideal (i.e. perfection) it is necessary to adopt the cause (i.e. learning). We express this *necessity* in terms of "ought". Therefore, my notion of human nature does not involve moral commitments but neither is it irrelevant to morality.

In any case, I believe in the sameness of human nature among different people. However, even if we accept that there are different human natures (that is, human beings are only biologically the same) and that people with different natures may have different ideals, it does not solve the problem for relativists. For people are bound to their nature and people with the same nature cannot adopt different moralities, yet the relativist has to show that people in the same condition can justifiably have different moralities. An analogy is health. People in different conditions may need different types of care or different types of food or vitamins. However, there is no doubt that human beings are biologically and physically almost the same and *in the same condition* they need the same nutrition and health care. Therefore, the difference in health requirements does not imply that health is not objective or that there are no general laws concerning health.

Thus, the objectivity of ethics or the denial of ethical relativism does not require that all people have to act similarly. Different people with the same nature may be morally expected to act differently. What a child is expected to do is different from what an adult has to do. The right things for a woman as a mother differ from the right things for a woman as a daughter or as a sister or as a wife. Even the same person with the same role may be morally required to act in an opposite way in different times or different places. For example, Mrs M as a mother should feed her son or daughter during his or her childhood, but she should not do so when they are grown up. Therefore, to assume that different people may have different natures or different obligations and responsibilities is no proof of relativism. An argument that could support ethical relativism would be that people with the same nature and in the same conditions may justifiably do different things.

I wish to note here that it does not suffice relativists like Wong to say that different people have the same nature, but that the plasticity of complexity of human nature "make[s] it possible for us to prize a variety of goods and to order them in different ways" (Wong, 1996, p. 446). As I argued earlier (Chapter Three, Descriptive Relativism), people's failure adequately to understand human nature or to put values in their proper order does not mean that there cannot be an encompassing morality that is faithful to all human values and puts them in the right order.

As long as relativists have not presented a good argument for ethical relativism, there seems to be no reason not to believe in absolutism, which is a common-sense view – as admitted by absolutists and nearly all relativists. However, I shall now try to build up my argument for absolutism using ideas that I have developed earlier in this chapter.

Characteristics of a true moral ideal

In practice, people may adopt different types of ideals in their lives. This adoption may partly or completely be shaped by factors such as religion, culture, training, professions and family upbringing. Ideals adopted in this way may vary and, indeed, may oppose each other. Yet they all have the same function, which is to define one's values and shape one's form of life. Every rational person should always think about his or her ideals and see whether they are worthy of being adopted as ideals or not. Therefore, we have to distinguish between what I call "a true moral ideal" and what has happened to be adopted as a moral ideal, that is, between an *ideal* ideal and an *actual* ideal.

Here, I try to list what I think to be the characteristics of a true moral ideal. Of course, there might be others that have not occurred to me. Those characteristics are:

1. Whether we recognize true moral ideals or not, there should be no disagreement that a true moral ideal has to be compatible with human nature.

2. A true moral ideal has to be conceivable by our reason; otherwise we cannot follow it.

3. A true moral ideal has to be supported by reason, because, as discussed earlier, no one decides to do something unless he or she believes in its usefulness for him/herself. If this is the case for a single action, how much more important must the criterion of usefulness or properness be for the ideals for all actions, indeed, for the whole of one's life? It is also clear that there can be no belief without rational assessment. It is part of human experience that we try to justify and argue for our beliefs, moral judgements and even emotional conduct. Even those people who think that there can be voluntary (or indeed arbitrary) beliefs or emotional beliefs or any other non-rational beliefs must acknowledge that there can be no belief that contradicts reason. Any such contradiction or conflict is against what we find in ourselves: the unity of our "self" and coherence of our faculties. No one can devote self and life to an ideal and sacrifice everything for it when there is any doubt about its truth, let alone when it contradicts his or her rational standards. The adoption of a true moral ideal has to fulfil all the requirements of a rational choice. As we saw earlier, a choice is rational if it is free, enlightened and impartial.

4. A true moral ideal has to be supported by our genuine desires; otherwise it cannot motivate us to act according to what we have discovered to be good for us.

5. A true moral ideal has to be achievable and practical; otherwise it is a dream and not a guideline for life.

6. A true moral ideal has to be able to encompass all other values and moral standards and to rank them correctly with the hierarchy, since it must be able to explain one's purpose or the intended value beyond each action. If you ask a person the reason for this or that action, any appropriate response has to involve an evaluative or normative element. For example, if you ask a teacher why she teaches, you do not expect her to answer simply, "because I teach" or "because there are students". None of these or similar facts explains why she teaches. An appropriate response may be, "It is good to teach" or "I should help people" or "I have to serve my country or people" or "I ought to do what I am paid for". Responses such as "I like to teach" or "My father advised me to teach" can be plausible only when

we consider the hidden premise/s in each case, such as, "It is good to do what you like" or "You should take your father's advice".

If we study carefully all evaluative or normative statements used by a person we can discover that person's system of values. One's ideal/s has/have the central and crucial place in that person's system of values.[1] Moral ideals first define values and second put those values in order. Regardless of what the moral ideals are or should be and regardless of whether "good" is definable or not, for each person the moral ideal is the highest good. If we successively ask any man his reasons for action, he goes step by step higher and finally he reaches a point at which he cannot any further. It is at this point that we can discover his ideals. For example, if we ask a student at high school why he goes to school, he might reply that he wants to go college. If we ask him why he think it is good for him to go college he might say because then he can go to the university. Successively we might hear these responses: "Because then I can become expert in management", "Then I can become a good manager", "Then I can develop my country", "Then I can help to create enough job opportunities and security for my people", "Then I can feel that I have been helpful to my nation and especially to needy people", "Then I feel happy, confident and pleased".

This series of goals finally comes to an end when one reaches the ideal or ultimate good. Other ends get their validity from this ultimate good. Closeness to or remoteness from the ultimate good defines the position of each end or value in a given moral system, that is, in a hierarchy of ends or values adopted by a person or a group or a society. Considering places or degrees of each end or value, the agent can decide what to do when faced with a practical conflict between some values. In such cases one has to distinguish between good and better or between bad and worse. Indeed, most of the moral disagreements invoked by moral relativists as candidates for moral disagreements arise here. Reflection on those cases shows that individuals or societies in principle agree on what is good or bad. Of course, the denial of this point does not refute moral absolutism, since moral absolutism allows other sources of disagreements, such as confusion, different conditions and the like.

Again, I should say that the whole debate between relativists and absolutists is reducible to this problem as to whether there is a single set of true moral ideals (or a single true moral ideal) or not. We are not now

---

1. Of course, we are concerned here with moral values and ideals.

concerned with the number of ideals. What is important is that a true moral system has to contain any ideal that meets all the requirements. Now, let us consider again characteristics of a true moral ideal: that it has to be in complete accordance with our desires,[1] with our rational standards and above all with human nature, that it has to be practical and that it has to encompass all other ends and values and put them in the right order or hierarchy. (We also saw that relativists cannot solve their problem by assuming that people have different natures.) I think this account of true moral ideals gives us objective criteria against which we can test different candidates. The ultimate end of our moral enquiry has to be to discover the most promising moral ideal or set of true moral ideals. Unlike Wong, I believe that there can be no rival moral systems built around different ideals. Thus, the debate between absolutism and relativism can be settled in favour of absolutism, and, since there are objective criteria or requirements for ideals and derivative values, the debate between objectivists and subjectivists too can be settled in favour of objectivists.

Although the above account is enough for the main purpose of this work, i.e. to settle the debate between relativism and absolutism, and there is no need to develop a detailed list of ideals and values, I should like to refer to different proposals. There are lots of candidates, such as life, consciousness, and activity; health and strength; pleasures and satisfactions of all or certain kinds; happiness, beatitude, contentment, and so forth; truth; knowledge and true opinion of various kinds, understanding, wisdom; beauty, harmony, proportion in objects contemplated; aesthetic experience; morally good dispositions or virtues; mutual affection, love, friendship, co-operation; just distribution of goods and evils; harmony and proportion in one's own life; power; experiences of achievement; self-expression; freedom; peace, security; adventure and novelty; good reputation, honour, respect.[2]

The main reason why there is such a huge variety of proposals is the complexity of human nature and its multi-dimensional capacities. Our previous discussion of how we become motivated shows that our basic drive is self-love and we seek what is useful for us or pleasant to us. Therefore, the

---

1. The most relevant desires here are abstract desires, which are in a real sense *human*.

2. This list of candidates for intrinsic good was originally made by William K. Frankena in his *Ethics*, (Englewood Cliffs, NJ: Prentice-Hall, 2nd edition, 1973), p.88, and later invoked by others such as Robert Audi in "Intrinsic Value and Moral Obligation", *Southern Journal of Philosophy*, Vol. 35 (summer 1997), and in *Moral Knowledge and Ethical Character* (New York: Oxford University Press, 1997), p. 251.

intrinsic good can be understood only after we discover what a human nature can be at best. We need to know human capacities and potentialities.

Of course, it is not now our concern to define what is exactly the intrinsic good and what are the derivatives ones. However, given that our basic drive is self-love, our intrinsic good is "larger quantity and greater quality of our life". This seems to involve all other candidates and therefore to be in a sense acceptable to all their advocates.

Conclusion

In brief, what I have done in this work as follows:

1. Conceptual clarification

Since one of the main problems in the debate on relativism in general and moral relativism in particular has been the ambiguity of the concepts and the lack of clear and standard definitions of the relevant terms, I have tried to clarify the theoretical context of the debate on ethical relativism within the more general discussion about relativism in philosophy. In this regard, I have also tried to clarify the conceptual context of the debate by defining key concepts and their divisions, such as ethical relativism, individual and social ethical relativism, methodological and non-methodological ethical relativism, ethical absolutism, ethical universalism and ethical objectivism. Whenever necessary, I have proposed certain names or expressions to be given to the concepts at issue. For example, I have argued that "absolutism" is better than "objectivism" as the opposite view to ethical relativism, and that "social relativism" and "individual relativism" are successively better than "conventionalism".

As far as I know, such an attempt has not been undertaken in any other single work.

2. Critical discussion about the historical development of the debate

To familiarize readers with the vast literature on the issue and with the various positions taken by different ethical thinkers (including philosophers and anthropologists) throughout the history of the debate, especially in the twentieth century and more especially in the 1980s and 1990s, I have devoted a whole chapter to discussion of the history of ethical relativism. One of the results of this survey has been to establish the fact that, unlike in the late nineteenth and early twentieth centuries, support for ethical relativism has recently declined. Ethical relativists of our time have developed more limited and moderate versions of ethical relativism. I have suggested three kinds of explanation for this phenomenon: the rational, the psychological and the sociological. The rational explanation of this phenomenon is that none of the previous forms of ethical relativism has survived criticisms. The psychological explanation of this phenomenon could be that moral philosophers who were considerably shocked by the mass of anthropological information about the diversity of morals gradually regained their confidence and realized once again that anthropological data cannot settle a philosophical debate, the debate about whether there is a single true morality or not. As regards to the effects of the social atmosphere of the mid-twentieth century onwards on the phenomenon of ethical relativism, I referred to a typical sociological account, from Whitaker (1997), who, inter alia, stresses the inadequacies of applying relativist tolerance to that period's bloodstained ideologies.

As far as I know, such a detailed discussion about the history of ethical relativism was missing.

3. Distinguishing different types of ethical relativism, discovering possible grounds for each and evaluating them

I distinguished between three different types of ethical relativism, the descriptive, the meta-ethical and the normative. Having discussed what each means, the different versions of each and the substantive differences between their claims, I tried to distinguish between the different grounds on which relativist theories may be developed. I believe that, despite the huge amount of work that has been published on ethical relativism, it was not treated like this before.

In respect to descriptive relativism, my conclusion has been that it is weak, both in its strong and moderate versions. Descriptive relativism in its strongest form (i. e. the claim that all basic moral values vary from individual to individual or from culture to culture) suffers from lack of evidence and, in fact, it is practically impossible to investigate its truth. I also argued that the strongest is also in conflict with the fact that many moral principles and values have been common to the majority of people and in some cases to all reasonable human beings and typical civilized societies. Descriptive relativism in its moderate form (i.e. the claim that some basic moral values vary) is more tenable, but it still suffers from the fact that many examples adduced by relativists are either irrelevant to morality or do not embody fundamental differences. In any case, descriptive relativism in either of its forms has no philosophical implications and can be accepted by objectivists or absolutists. For their belief in a single true or most justified morality does not require any level of agreement, just as physical facts may be both true and disputed.

In respect to meta-ethical relativism, I studied eleven different arguments, along with my own objections and comments. I also stated either the standard objections to those positions or some of the objections made by others. In some cases, I had to discuss at some length other important topics in philosophy, such as the concept of relative truth. In other cases, further assessment of arguments for meta-ethical relativism was shown to depend on other discussions in the present work, such as those dealing with descriptive relativism and the foundations of morality. I indicated that certain aspects merit independent work, such as the possibility of knowledge and Quine's theory of translation, but I gave relevant references to existing other works. In general, I argued that none of those eleven arguments for meta-ethical relativism works. Indeed, the aim of the next two chapters, Chapters Four and Five, was to consider whether the modifications or supplementations made by Harman and Wong to the last two arguments can make them good or not.

I argued that normative relativism is more dubious and controversial than meta-ethical relativism, just as meta-ethical relativism is more dubious and controversial than descriptive relativism. Besides difficulties in both descriptive and meta-ethical relativism, it was argued that neither of them entails normative relativism. Moreover, I argued that a combination of ethical relativism and Western liberal contractualist ethics does not solve the problem. I also emphasized that there is a sharp difference between normative relativism and the principle of tolerance. An absolutist also may support the principle of tolerance or reject the enforcement of moral norms. On the other hand, a relativist may not recognize tolerance as a value in his moral system.

4. A full account of the different non-relativist (absolutist) explanations of moral diversity and disagreements

In the second part of Chapter Three, I tried to present a short but comprehensive account of the absolutists' policy in dealing with the issue of ethical relativism, because moral diversity and moral disagreements have always been seen as evidence, or for some relativists as a reason, for ethical relativism. The main result was to discover that a non-relativist account of morality is capable of explaining our moral experiences, including moral diversity and disagreements, without having the undesirable implications of ethical relativism. Although non-relativist philosophers have previously dealt with this issue and attempted to give an absolutist account of moral differences, I think the issue has never been separately and exhaustively discussed as here.

5. A study of two of the most important recent theories of ethical relativism
In Chapters Four and Five, I studied two of the most recent and important versions of ethical relativism, which are developed by Gilbert Harman and David Wong. In each case, I explained the main features of their moderate theories of relativism, including both central and derivative elements. I argued that their moderate theories have seven advantages. However, I concluded that they are both still subject to criticisms. Comparing these two theories with each other, I argued that Wong's theory has seven additional advantages, though this has made his proposal less relativist. The further he moved from stereotypical relativism, the better the results he achieved!

My main objections to Harman's theory concern his internalism, his moral conventionalism, the distinction between evaluative ought and moral ought, the notion of quasi-absolutism and the ambiguity of his argument in some of his works. I also disagree with him about explaining moral disagreements and aspects of our moral experience, which he takes to serve as evidence for his theory of moral conventionalism, such as the relative strength of the duty not to harm others compared with the duty to help and the fact that in most moral views animals are ranked lower than people.

As regards Wong, although on many points I agree with him, especially in the way he describes and defines actual morality and conforms better to common sense and human moral experience, I observe six problems in his theory, such as his view about "inference to the best explanation", his position about the origins and ends of morality and his explanation of differences between rights-centred and value-centred.

6. Defining the best policy for settlement of the debate on ethical relativism and
    developing the appropriate theory
I argued in Chapters Three to Five that the essential problems of ethical relativism cannot be avoided unless relativism is totally left aside. Modification of ethical relativism may lessen those problems. For example, Harman's theory was shown to have fewer problems than stereotypical relativism and Wong's had fewer still, since it was more modified. As long as relativists have not presented a good argument for ethical relativism, there seems to be no reason not to believe in absolutism, which is a common-sense view (as admitted by absolutists and nearly all relativists). But the final solution for essential or substantial problems is to develop a substantially different theory about the foundations of morality, which discovers the nature of morality, appreciates all aspects of our moral experience and locates morality in its real place. In Chapter Six, I started to develop such a theory about the foundations

of morality. Without engaging in complicated discussions about the objectivity or subjectivity of morality, I have taken into account the nature of morality, moral ideals and their characteristics, the different factors involved in the process and in the outcome of decision-making.

I argued that every moral system is based on some moral ideals. Moral ideals first define one's values, and, second, put those values in order. Regardless of what moral ideals are or should be and regardless of whether "good" is definable or not, we can say that for each person his moral ideal is the highest good or final end. Our moral ideals are in turn defined by our self-love and they can be summed up as desire for life in the largest quantity and the greatest quality. The moral status of every act depends on the relation between that act and those ideals. An act is good if it can lead to our ideals. Our self-love also establishes a cluster of desires that may give us sufficient motivation to perform what practical reasoning instructs us to be a good means for achieving our ideals, our goals and objectives. Whatever is demanded by our genuine desires (i.e. the real and irreducible desires) is a natural value for us and gives us pleasure. This fact is closely related to another fact, namely, that "good" and "bad" are not conventional or contractual, but rather that they really exist and can be realized and discovered by human reason through consideration of human nature, human talents and potentialities and their perfection.

Then I argued that the only plausible strategy for relativists would be to show *that different individuals or societies can adopt parallel ideals that are equally justified*, but to be able to show that there are those parallel ideals, the relativist has to show that there are different types of human nature, since my account shows that there is a *real* relation between our ideals and our nature. People or individuals with different moral systems must be supposed to belong to different species and not to possess what we usually conceive of as the same human nature. Referring to the implausible implications of this assumption, I argued that even the acceptance of different human natures does not support relativism. For people are bound to their nature. The same person cannot adopt different moralities, while the relativist has to show that the same people in the same condition can justifiably have different moralities.

Suggestions for further works

I hope that the present work, if it achieves the above six objectives, will help to put an end to some of the misunderstandings recurring in the discussion of ethical relativism. However, the arguments can be further developed by studying the following three areas.

1. A psycho-philosophical analysis of human nature, faculties and desires:
   Such an analysis would help:

   a. to determine whether human nature is the same in all human beings or
      whether it differs;

   b. to discover the potential aspects of human nature, what stages they can
      reach and what perfection they can acquire.

2. Developing a comprehensive system of morality based on the theory
   developed in Chapter Six: Three main characteristics of such a system can
   be described as follows.

   a. Such a system would have to work out a list of moral values and put
      them in order, in such a way that the highest one comes immediately
      after our ideals, i.e. having a longer life and a greater quality of life.

   b. To be practically efficient, such a moral system would have to tell us
      what to do when two or more moral values are in conflict. Obviously,
      if one is in a higher position in the hierarchy of values, we should give
      priority to it. For example, saving an innocent life takes precedence
      over helping a needy person, but if they are at the same level what
      should we do? Are we always free to do whatever we choose in such
      situations, and, more importantly, what should we do if we are in
      doubt whether this value is more important or the other, as in the case
      of Sartre's pupil?

   c. Such a system would also have to define the moral status of different
      sorts of action. Some actions have a necessary relation to our ideals, so
      that they are always good, such as justice, or bad, if they have negative
      relation to our ideals, such as oppression. Some actions tend to lead to
      our ideal and, if there is no conflicting element, will certainly bring
      about the attainment of that ideal, such as telling the truth. Telling the
      truth is, in itself or other things being equal, good, but there may be
      circumstances or factors that may prevent telling the truth from
      bringing us nearer to our ideal or may even take us further from it, for
      example telling a truth that endangers an innocent life. There may be
      some actions that are neutral, that is, they have even no tendency
      towards our ideals or their opposites. In such cases, an additional

element is needed to tip them in one direction or the other, towards good or towards bad. Speaking to a child who feels lonely in order to make him or her happy, for example, turns a neutral action, that of speaking, into a good one, that of helping another person.

Having such a moral system instructs us what to do in complicated cases and helps us to understand how people may come to different judgements when they have no such comprehensive moral system.

3. Developing a theory on intercultural actions: I argued earlier that an absolutist account of morality may encourage tolerance and condemn enforcement of moral values on those who have different moral systems. I also argued that there may be cases in which even relativists feel it necessary to pass judgement or even interfere in the practices of people from substantially different cultures, such as slavery or torture or mass murder.

In the light of a general non-relativist theory of morality further discussion is needed on the proper course of action when two cultures with fundamentally different moral values want to co-operate. Of course, it cannot be suggested that one culture has simply to give up its values in favour of the other. Neither can it be suggested that the standards of both cultures be followed completely, since this is not practically possible.

It seems to me that the proper policy is to conduct a theoretical dialogue among the people in the two cultures to discover the most justified way of behaving or of combining values.

Until a common understanding is reached, a practical solution based on mutual respect should be devised. This should establish rules concerning what to do when some fundamental values in the view of one culture are overlooked by the other, such as respect for innocent life, i.e. innocent in the view of the former. Criteria also need to be devised by which to judge whether the offending values outweigh the value of mutual respect and non-interference. To interfere or protest without having such criteria as a basis may do more harm than silence. Until those criteria are defined no culture has the right to impose its values on another.

On a smaller scale, a suitable policy has to define what to do when a person or a group of people or a community live in a larger society with fundamentally different moral values. In this case, we again have a conflict of two cultures: the culture to which that person, group or community belongs and the culture of the larger society. However, the two cultures do not have the same weight. Therefore, adequate answers are needed to questions such as: Should the individual or group or community always compromise and give priority to the values of the larger society? Does the number of people have any bearing on the plausibility of their values and the respect that is due to them? Are there some values of the person, group or community that the larger society has to recognize and respect under any condition? It has to be noted that this is not the same issue as that of the rights of minorities, but it can be a moral enquiry about the issue of minorities, if we suppose that the minority has a radically different culture from the culture of the majority and if we suppose that moral values are concerned and not just legal rights.

Bibliography

Here I include the books by Gilbert Harman and David Wong to which I have referred in this work. For a more detailed list of their works on ethical relativism, see pp. 127 and pp. 173.

Arrington, Robert (1989), *Rationalism, Realism and Relativism* (Ithaca: Cornell University Press).

—— (1983), "A Defense of Ethical Relativism", *Metaphilosophy*, 14.

Becker, Lawrence C. (1992), ed., *Encyclopedia of Ethics* (New York and London: Garland Publishing, Inc.).

Benedict, Ruth (1934), *Patterns of Culture* (New York: Penguin).

Benn, P. (1998), *Ethics* (London: UCL Press).

Billington, R. (1993) *Living Philosophy: An Introduction to Moral Thought* (London: Routledge, 2nd edition).

Blackburn, Simon (1998), "Moral Relativism and Moral Objectivity", *Philosophy and Phenomenological Research*, Vol. LVIII, No. 1, March, pp. 195–8.

—— (1993), *Essays in Quasi-Realism* (New York: Oxford University Press).

Botton, Alain (1999), *The Essential Plato* (UK: The Softback Preview; special edition of the Benjamin Jowett translation of Plato, published in 1871).

Brandt, Richard B. (1959), *Ethical Theory: The Problems of Normative and Critical Ethics* (New Jersey: Prentice-Hall, Inc., Englewood Cliffs), reprinted in Wilfrid Sellars and John Hospers (1952, 2nd edition 1970), eds, *Readings in Ethical Theory*, (New York: Appleton-Century-Crofts).

Bunting, Harry (1996), "A Single True Morality? Challenge of Relativism", in David Archard, ed., *Philosophy and Pluralism* (Cambridge University Press).

Cooper, John M. (1992), "History of Western Ethics 2: Classic Greek", in Lawrence C. Becker (1992), ed., *Encyclopedia of Ethics*.

Copleston, Fredrick (1970), *Greece and Rome*, Vol. 1 of *A History of Philosophy* (London: Search Press).

Darwall, Stephen (1998), "Expressivist Relativism", *Philosophy and Phenomenological Research*, Vol. LVIII, No.1, March, pp. 183–8. [This article is on Harman (1996).]

—— (1998), *Philosophical Ethics* (Oxford: Westview Press).

Donagan, Alan (1992), "History of Western Ethics: 12, Twentieth-Century Anglo-American", in Lawrence C. Becker (1992), ed., *Encyclopedia of Ethics*.

Donaldson, T. (1989), *The Ethics of International Business* (New York, NY: Oxford University Press).

Fieser, James (1996), "Moral Relativism", in *The Internet Encyclopedia of Philosophy* (hosted by University of Tennessee at Martin, www.utm.edu/research/iep).

Fletcher, Joseph (1966), *Situation Ethics* (London: SCM Press).

Foot, Philippa (1982), "Moral Relativism", in J. W. Meiland and M. Krausz, eds, *Relativism: Cognitive and Moral*.

—— (1978), *Moral Relativism*, The Lindley Lectures (KS: University of Kansas Press).

—— (1961), "Goodness and Choice", *Proceedings of the Aristotelian Society*, Supplementary Vol. 25.

Gauthier, David P. (1969), *The Logic of Leviathan: The Moral and Political Theory of Thomas Hobbes* (Oxford: Clarendon Press).

Geertz, C. (1988), "Anti Anti Relativism", in Michael Krausz (1989), ed., *Relativism: Interpretation and Conflict*, pp. 12–34.

Jeffery A. Gray and Roy Porter (1999), "Emotion", in Allan Bullock and Stephen Trombley, eds, *The New Fontana Dictionary of Modern Thought* (London: HarperCollins, 3rd edition).

Hare, R. M. (1993), "Universal Prescriptivism", in P. Singer, ed., *A Companion to Ethics* (Oxford: Blackwell), pp. 451–63.

—— (1991), *Moral Thinking: Its Levels, Method and Point* (Oxford: Clarendon Press, 6th impression, first published 1981).

—— (1988), "Comments", in Douglas Seanor and N. Fotion (1990), eds, *Hare and Critics: Essays on Moral Thinking* (Oxford: Clarendon Press).

—— (1963), *Freedom and Reason* (Oxford: Clarendon Press).

—— (1952), *The Language of Morals* (Oxford: Clarendon Press).

Harman, Gilbert (1998a), "Precis of Moral Relativism and Moral Objectivity – Precis of Part One", *Philosophy and Phenomenological Research*, Vol. LVIII, No. 1, March.

—— (1998b), "Responses to Critics", *Philosophy and Phenomenological Research*, Vol. LVIII, No. 1, March.

—— and Thomson, J. J. (1996), *Moral Relativism and Moral Objectivity* (Oxford: Blackwell).

—— (1978), "What Is Moral Relativism?", in A. I. Goldman and J. Kim, eds, *Values and Morals* (Dordrecht and Boston: D. Reidel).

—— (1977), *The Nature of Morality* (Oxford: Oxford University Press).

—— (1975), "Moral Relativism Defended," *Philosophical Review*, 84, pp. 3–22.

Harre, Rom, and Krausz, Michael (1996), *Varieties of Relativism* (Oxford: Blackwell).

Herodotus (1972), *The Histories*, translated by Aubrey de Sélincourt, revised by

A. R. Burn (Harmondsworth, Middlesex: Penguin Books).

Hudson, W. D. (1990), "Development of Hare's Moral Philosophy", in Douglas Seanor and N. Fotion, eds, *Hare and Critics: Essays on Moral Thinking* (Oxford: Clarendon Press).

Hume, David (1965, first published 1751), "A Dialogue", in Alasdair MacIntyre, ed., *Hume's Ethical Writings* (New York: Macmillan), pp. 157–74.

—— (1857), in T. H. Green and T. H. Grose, eds, *Essays Moral and Political*, four vols (London), ii. 68.

—— (1752), *An Enquiry Concerning the Principles of Morals* (London: T. Cadell).

—— (1739), *Treatise on Human Nature*, Book III, Part 2, Section 2.

Kahn, Charles H. (1992), "History of Western Ethics: 1. Presocratic Greek", in Lawrence C. Becker (1992), ed., *Encyclopedia of Ethics*.

Katz, Jerrold J. (1964), "Semantic Theory and the Meaning of 'Good'", *Journal of Philosophy*, Vol. 61.

Kenny, Anthony (1998), *A Brief History of Western Philosophy* (Oxford: Blackwell).

Kockelmans, Joseph (1992), "History of Western Ethics: 11, Twentieth-Century Continental, Part 1", in Lawrence C. Becker (1992), ed., *Encyclopedia of Ethics*, pp. 522–8.

Krausz, Michael (1989), ed. and writer of introduction, *Relativism: Interpretation and Conflict* (Notre Dame: University of Notre Dame Press).

Krausz, Michael, and Meiland, Jack W. (1982), eds, *Relativism: Cognitive and Moral* (Notre Dame: University of Notre Dame Press).

Lukes (1991), "Making Sense of Moral Conflict", *Moral Conflict and Politics* (Oxford: Clarendon).

MacIntyre, Alasdair (1989), "Relativism, Power and Philosophy", in Michael Krausz (1989), ed., *Relativism: Interpretation and Conflict*.

—— (1988), *Whose Justice? Whose Rationality?* (Notre Dame: University of Notre Dame Press).

—— (1984), *After Virtue* (Notre Dame, Indiana: University of Notre Dame Press, 2nd edition).

Mackie, J. L. (1977), *Ethics: Inventing Right and Wrong* (Harmondsworth, Middlesex: Penguin).

McNaughton, David (1998), *Moral Vision: An Introduction to Ethics* (Oxford: Blackwell, first published, 1988).

Margolis, Joseph (1989), "The Truth about Relativism", in Michael Krausz (1989), ed., *Relativism: Interpretation and Conflict*.

Matilal, Bimal K. (1989), "Ethical Relativism and Confrontation of Cultures", in Michael Krausz (1989), ed., *Relativism: Interpretation and Conflict*.

Nagel, Thomas (1986), *The View from Nowhere* (Oxford: Oxford University Press).

—— (1970), *The Possibility of Altruism* (Princeton: Princeton University Press).

Neimark, M. K. (1995), "The Selling of Ethics: The Ethics of Business Meets the Business of Ethics", in *Accounting, Auditing and Accountability Journal*, Vol. 8, No. 3, pp. 81–96.

Nielson, K. (1982), "Problems for Westermarck's Subjectivism", *Acta Philosophica Fennica*, 34, pp. 122–43.

Nietzsche, F. (1887), *On the Genealogy of Morals*, translated by Kaufman and Hollingdale (New York: Random House, 1967).

Norton, David Fate (1996), "Hume", in Robert Audi (1995, reprinted 1996), ed., *The Cambridge Dictionary of Philosophy* (New York: Cambridge University Press), pp. 342–7.

Plato (1973), *Theaetetus*, translated by J. McDowell (Oxford: Clarendon Press).

Pojman, Louis P. (1998), *Ethical Theory: Classical and Contemporary Readings* (USA: Wadsworth Publishing Company, 3rd edition).

—— (1996a), "Relativism", in Robert Audi (1995, reprinted 1996), ed., *The Cambridge Dictionary of Philosophy* (New York: Cambridge University Press), pp. 690, 691.

—— (1996b), "Westermarck", in Robert Audi (1995, reprinted 1996), ed., *The Cambridge Dictionary of Philosophy* (New York: Cambridge University Press).

—— (1990), "Gilbert Harman's Internalist Moral Relativism", in *The Modern Schoolman*, LXVIII, pp. 19–39.

Popkin, Richard H. (1996), "Montaigne", in Robert Audi (1995, reprinted 1996), ed., *The Cambridge Dictionary of Philosophy* (New York: Cambridge University Press), pp. 505, 506.

Rachels, James (1998), *Ethical Theory* (New York: Oxford University Press).

—— (1996), "Subjectivism", in P. Singer, ed., *A Companion to Ethics* (Oxford: Blackwell), pp. 432–41.

—— (1993), *The Elements of Moral Philosophy* (New York: McGraw Hill, Inc., 2nd edition).

Radcliff-Brown, A. R. (1952), *Structure and Function in Primitive Society* (London: Cohen and West).

Railton, Peter (1998), "Moral Explanation and Moral Objectivity", in *Philosophy and Phenomenological Research*, Vol. LVIII, No. 1, March.

Rand, Ayn (1964), *The Virtue of Selfishness* (New York: Signet).

Rorty, R. (1989), *Contingency, Irony and Solidarity* (Cambridge: Cambridge University Press).

—— (1980), *Philosophy and the Mirror of Nature* (Oxford: Blackwell).

Sartre, J. P. (1970), *Existentialism and Humanism* (Frome and London: Butler and Tanner, 1st English edition 1948).

Sayre-McCord, Geoffrey (1996), "Fact-Value Distinction", in Robert Audi (1995, reprinted 1996), ed., *The Cambridge Dictionary of Philosophy* (New York: Cambridge University Press).

Scanlon, Thomas (1999), *What We Owe to Each Other* (Cambridge and London:

The Belknap Press of Harvard University Press, 1ˢᵗ published 1998).

Schacht, Richard (1996), "Nietzsche" in Robert Audi (1995, reprinted 1996), ed., *The Cambridge Dictionary of Philosophy* (New York: Cambridge University Press), pp.532–6.

—— (1992), "History of Western Ethics: 10, Nineteenth-Century Continental", in Lawrence C. Becker (1992), ed., *Encyclopedia of Ethics*.

Schneewind, J. B. (1996), "Modern Moral Philosophy" in P. Singer, ed., *A Companion to Ethics* (Oxford: Blackwell), pp. 147–57.

—— (1992), "History of Western Ethics: 8, Seventeenth and Eighteenth Century", in Lawrence C. Becker (1992), ed., *Encyclopedia of Ethics*.

Schroder, William R. (1992), "History of Western Ethics: 11, Twentieth-Century Continental, Part II", in Lawrence C. Becker (1992), ed., *Encyclopedia of Ethics*.

Schweder, Richard A. (1989), "Post-Nietzschian Anthropology: The Idea of Multiple Objective Worlds", in Michael Krausz (1989), ed., *Relativism: Interpretation and Conflict*.

Shomali, Mohammad, A. (1996), *Self-knowledge* (Tehran: International Publishing Co.).

Sidgwick, Henry (1967), *Outlines of the History of Ethics* (London: Macmillan, 1ˢᵗ edition 1886, 6ᵗʰ edition 1931).

Siegel, Harvey (1987), *Relativism Refuted* (Dordrecht: Reidel).

Singer, Peter (1988), "Reasoning towards Utilitarianism", in D. Seanor and N. Fotion (1990), eds, *Hare and Critics: Essays on Moral Thinking* (Oxford: Clarendon Press), pp. 147–59.

Snare, F. E. (1980), "The Diversity of Morals", *Mind*, Vol. 84, No. 355, July, pp. 353–69.

Stevenson, Charles L. (1967), *Facts and Values* (New Haven and London: Yale University Press, 1ˢᵗ published 1963).

—— (1944), *Ethics and Language* (New Haven and London: Yale University Press).

Stewart, Robert M. and Thomas, Lynn L. (1991), "Recent Work on Ethical Relativism", *American Philosophical Quarterly*, Vol. 28, April, pp. 85–100.

Sturgeon, Nicholas L. (1998) "Thomson Against Moral Explanations", *Philosophy and Phenomenological Research*, Vol. LVIII, No.1, March.

Sumner, William G. (1906), *Folkways* (Boston: Ginn).

Taylor, Paul (1970), "The Justification of Value Judgments: Rational Choice", *Readings in Ethical Theory*, reprinted from Paul W. Taylor (1961), *Normative Discourse* (Englewood Cliffs, New Jersey: Prentice Hall).

Unerman, Jeffery (1996), "Ethical Relativism: A Reason for International Differences in Social and Environmental Accounting", online article.

Walzer, Michael (1987), *Interpretation and Social Criticism* (Cambridge, MA: Harvard University Press).

Watt, W. Montgomery (1983), *Islam and Christianity Today: A Contribution to Dialogue* (London: Routledge and Kegan Paul).

Westacott, Emrys (1999a), "Cognitive Relativism", *The Internet Encyclopedia of Philosophy* (hosted by University of Tennessee at Martin, www.utm.edu/research/iep).

—— (1999b), "Relativism", *The Internet Encyclopedia of Philosophy* (hosted by University of Tennessee, Martin, www.utm.edu/research/iep).

Westermarck, Edward (1932), *Ethical Relativity* (London: Kegan Paul, Trench, Trubner).

—— (1906-1908), *The Origin and Development of the Moral Ideas*, 2 vols (London: Macmillan).

Whitaker, Mark P. (1997), "Relativism", in Alan Bernard and Jonathan Spencer, eds, *Encyclopedia of Social and Cultural Anthropology* (London and New York: Routledge).

Williams, Bernard (1997), "Ethics", in *Philosophy: A Guide through the Subject* (Oxford: Oxford University Press).

—— (1974-75), "The Truth in Relativism", *Proceedings of the Aristotelian Society*, 75, pp. 215-28.

Wong, David (1998), "Moral Relativism", in Edward Graig, ed., *Routledge Encyclopedia of Philosophy* (London and New York: Routledge).

—— (1996), "Relativism", in P. Singer, ed., *A Companion to Ethics* (Oxford: Blackwell).

—— (1992), "Moral Relativism", in Lawrence C. Becker (1992), ed., *Encyclopedia of Ethics*.

—— (1984), *Moral Relativity* (Berkeley: University of California Press).

Wood, Allen (1995), "Relativism", online article from Cornell University.

Index of Concepts

Index of Names